RON GOSBEE

NO ESCAPE

WITNESS TO A
CANADIAN GENOCIDE

**Memories from St. Anne's
Indian Residential School**

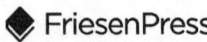 FriesenPress

One Printers Way
Altona, MB R0G 0B0
Canada

www.friesenpress.com

Disclaimer
This book is a memoir that depicts actual events in the life of the author and fellow
contributors, as truthfully as recollection permits. The author, fellow contributors, and
publisher do not assume and hereby disclaim any liability to any party for any loss,
damage, or disruption caused by errors or omissions, whether such errors or omissions
result from negligence, accident, or any other cause.

**Cover photo: Ron, front row left; his sister Lou, front row middle; and their fellow
students at St. Anne's, circa 1960**

All photos courtesy of Donovan and Margaret Gosbee Archives unless otherwise stated.

ISBN
978-1-03-919833-3 (Hardcover)
978-1-03-919832-6 (Paperback)
978-1-03-919834-0 (eBook)

1. BIOGRAPHY & AUTOBIOGRAPHY, PERSONAL MEMOIRS

Distributed to the trade by The Ingram Book Company

TABLE OF CONTENTS

TABLE OF CONTENTS

FOREWORD

by Charlie Angus,

Federal Member of Parliament for Timmins-James Bay

ST. ANNE'S RESIDENTIAL SCHOOL HAS been closed for nearly half a century but its dark shadow still lingers over the vast region of Treaty 9 in Northern Ontario. You can track the movement of this shadow through the lives of the elder generations who suffered staggeringly high levels of addiction and self-destructive behavior. It is there in the suicide waves that continue to engulf children as young as 12. And I have learned to recognize the shadow in the faces of many that I have served as an elected representative. I see it in the tenseness of the jaw and facial muscles. It is the permanent tattoo of trauma marked on them when they were mere little children.

My office is full of binders of evidence on St. Anne's residential school – police reports, affidavits, countless letters to justice officials. I also have thousands of pages of blacked out documents – a process of deliberate erasing that has been done in these times by government officials determined to protect the Catholic Church and the officials who continue to deny justice for people whose only crime was that they were First Nation children.

And yet, knowing what I know of this house of horrors, I still felt great trepidation opening Ron Gosbee's powerful book No Escape. Ron's story is unique – he and his two sisters were the three white students in an institution designed to destroy the identity of the Indigenous children of the James Bay region. Ron's parents worked at the Hudson's Bay Post in Fort

Albany in the late 1950s and 60. They naively thought that since the institution was run by nuns and priests their children would receive a good education at a caring institution.

Gosbee brings a powerful perspective because it is an eye-witness account rendered through the eyes of a child. He fills in the details that are missing from the police reports and studies – the smells, the sounds, and the palpable fear as experienced by children. This book will help a new generation understand the systemic abuse and violence that was Canada's state policy for Indigenous children for over a century.

Gosbee shines a brave light on a dark time. It may help us to finally rid our nation of the dark shadow of the nightmare institutions like St. Anne's.

AUTHOR'S NOTE

MY TWO SISTERS AND I were part of the Indian Residential School experience that so profoundly affects Canada today. It is not common knowledge that this hellish system of religious schooling, created to "get rid of the Indian problem" (Duncan Campbell Scott, 1920), swept up a few of us "white" kids too. We were witnesses: three little white kids who managed to keep written and personal photographic evidence, unlike many of our residential school friends.

My sisters and I lived in Northern Ontario in the 1950s, as my father was a post manager of the Hudson's Bay Company. Our parents were given many of the same deluded and even false promises that Indigenous parents were given. They were led to believe that a better education, thoughtful care, and a spiritual life awaited their children within the walls of St. Anne's Indian Residential School.

This was not the case.

The purpose of the residential school system in Canada was to educate and convert Indigenous youth and to assimilate them into Canadian society. It was a horrific system, rife with abuse and doomed to failure from the start. Regardless of any good intentions, these schools destroyed their culture by taking children away from their parents, integrating them into the dominant "white" culture at the time, and thereby removing land claims as well.

The story of what happened to Indigenous children in these residential schools has been told, and must be retold, especially by Indigenous Peoples. I want to be careful not to create a second colonization of people's pain with this book.

This memoire was initially just meant to be a record of our time at St. Anne's with our fellow students. But the school is also part of a larger story, so I hope that by illuminating the experience, it can also act as a bridge for "settler culture" to grasp the enormity of the crime done in their name. One shouldn't have to speak or write about this. A crime against the children of one people should be a crime against all children, and everybody should react the same. But they don't. I hope that this account, therefore, can also pierce the prejudice of "settler culture" that is impervious to the cries of children who simply have the "wrong" skin colour, ethnicity, religion, etc.

As a child, I did not realize that our common residential school experiences would be locked away in memory, in fact, in history, and be of interest to the world so many years later. During the writing of this memoir (almost sixty years later), the Canadian Broadcasting Corporation (CBC) aired an interview on me and my family about our experiences at St. Anne's.

The interview illustrated to me how fragmented my memory was of the experience. The process of recalling these fragments was like doing an archeological dig, or more precisely, like trying to recover DNA evidence at a blood-spattered crime scene in order to determine what happened. As I began to piece the fragments together, I realized I needed help to tell more of the story.

Thankfully, as a result of the CBC interview, some fellow inmates from St. Anne's, now adults, contacted me to share memories of our time at that school. Their willingness and non-judgmental support were similar to when we were children at the school. I was grateful to reconnect with these fellow students, once drawn together by an unseen force and still bound together through common experience.

Although my sisters helped to flesh out some of our memories, due to the segregation in the school, some of our experiences were different. It was only through the sharing of memories with my fellow dorm mates that I was able to verify and reconcile a lot of those troubling times.

One of those boys was Tony Tourville, who contributed significantly to this book. It was through the process of talking with other survivors, especially Tony, that I came to the important realization that my writing was polite and sanitized compared to their recollections. It was as if I had developed a protective layer of neutral words to guard against having to face such painful memories again.

For example, in my initial writing, I would use words such as "school" while they used words such as "prison." And I used the words "dorm supervisor," while they used the words "prison guard." I would describe our meals as "breakfast" or "dinner," but they used words such as "slop fest."

As I continued on this story of self-discovery, I began to use words that were more in line with the emotions I was feeling. I would even say them out loud, which turned out to be a surprisingly cathartic experience.

An inability to find the words, or even exploding in a tornado of words, could be a sign of dragging unprocessed, unresolved trauma and that you have not made peace with whatever is boiling inside you. I had the emotions but no adequate words to go along with the experience, until hearing those expressed by my dorm mates. They have not only helped me tell the full story, but have also helped me to find my voice. There is something to be said for identifying and naming one's demons as a first step in the healing process.

During the writing of this book, it also became apparent to me that the experience of going to a residential school existed within a larger context. Referring to the experience with such words as "tragic" did not fully encompass the larger picture of what happened. It was only when I heard the word "genocide" used to describe the Indian Residential School system that a clearer picture of the crime emerged.

Such a strong word has sparked discussion and division, and it was an important moment, therefore, when the Canadian House of Commons gave unanimous consent in June 2021, in favour of a motion calling on the federal government to recognize Canada's residential schools as genocide (Sean Kilpatrick/Canadian Press).

For those who think that such a system does not warrant the word "genocide," I say that comfortable people want to remain comfortable.

On a broader note, this memoir is an example of what unchecked power creates. The more light that we shine upon such danger, the better off we will be as a society. Hopefully, it can be a call to action against all such terror forced upon the powerless by the powerful.

HISTORICAL PERSPECTIVE

ACCORDING TO CHARLIE ANGUS IN *The Broken Treaty* (Angus, 2017), the Oblate Missionaries of Mary Immaculate were a band of militant Catholic priests and brothers who had arrived in the James Bay region by 1850, having arrived first in Montreal in 1841. The Oblates' intent was to aggressively replace all other religions in Aboriginal territory.

St. Anne's Residential School had been a Catholic stronghold since Treaty 9 was signed between Indigenous groups and the federal government in 1905. Treaty 9 was the basis of the educational structure laid out for Native children in the North. It gave the government the right to use force to remove these children from their parents and their homes and to place them within institutions. It also, and most importantly for the governing body, signed away Native lands to government ownership.

By all accounts, the government showed little concern for the welfare of the young people in their charge. The quality and type of education and care to be provided was not described in any detail within the treaty. The children were simply a cost: the Catholic brothers' "bid" undercut the Anglicans by 25% per child. They also provided a building, which, in their estimation, needed minimal improvements.

This became St. Anne's Residential School.

Note: St. Anne's (Fort Albany) Indian Residential School (IRS) was initially located on Albany Island from 1906 – 1932. In 1932, it was relocated to the same Roman Catholic Mission site where this story takes place. In the mid 1950s the wooden (IRS) structure burned down and a new building took its place. This new school was constructed with non-combustible materials. It was being renovated and enlarged during the time of this account.

PROLOGUE

WHEN I SLOWLY OPEN MY eyes, the faint morning light from the windows reflects on the ghostly white pillars standing silently on guard in regular rows around the dormitory. The sighs and snores of the other boys roll across my bed.

The air in the room smells like a litter of puppies. Something ruffles my hair. It's the foot of the boy in the bed behind me. We are lying in packed rows, in the boys' dorm room. I am in a bed in the middle of the room – the only white boy – jammed in with a hundred or so Native boys.

As I look out from under my pillow, a shape floats by me. It is our dorm supervisor on the hunt for any boy who deserves a reprimand. I freeze in fear as she moves past, reeking of starch and Noxzema. The sound of sniffs from other boys gives dimension to the darkness. But not all are crying. Some are smelling for her presence. Some are sick. Others are just whimpering from sadness.

I can hear the boy beside me. He wants to go home to his family, now miles away in their hunting grounds. I want to go home too, and my family is only about five miles away, across the river.

We saw an older boy struck on the head with the heel of a shoe the day before. His infraction was minor. It doesn't seem to matter what we do. The threat is always there. He made no sound as our supervisor, a Native nun, struck him. We all knew shouting out might result in more hits and a loss of status in the pecking order.

I turn on my side and brace for the loud clank of the handheld bell, the signal that it is time to get up. *When, oh when, will Mom and Dad ever come again? Will I ever be rescued? How long will this last? How long can I last?*

CHAPTER ONE:
PRESCHOOL YEARS, LIVING IN A BUBBLE

TO UNDERSTAND WHAT MADE THE residential school experience so unique for me and my two sisters, we must first travel back to the mid 1950s. My dad was the post manager for the Hudson's Bay Company (HBC) trading post on Albany Island, Northern Ontario, on the west side of James Bay.

The HBC post store and house on Albany Island, circa 1956.

My family consisted of me; my dad, Donovan Gosbee; my mom, Margaret; and my sisters, Ruth and Lou.

It was there that we kids lived prior to going to school, enjoying an idyllic, rustic life that many people can only dream of. We didn't have a care in the world because all our basic needs were being looked after by the HBC, and we had the nurturing love of our parents as well.

Mom remembers me as being a little hellion at times as compared to the more gentle nature of my sisters. Although we had our differences, as all kids do, we banded together through play, naturally figuring out the world around us and our place in it.

Ruth and Ron at home, at the HBC post on Albany Island, circa 1956.

Most days, we went outside to our yard. It was such a wonderful playground. The air would blow in off the river, bringing with it wild, rich smells that created an intriguing sense of possibility. The yard was a perfect place for kids with imaginations like ours. It always seemed to be waiting for us to come out to play, to imagine, and to dream.

Even though our house was in the wilderness, in the middle of nowhere, about a mile from our nearest neighbour, and hundreds of miles from any large city, it was surrounded by a white picket fence, the ultimate symbol of colonialism. We stayed behind that fence in those early days, and made our own fun from the resources we had at hand.

Ruth and Ron making their own fun with the HBC store
in the background, circa 1956.

The HBC store, located beside our home, hinted at a larger world but it was off limits to us kids unless accompanied by an adult. Dressed up with white paint and with its signature red roof, the store looked shipshape, although the smell inside suggested a much older past.

On the rare occasion that we kids got to go to the store, those smells were more interesting to me than the supplies displayed on the shelves.

The air within the store hung heavy with the aromas of wood smoke, linseed oil, and animal fur (from trading with the Native hunters). There was also a dustiness in the air, the residue of decades of cigarette and pipe smoke. These extreme odours mixed together were mesmerizing to a child.

The sparse, tidy interior of the HBC store with
its wood-burning stove, white shelves, and bare lightbulbs, circa 1956.

Although we enjoyed a sense of security, with the HBC supplying our lodging all our food, and even some modernity, such as a generator, we three kids didn't know anything about the world and really did not know anything about the world outside of our picket fence. If ignorance was bliss, we were blissfully ignorant, and it was great.

The more accurate description, however, is that we were insulated. We were living in a bubble. I was a bubble boy, and everything I understood about myself and the world around me happened inside that bubble. For example, Mom got into trouble once with Dad when she tried to befriend some of the Native customers by inviting them in for tea – someone for us kids and for her to interact with – which she desired because she was going out of her mind from the isolation. But Dad intervened and sent them away, saying to Mom, "You'll have every Native stopping in here for tea when they come in to trade at the store. They will get to expect it, and you won't be able to keep up." The rule was that we were not to get too friendly with the Natives because we were there to trade with them and make a profit for the HBC – not to make friends with them.

Therefore, as a boy under five years old, with an impressionable mind, I was conditioned to think of the Natives as somehow inferior and not to be associated with. Since there were no other white kids around for about a hundred miles, my sisters and I just learned to play amongst ourselves. Sure, on a few occasions, a couple of Native children were presented to us to play with, but these were really staged affairs. They were the children of the Native Anglican lay minister, who my parents had met at church and approved of. But their visits were brief and rare and so did not condition me to have a positive view of them or to be socially adjusted to play with kids other than my two sisters.

The Native kids spoke some English, often with Cree words mixed into an English sentence. Ruth attempted to find common ground with them, but I would have none of it. I found their treatment of my toys rough, and I looked forward to them leaving.

I quite enjoyed the fact that I could leave my playthings strewn in the yard, and they were not "touched" by the local Natives. They did not dare to cross the social border, the white picket fence, between us and them. I felt safe in my world and happy that they seemed to know their place and did not try to enter our world of plenty without a formal invitation. At that point, I didn't think about the lives and suffering of the people around me, as long as I was in my yard playing make believe with my toys.

My favourite toys were boxes, and because all our goods were shipped in, there was no end to boxes. A kid's paradise! Having control of all the cargo boxes to do with as we wished must have sent a message to the local Native kids that my two sisters and I were very privileged.

Boxes in our yard at Fort Albany, circa 1957.

A good cardboard box was considered better than any other toy: it was the top of the toy line. A big cardboard box could be anything you wanted it to be. My favourite activity was to join boxes together and create a tunnel to the box that felt the strongest and safest, rather like an igloo. It was a safe, quiet place for a child to hide and imagine.

As time went on, we kids would occasionally venture outside our picket fence with Dad or Mom, but life outside of our safe place was always a concern, for me at least.

Lou, Ruth, and Ron venturing outside of their white picket fence, hoping that the sky would not fall on them. Albany Island, circa 1957.

There was not really any place to go, though, except to the store or else to the Anglican church about half a mile away, where we would either attend religious services or else attend the occasional lessons where the lay minister would teach us our A,B,C's.

Since these lessons were not adequate for formal schooling, Ruth was eventually sent to relatives in southern Ontario to attend school.

This left Lou and I to play in our protected environment on our own, with little understanding of the world around us, or the perspective that the Natives had of us either.

It must have been maddening for the Natives to see the privileged life we HBC people were enjoying. At certain times of the year, they would arrive with heavily laden sleds of freshly stretched skins to trade at the store for supplies. But after a short period of "feast time," they had to struggle till the next haul of furs while the tantalizing goods on the shelves lay just out of reach. It did not seem fair, since they had no say in what the value of their skins were, the price being set by the HBC.

The fact that a few bullets were fired into our chimney by some of the local Natives might have given us a clue that they were not happy. Each year, a group of them would gather and troop from their community about a mile away to shoot at the chimney of the trading post at midnight to mark the beginning of the New Year. One time, they shot at the chimney of our home as well. The pings of their bullets above our heads did not raise much of an alarm, though. We just thought the community was including us in their celebrations. Although the perpetrators were not bloodthirsty, it should have been a wakeup call that we "whites" were seen, at least by some, as an invading force.

My world at home and the bubble that I lived in, finally burst and came to an abrupt end when I reached school age and my formal education had to be considered.

Although Ruth was already attending school in southern Ontario, Mom and Dad thought it might be better to have me closer to home by attending the local Native residential school of St. Anne's instead. It was located only about eight kilometres from where we lived. And so, wanting to have us closer to home, they decided to enroll me there first, with plans for Ruth and Lou to attend in the following years.

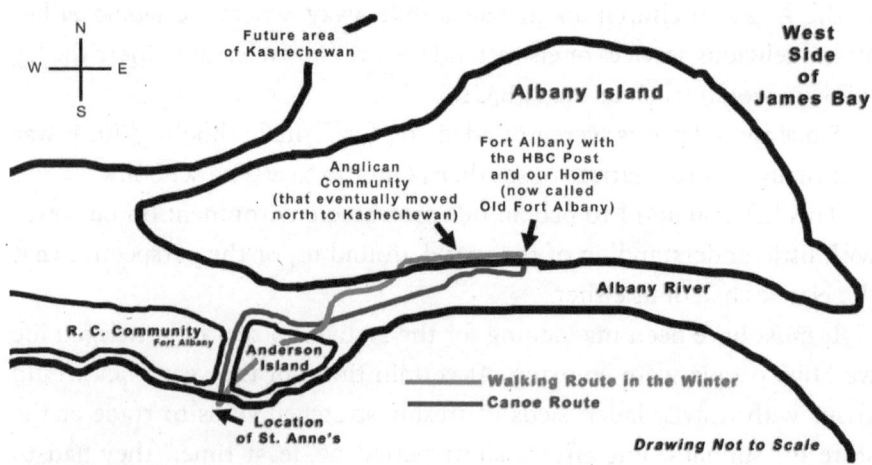

Map drawing of Fort Albany area during the time of this story (1955 to 1961).

Prior to my enrolment, Mom visited St. Anne's on a fact-finding mission and asked about the quality of education provided by the school. Although Dad wanted to be present as well on such a visit, he was not able to because he had to mind the store.

In response to Mom's questions, the Mother Superior informed her that the teachers there had teaching degrees and were the best of the best. Although Mom could have homeschooled us, (after all, she had already taught us kindergarten from lesson books sent in by the HBC), she thought, "Why not leave my children's formal education to these professionals?"

Mom was also assured that, although my two sisters and I were Anglican and St. Anne's was Roman Catholic, we would not be required to convert in order to attend the school – which was a relief and a surprise to her, since religious denominations were very competitive and insular in those days.

A priest then gave Mom a tour of the grounds of St. Anne's. With its sawmill, a big garden, bakery, and even a nursing station, St. Anne's looked like a Mennonite village like she had heard about from her mother, who had lived in such a village back in Russia. In those stories, everyone had lots of work to do and lots of good food to eat, prepared by people who knew all about baking. Mom thought St. Anne's was likely a good place to send us kids for school, as it seemed like an ideal environment to her.

A Red Flag

Unfortunately, she was not given a tour of the children's dormitories or even introduced to the dorm supervisors or the teachers. The priest however, took the time to give her a tour of the nuns' quarters. He proudly presented a large ring of keys, indicating that he had a key for each of the nun's rooms, and unlocked the door to one of them to show Mom the layout. However, he did not knock when entering, giving our mother a sly look that stuck with her. He simply said that it was the room of one of the nuns who was also a teacher. It was a plain room with a bed, dresser, bookcase and rocking chair. Mom thought it odd that the priest would have all the keys and that he would exhibit such a lack of consideration when entering a nun's private area without knocking.

Interesting that he showed Mom the room of one of the teachers but did not introduce her to an actual teacher. In fairness, maybe all the teachers were away on holidays since it was still summer before school was in session.

The priest's decision to show her the nun's bedroom may have been because he might have thought that the neatness of the nun's room, was next to godliness, and might have meant something to Mom as a homemaker – indicating the relative short sightedness of the priest and social norms at the time. Who knows.

It is unfortunate that she did not have the opportunity to see the classrooms and what might be written on the black boards, or actually see a teacher in action.

It was also unfortunate that she was not shown the dorm where I would be living or allowed the opportunity to meet any of the staff that would be directly in charge of looking after me.

As Mom was on a fact-finding mission, the minimal glimpses into the place and the priest's sly looks caused her concern but since she had been assured by the Mother Superior that her kids would receive a good education while still being close to our home, she buried her unease at the actions of the priest.

So, at the age of five, in 1958, I was duly enrolled at St. Anne's.

St. Anne's Residential School. Extract. Source: Archives Deschâtelets-NDC, Fonds Deschâtelets, Fort Albany residential school.

CHAPTER TWO:
RON IS ENROLLED IN ST. ANNE'S RESIDENTIAL SCHOOL

THE DAY I WAS ENROLLED at St. Anne's changed my life. Mom got me up early, made me breakfast one last time, and dressed me in my Sunday best. Then with a big sigh, she took hold of my hand while Dad picked up my sister Lou in his arms. We then all walked out of the safety of our white picket fence and down to the river to our big, trusted, grey freighter canoe to journey to St. Anne's.

Although the fresh fall air was invigorating, the purpose of the trip dulled any excitement of a family excursion. This was to be my first day of school, but also because of the distance (about five miles upriver), arrangements had been made for me to live at the school. I was leaving home to live somewhere else for the first time.

Mom took her place in the canoe with her head bowed in an act of resignation, maybe even praying, her pensive look indicating the pain and concern she was feeling for the decision that had been made.

I was also apprehensive, filled with fear and dread of the unknown, but what could I do? At my young age, I just saw life through my eyes. The situation I faced was bigger than I could comprehend – I did not understand why I had to leave home. Why could I not just stay home and be taught by Mom and Dad? Obviously, I had lots of questions and uncertainty, but I had no say in the matter.

I stood on the dock, waiting for Dad to help me take my place, but first he lifted the heavy red gas tank into the canoe, connecting it to the motor with one smooth, skillful motion. His movements were not lost on me. Would I ever get to learn all that Dad knew? Was being sent away to school marking the end for me as a member of the family? I looked for any emotions coming from him that might indicate that he was sad about me leaving home, but he just concentrated on preparing for the trip. Likely he was just trying to look strong for us all, but I wasn't quite sure. Wasn't Dad all-powerful, after all? Why could he not just let me stay at home?

Preparations now complete, Dad picked me up and lowered me into the canoe beside my little bag of clothes. I clutched at the bag as if seeking comfort, but there was none. For some reason, I had not been allowed to bring any toys with me, not even my stuffed guard dog.

Dad then pushed the canoe out into the river, and with his cigarette firmly clenched in his teeth, began yanking on the starter cord of the motor. His actions were slow and deliberate, taking great care to coil the cord just right so as not to get it tangled. Each time he yanked, I prayed that the cord would break, but unfortunately, it held firm. Then, with one extra powerful pull, the motor came to life, its roar punctuating the moment for us all. We proceeded out into the flow of the river with the smell of gasoline and cigarette smoke filling the air.

I knelt on the floor of the canoe, my little head peeking out like a chick about to leave its nest for the first time. My sister Lou, nestled between Mom's knees, observed me with her all-knowing stare, still too young, at three years of age, to be considered for school herself.

The loud roar of the motor prevented any conversation, so we all just sat in silence, alone with our thoughts. Maybe it was just as well, as it allowed the wind whistling through my hair to catch my attention. I welcomed the wind and its soothing effects. There was a comforting gentleness to it, but also a strength in its buffeting that shook at me as if trying to wake me up. The thought came to mind that the wind might actually be alive. This playful interaction helped distract me from my concerns, and I began to feel a sense of internal peace – perhaps like the kind where wisdom is born.

Eventually I emerged from this peaceful state of mind, a place without time, and wondered if I had been daydreaming or experiencing something bigger – like a vision. Where could such an immediate feeling of peace have come from? This glimpse came from somewhere beyond my years, and I hung onto it like a token of comfort, a little potion of strength, from unknown origins as we journeyed onward.

I wanted to let Dad know what I had discovered, but since I was still not sure what it was and the extent of its power, I thought better of it. I was concerned he might think I had just been daydreaming. Heaven forbid! I always had to guard against daydreaming because Dad did not like it when I did. Although this felt like something more, the sound of the motor was too loud anyway to even attempt to describe the experience. This would just have to be my secret power, but I hoped I could activate it again if and when I might need to.

We continued up the river, over water smooth as glass, skimming past wilderness so unique to the North, each tree twisted and shaped from its struggle for survival. As those tortured trees passed before me, I felt a strange connection to them, given my state of mind and concern for the future. They were disturbed, deformed, but defiant in the face of unyielding power and were now the remains of the struggle with their lot in life. They took their place in the distance as our canoe motored onwards, leaving just a trail of swirling reflections in the water, the only hint of our passing.

Then, from somewhere ahead, the river exploded into a flurry of frenzied movement as a flock of geese scrambled to avoid us. High-pitched honks echoed over the water like an early warning system of some sort, snapping me out of my thoughts. Pushing past them with the roar of our twelve-horsepower motor, we continued on our way.

Travelling on the Albany River toward St. Anne's, with the tortured trees in the background.

We travelled past Anderson Island, then around the curve of the river, passing the early-warning military radar site and then a further mile south to our destination. Years later, I learned that this radar site had been established by the government to protect us by watching the skies for the enemy. I wish now that they had been watching the land for the enemy that was hiding in the school right beside them.

We came ashore on the south side of the river, in front of St. Anne's, and tied up our canoe. Dad lifted me out and set me carefully on the rock-studded muddy shore while Mom cautioned me to be careful not to get my little shoes dirty. I noticed that some of the rocks looked strangely like the white, bleached bones of some long-dead animal.

We walked hand in hand up the riverbank past the sawmill on our left, its big scary saw screeching and filling the air with a sense of danger. The sound travelled with us as we walked across the grounds toward the school, its high-pitched screech sounding like another warning. It was so unsettling, but there was no turning back. With our emotions controlled as much as possible and me full of five-year-old dread, we walked across the little foot bridge in front of the school and up to the big front door. When we crossed that bridge that day, our lives would be changed forever, and not for the better.

Tony:

"I read a passage from Dante that said, 'Lose all hope ye who enter these gates.'
That would have been an appropriate sign over that bridge."

The bridge in front of St. Anne's. Extract. Source: Archives Deschâtelets-NDC, Fonds Deschâtelets, Fort Albany residential school.

As we entered the school, we were confronted by a noticeable rotten stench. It was a foul smell, similar to our outhouse back home, but it was everywhere. It bit into my senses. I caught my breath as we waited for someone to greet us.

A few girls – all Native and of various ages – stood in the gloomy dark hallway. It was odd how silent they were. As a young child used to playing freely, I thought it odd that they were just standing around, some leaning against the walls, as if they had no place to go and had nothing to do. Some of them seemed to melt into the background through lack of movement, as if trying to hide. The girl closest to us in the hallway, about twelve years old, offered a friendly, welcoming smile and a little wave. Then, with a slight spring in her walk, she came toward us like an unofficial greeter. It looked like she had been waiting for someone – maybe even someone special. I wondered if she knew that we were important people from the HBC trading post.

A white woman then appeared, dressed in a light-blue and white uniform. She greeted us with smiles and showed us into a room by the front door. There were two Native girls (a little older than me) in the room, who she shooed out with a hushed command, promising them that they could return later to play.

This woman was very personable and friendly but appeared to be rushed, as if she had lots of chores to do. There was a cross hanging from her neck, which I presumed meant that she was a nun of some sort. There were also a number of badges pinned on her uniform, including a badge with a red cross on it, that I found intriguing. She did not seem comfortable in that uniform and pulled at the sleeves, as if it were a new stiff dress that she was not used to wearing.

She was a surprisingly big woman – not fat, just big and wholesome looking. I also noticed how energetic and caring she was, sort of like our mother. This made me feel that she must be okay and well-meaning. Sadly, not all the nuns I was to meet there had this quality.

It's surprising how much a child can remember when faced with uncertainty and looking for signs and signals for the sake of self-preservation. I would soon learn that there were different kinds of nuns with different duties at St. Anne's. These friendly nuns were like their public relations nuns.

The nun offered chairs to Mom and Dad and got directly to business with friendly but direct questions, while my sister Lou and I were left to stew on our own. The room was a children's playroom of sorts, multipurpose, with items in disarray; indeed, it looked like a confused, unhappy, and dusty place. It had a heaviness to it. It did not have the same warm, golden light as our home. Here, the light was stark and cold, like the interior of our HBC store, a place of business. The few toys strewn around were worn and scratched, their colours fading away. They looked like old, tired workhorses waiting to be put out of their misery, and their condition gave clear warnings to me that something was not quite right.

Since I came from a relatively modern home at the HBC post, the decor and construction of the room was not unusual to me, but the odour in the air, the lifeless, worn toys, and the businesslike manner of the nun were of such great concern that I began to feel a mounting sense of dread.

As the adults talked in serious tones, the nun looked toward me with a critical eye, as if evaluating me. I had seen that look before. It was the same kind that Dad had when grading furs at the store. This realization only heightened my already fearful state of mind, and I began to feel trapped. I experienced a mounting shortness of breath, to the point of choking, like an animal caught in a snare. I thought of animals caught in snares, whose skins were then brought into our HBC store for trade.

I wished in that moment that I knew how to be invisible, or at least be able to summon the power of the wind to calm me down, but none of my child magic powers came to my aid in that moment. Fearful thoughts exploded in my mind, thickening and trickling through me, paralyzing me. I stood in shock, about to pee my pants. The thought crossed my mind that if I peed my pants, I might not be worth keeping, and then I might get to go home.

My mother must have sensed the extent of my fear. She and I had a very close, intuitive emotional bond. Thankfully, she took a moment and came over to comfort me and calm me down. She led me to a crudely made rocking horse and suggested I get on it, which offered a distraction. The movement of the horse helped loosen up the fear hardening in my joints.

This was my first rocking horse ride ever, and yet I knew how to ride it as if a natural understanding kicked in. Kids have the ability to know just what to do when playing with toys, even unfamiliar ones, if given the chance. Realizing that I could move forward by rocking with extra force, I rocked over to where my sister Lou was on another rocker and whispered my plan to escape. Together we began rocking ever so slowly toward the door. Little did I know at the time that I and many other students would feel the urge to escape.

As I neared the door, the nun jumped out of her chair with surprising speed to catch me. I looked around for support, but neither Mom nor Dad came to my aid. They just sat there as if under the command of the nun. Dad told me to behave and calm down, and Mom tried to console me with words of comfort, but from afar.

Feeling more alone than ever now, and looking for any kind of help, I began rocking that wooden horse closer to Mom as subtly but as quickly as possible. Although I knew Dad cared, I thought Mom was the best bet to hear my pleas. As it turned out, my efforts were in vain. I was still too young to understand what was being discussed by the adults, but I sensed that I was about to be abandoned to this nun.

When the moment came, it was sudden. The nun knelt down and put her arm around me as I reached out to my parents. I managed to escape her hold and grab at my parents' clothes as they prepared to leave. As I cried and hung on, my hands were gently but firmly unpeeled. Then the nun's demeanour changed and became firmer and hurried, as if she had no more time for us. She tried to mask this with smiles, but I knew what was happening by her unyielding grasp. She was trying to separate me from Mom and Dad – but I still resisted. I was surprised at myself for grabbing onto my parents, as I had never in my life demonstrated so much physical expression before.

Then another more aggressive nun (who I refer to now as an "enforcer" nun), entered the room. She was older than the first nun. It was all business with her. Even the look of her black uniform meant business. She lost no time in swooping up behind me and sinking her fingernails into my arms and shoulders in one controlling grip, while she flashed a toothy, reassuring smile at my parents. The pain from her claws clutching me with unspoken aggression was a shock. There was something threatening, insensitive, and perhaps even evil here.

As this nun held me firmly, Dad, with Lou in his arms, kneeled down to give me a hug. He then told me to be good and made his exit with Lou. Then Mom wrapped her arms around me as I began to shake from crying. I could feel her loving support enveloping me like a protective blanket of love, as only mothers are able to do. With both of us now sobbing, and with a promise to come and visit me soon, she pulled herself away and was gone.

Then the nice, friendly PR nun said goodbye and disappeared, leaving me in the business grip of the enforcer nun. I was never to see that friendly nun again. The mean nun began to propel me down the hall with her claws still firmly clutching my shoulder. She was an adult, so I knew I was supposed to obey her. But it was such a dark and stinky place that I naturally dug in my heels, fighting against her unyielding grip dragging me into that black hole. I was so terrified. Was I just acting like a little hellion again or did I have grounds to fight her? I just did not know the right thing to do at that moment.

The nun was no-nonsense and had an agenda to follow that left very little consolation for a young, confused, and traumatized child.

My struggles must have triggered her meanness because she abruptly stopped and gave me two hard whacks on my bottom. It was my first spanking ever, and the force sent me forward and off balance. Her grip on my arm and her strength kept me from stumbling to the floor. It was a shock, and I was jolted with the realization that my freedom was being stripped from me.

The fear of being skinned alive came to mind. I had never experienced such an attack before, and coming from the HBC trading post, all I could think of was the shock the animals must have felt when caught in traps prior to being brought into the HBC all perfectly stretched into shape.

But I did not want to be changed. I wanted to be just the way I was. I tried to wiggle out of her grip, fighting with all of my little strength. I banged up against the wings of her head bonnet and felt it crumple a bit as its starch cracked under my weight like the wings of a dragonfly being crushed. This roused her anger even more. She took hold of my left ear and wrenched it around while pulling me forward. The searing pain in my ear burned itself forever into my memory.

This incident would mark the point at which I was pulled kicking and screaming into the folds of St. Anne's.

CHAPTER THREE:
ALONE

EVERYTHING WAS HAPPENING SO FAST now that I could not keep up with all the shocks to my system and sensibilities. I tried to summon my courage and find some sort of comfort from within, but the physical struggles had heightened my agitation to the point of no control. I could not calm down. Through it all came the crystal-clear understanding that I was being imprisoned in a controlling, confining, and stinking place.

The nun propelled me up the stairs and into the boys' dormitory. There looked to be about one hundred little beds with metal frames packed tightly together, with all the beds positioned in tight rows, each covered with uniform white bed coverings. It looked like a very strict and lifeless place. In my child-like mind, it seemed like a place for kids who were sick or who had been bad, but it felt more like a prison, given the treatment I had received.

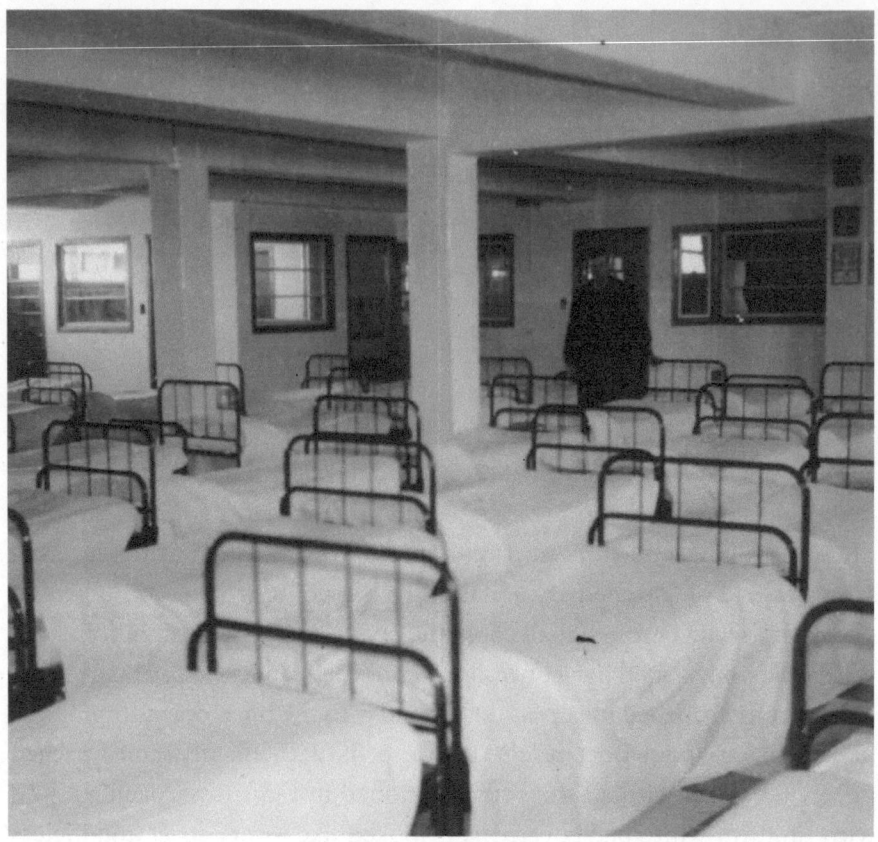

The boys' dorm at St. Anne's. Source: Archives Deschâtelets-NDC, Fonds Deschâtelets, Fort Albany residential school.

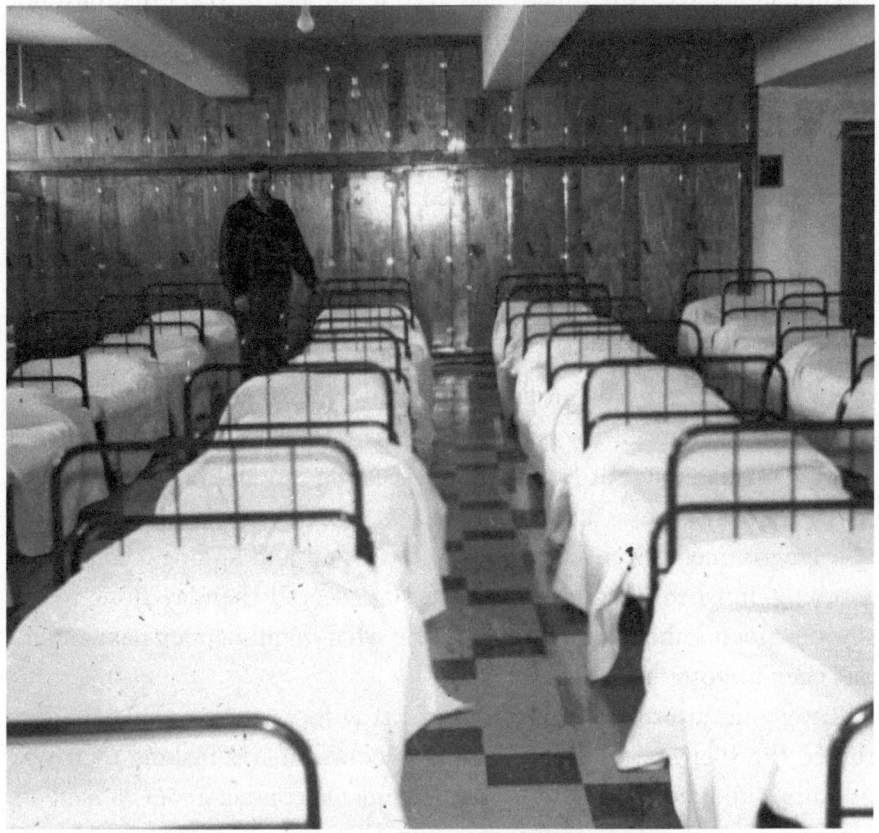

The boys' dorm at St. Anne's. Source: Archives Deschâtelets-NDC, Fonds Deschâtelets, Fort Albany residential school.

With her fingernails firmly dug in, the nun led me to one of the beds in the centre of the room and told me to sit and calm down. I sank onto the bed feeling vulnerable and frightened. I wondered what would happen next. It was overwhelming.

I noticed that the nun was breathing heavily and sweating from her struggle with me. I was glad to see her discomfort. It showed me she was vulnerable and human after all – and I had gotten through her defences. With a stern command to lie on the bed, the nun left me to my thoughts.

I lay there for a long time, as if suffering with an illness. I had been ripped out of my family and transplanted into a foreign, confining environment full of antiseptic and horrid smells. There was also a deafening unfamiliar silence. It felt like I had aged a number of years that day, but I was still only five years old. All I had to hold onto was the memory of Mom's promise to come and visit me. I sucked on this thought to help calm me down.

Sometime later, a nun dressed in white and carrying a glass of milk swished in and glided over to my bed as if floating on air and asked if I was feeling better now. I looked at her in disbelief. I was confused. She was nicer, compared to the brute who had dragged me into the dorm. (It seemed to me that the nuns dressed in white were nicer than the nuns dressed in black.) However, I did not know who to trust after the trauma of my morning's enrolment. I just looked away, resigned. She set the glass of milk on the floor by my bed and withdrew. It was a comforting gesture and I appreciated it, but I was not in a trusting mood. I just stared at the milk for a long time, as a puppy might react when being introduced into a new environment. Eventually, I began to sip at it and finding it somewhat soothing, finished it right down to the last drop. I then lay alone in the silence for a number of hours, wondering what might happen next and if I had been forgotten.

Later that afternoon, the sound of many footsteps on the stairs disrupted the silence. I presumed it was my dorm mates making their way upstairs, and braced myself for the unavoidable contact about to happen. Uncertain whether to lie still or stand up, I sat up and waited.

Aside from the sound of their footsteps, it was surreal how quiet and subtle their entrance was. About one hundred boys – all Native – of various ages, shapes, and sizes came in, but without speaking. Their combined pent-up power was noticeable, and their silence was unnatural and even frightening to me. I was used to talking and even being loud and boisterous back home if I felt like it – unless I was sad or afraid. Could all these boys be sad or afraid? The situation did not seem normal.

As they filed in, I tensed for what might happen. Although there were some surprised looks as they saw a lone, little white boy sitting on a bed in the middle of their dorm room, they did not threaten me. All eyes were on me, though, and some of the more aggressive ones pointed at me and snickered, which made me feel very small and vulnerable.

I realized at that moment that I was no longer protected by the power of the HBC or my parents. That realization almost made me throw up. Up to that time in my life, I was used to playing in my own yard with just my sisters. Since we three were the only "white" kids for about one hundred miles around, I was not used to associating with any kids other than my two sisters.

Now, here I was in the same dorm with about one hundred Native boys and no fence to separate us; no fence to protect me, as I had enjoyed back home. I did not know what to do. Was I to be their victim? Was I to be their prisoner? Or was I like them now, whatever that meant? I was at a loss.

From my previous conditioning, we were not to mix, and yet here I was being mixed in with the very people that I had come to understand as inferior. This truly magnified my sense of abandonment and confusion that day. It was also the day, though, that I was to begin a long path to gaining an understanding and empathy for the plight of these people.

Although the boys were relatively quiet, the force of so many children in one room enveloped me, not so much like an embrace but more like a shockwave. I was scared and felt alone and different than these Native boys, pressed into a strange and controlling world where mean-spirited women in weird-looking outfits had treated me so roughly.

Who was I now? What was I now? How was I expected to act? How was I to fit into this group, my first group ever? I was overwhelmed. I needed a hiding place at that moment, but there wasn't one anywhere in that dorm room.

Quiet Time

As I struggled with this anxiety, the boys claimed their assigned beds. Although their skin and hair colour were different from mine, their actions caught my attention. Some of the older, bigger boys pushed some of the younger boys around playfully, but firmly. Thankfully, they did not focus their attention on me, though I felt no peace of mind.

Some of the younger boys about my age began to make their way through the maze of beds toward me. A few of them greeted me with simple words like "hey" and "hi," as they climbed up onto their beds. Others just looked at me or disregarded me.

Then one of them asked me the inevitable question: "Where you from?"

"The HBC post," I answered. He replied with a shrug of his shoulders, as if it didn't matter, or he didn't understand. I felt relieved and deflated all at the same time. I must have been accepted at that moment, though, because the boys did not challenge me. I was relieved. The nun in the room then clapped her hands sharply and, as if on command, all the boys lay down on their beds, and some even assumed a prone, face-down position. I was used to having quiet time back home when I was upset about something or had done something bad, and yet here everyone was lying down. Could it be that they had all been bad, or that they were all upset at the same time? This quiet time, I was to learn, was a regular occurrence when the boys were expected to decompress from the activities of the day.

I noted that no one had asked my name. I was to learn that names were not important in such an environment. Expressions of empathy were more important. A name was a badge, a label, and in such an environment, the less known the better, so names were avoided. They were dangerous labels. That sense of nonentity would continue as I disappeared into that mass of boys, to be stirred only by the routine that I would come to experience that controlled our lives. I cannot remember ever hearing my name in that school.

I followed the movements of my dorm mates and lay down on my bed as well. However, there was obviously a rule in place because they also put their pillows over their heads. I did the same, with my eyes open under my pillow, listening intently for a hint of what activity was to come next. It seemed like a strange rule to me. Maybe it was a game, like hide-and-seek. But it was different. I could hear a nun warning everyone to keep their heads covered, and occasionally she would yell at one of the boys who obviously wasn't doing it right. I hoped I was. We were now motionless under our pillows.

About half an hour later, the game, or whatever it was, came to an end when the nun clapped her hands and shouted to us all to get to our feet. She then directed us to get into line with the youngest at the front. With loud, sharp handclaps, the nun spurred us all forward, and we trouped downstairs for dinner.

After my shock at my first experience with the food there, which I will describe later on, we were herded through a confusing maze of hallways and stairs to the chapel for evening prayers. Not knowing what to expect, I just followed the others, swept along according to the agenda of the moment.

Upon entering the chapel, an intense smell of incense stung my senses and disoriented me. It was like time stood still, and I was unexpectedly transported out of myself. After all, this was a holy place where one came to pray and be with the Almighty – so some disorientation was to be expected. It was also comforting, though, because it reminded me of the rich smell of linseed oil back home when I visited my dad in the HBC store. In my child's mind, I would come to regard the chapel, with its unique smell, as a place of business where we came to visit God, the Almighty Father.

The attitude of the nuns who had acted like our guards changed, and their focus toward us kids softened, like we were more of one body and mind now. The mood of some of the boys changed from resignation to anticipation as they focussed on the girls' side of the chapel, as if looking for someone.

I was to learn that they were brothers and sisters stealing a glance at each other, hoping to keep their family bonds somehow alive. So much can be communicated in the blink of an eye, in a look, even from afar. No one dared to wave, though. I did not understand until later that it was against the rules to talk or even wave at loved ones. I wished I could have just seen my sisters, even if it was from across the aisle in the chapel, but they were not enrolled in the school yet, which made me feel even lonelier. I felt their absence and wondered how long it would be until I would get to see them, if ever.

After experiencing a mixture of singing and praying in various languages: Latin, English, and Cree, we were herded back to our dorm in a long, silent line. I just followed along ... there had been no orientation, so I watched for any clue that would inform me what I was to do next.

I do not remember much else from that first day at the school. After the terror of my arrival, the horrid food, praying for forgiveness for my five-year-old sins, the washroom, and saying bedtime prayers, I was tired out. I crawled under the unfamiliar blanket on my bed to drift off to sleep. I was to learn that sleep provided a way of escape from this prison, a time to imagine home and loved ones. We were essentially inmates, but because of our ages we were really just a mass of whimpering puppies, most brown in colour, except for one little white one, all feeling pain and loss, all just wanting to go home.

As I drifted off to sleep that first night, the significance of how the beds were arranged did not hold any meaning to me, with the youngest and most vulnerable in the middle of the room. Eventually, I was to learn that another world came alive at night, and being in the centre of the dorm with the others of my age was likely the safest place to be.

CHAPTER FOUR:
MORNINGS AT ST. ANNE'S

IN THE EARLY MORNING, WHILE all were still quiet and sleeping, I would sometimes dream that I was back at my home and in my own bedroom. While enjoying such a peaceful dream, the dorm would suddenly erupt like all holy hell was exploding. This happened each day with the clanging of a big handheld bell by our dorm supervisor, Anna Wesley.

The sound of the bell was so sudden and intense that it jolted us all out of our sleepy state, leaving us momentarily stunned. Then, for added measure, another nun would start smacking two wooden paddles together, making a hideous clacking noise that sounded like an unfortunate, trapped, wounded bird. The combination of the bell, the clacking, plus the yelling from these nuns to "get up, up, up" was a horrendous experience. It also set a tone for the day.

This was not like getting up at home, where one might enjoy the sunlight bathing one's bedroom or smell the glorious smells of breakfast. Here, life was institutionalized, basic, and strict, which did not leave any room to enjoy the day's arrival.

As Tony would later recount:

"A typical day in the life of the boys would begin at 7:00 a.m. with the maniacal ringing of a handheld bell by Anna Wesley, and the bright incandescent light bulbs coming on. It was expected and strictly enforced that us children would immediately assume a kneeling position on our beds. Any

child not quick enough to assume the prayer position would
be immediately slapped around."

For some who were not quick enough, the supervisor would stop by their bedside and ring that hated bell above their head. She seemed to enjoy torturing some of the slower ones in this way, sometime even smiling as if it was a game, before administering a morning slap. The first slap was usually on their bottoms. Then she would shake their shoulder and administer more slaps and spanks if necessary. I looked away when hearing such slaps. Some of the boys were much bigger than this relatively small woman, and yet no one ever challenged her. Shaking that bell while all prim and proper in her perfectly starched religious uniform, she appeared to be backed by the power of God Almighty himself – not to mention the unspoken threat of a leather belt or some such punishment waiting behind closed doors for anyone who objected too much. Her position and presumption of power allowed her to act with impunity.

One would think that given the importance of such tasks as snapping to a prayer position on our beds, newcomers like myself would have had some prior warning, some sort of orientation of what was expected of them – but no, we had the added pressure and fear that we might miss any hint of what to do and be punished as a result. I am reminded of the few times my dorm mate beside me would give my bed a shake to get me moving before the supervisor spotted me.

There were times when I would have preferred to just stay in bed because I was not feeling well but thought better of it for fear of receiving one of those wake-up slaps. I was to learn that we had to get out of bed no matter how sick we were, unless it was life threatening like measles, chicken pox, or mumps. (See "The Quality of Care" further on in the book, which describes how the unfortunate ones who had these diseases were cared for.)

Once all of us hundred or so boys were assembled in the prayer position on our beds – like little soldiers of God at attention – we began saying our Hail Marys and the Lord's Prayer out loud in Cree. The supervisor walked along the rows of beds, listening for any mistakes and ready to give us hell if necessary. We were expected to say these prayers as loudly as possible

30

for her to hear, which made it feel more like a chore than an act of reverence. Not knowing Cree or even all the words, my prayers all came out in a mumble. I feared I would be slapped for just mumbling, but the sounds of the other boys and my alert kneeling position must have saved me from her scrutiny.

Upon finishing our prayers, we proceeded row by row to the bathroom to wash ourselves and brush our teeth. The boys' washroom was surprisingly clean and designed to process a lot of little kids efficiently. It had an industrial smell of Javex and a hint of soap. Even though it was clean, it certainly was not the comfortable, "old English" smelling bathroom that I was used to back home. However, it turned out to be the freshest-smelling area for us boys, and I came to appreciate it.

The attention to our hygiene was a priority in the morning. Washing our hands and faces and brushing our teeth was encouraged. We also had the option to shower. Showering was a relief for me, as it helped to soothe some of my troubled thoughts. Mixing with all the brown bodies in the steamy washroom each morning was a challenge for me initially because it was a reminder that I was different and might not belong there. I was a minority and would try to keep myself covered in my pajamas right to the last minute, when I would slip into the privacy of one of the shower stalls.

While in the privacy of a steamy shower, as if hiding in a waterfall, I would drift away and imagine my past again. Yells from the nuns to "hurry up" would disrupt my thoughts, though, leaving little opportunity to drift away for long.

Some of the other boys taking showers would also stay in longer than it took to wash – like me, snatching a few minutes to be alone with their thoughts. Others seemed to walk in and out of the showers as if mindless of the opportunity to escape, even for just a moment. They just plodded through the mist wearing masks of stunned resignation on their faces. Likely, these were the ones already ground down from the controlling environment. If one looked closely, though, they still had the physical tension of a coiled spring in their walk – the mark of a hunter – but the spirit seemed to be absent in their eyes.

Wallowing in one's emotions was a luxury. Over time, most of our sense of identity would be washed away, leaving us all empty and numb inside to varying degrees. We were under constant pressure to hurry up in the washroom because the rest of the boys were waiting for their turn to wash up.

I detested being herded around without any say in the matter. It was the lack of power and loss of status that troubled me the most. No one seemed to acknowledge my privileged background there. My connection with the HBC counted for nothing and might even be a mark against me.

I was now mixed in with the very people who I had been conditioned to regard as somehow subservient and now I even had to wait in line with these same people to just wash myself in the washroom.

I was expected to bend to the rules and not question or challenge anything. Like all the other boys, I was expected to say "yes" to everything. There was no tolerance for anyone who tried to say "no."

My loss of status felt unbearable to me. Of course, I had no way of knowing the extent of what the other boys had lost, but I could identify with the fact that we had all lost our freedom and were missing home. However, it felt so maddening to me that no one around me seemed to care or know who I was. On the one hand, I did not want to fit in and felt that I was still entitled to the rights and privileges of the local HBC, but on the other, I did not want to stand out.

It is ironic that I was fighting the controlling atmosphere of St. Anne's while at the same time enjoying the benefits offered there. The fact that the residence had flush toilets and running taps and showers was a luxury and another indication to me that this Roman Catholic school might be more powerful than the HBC. It was more than we had at home, where Mom had to carry all the water.

This was my internal dilemma. I was fighting to keep my individuality, my status, my memories of home, and would revisit them each time in the privacy of the shower, while all around me there was an insensitivity to personal feelings and a push to make us kids all the same.

Upon finishing our business in the washroom, we proceeded to our little lockers to change into our clothes for the day. Thankfully, I had the few clothes that Mom had packed for me, which gave me a tangible sense of home every time I opened my locker door. I would rub the fabric a little as I was putting them on in order to feel the essence of home for a moment again. I did this secretly, for fear they might be taken away from me if it was discovered I still treasured something special from the past. Others were not so fortunate.

> **Tony:**
>
> *"Our clothes, for the most part, came from donations sent from Catholic charities in the South, so the kids were dressed in all manner of cast-off clothing ... Our lockers in the boys' dorm were only meant for our pajamas, towel, and toothbrush, and that's where we would also hang up our day clothes before going to bed. We never personally owned anything except for rosary beads, which we mostly kept in our pockets so we would always be on a moment's notice ready to pull them out and start saying our Hail Marys and Our Father prayers. Oh yeah, we also kept holy pictures in our lockers, which were given to us on special holidays and which we would trade amongst ourselves (much like kids down south were trading baseball cards). Some of these cards were very ornate, so they traded for much more than a regular Virgin Mary or Saint Whoever card."*

As we boys concentrated on getting ready for the day, the nuns would continue to spur us on with constant shouts and handclaps. It was confusing to me that Anna Wesley, the boys' supervisor and the symbol of authority, was Native. And though there was usually a white nun helping her in the mornings to get us boys ready, this nun did not appear to have any administrative power over Anna Wesley. She did not even display any outward acknowledgment of me as being similar to her in colour. She just treated me like the rest of the boys.

St. Anne's Residential School may have attempted to make us all the same – like good, little Christians in the image of the white culture – but I think it was when we trouped out of that washroom with all our dirt washed away that we were as close as we would ever come to being of one mind. We were clean, smelled the same, and hungry. But first we had to line up, with the youngest in the front of the line, and troupe down to the "prison" chapel for morning prayers.

Tony:

"Everything we did entailed having to line up with the smaller kids in front and the bigger kids at the back. During lineups, it was strictly forbidden to talk or look sideways as at all times we had to look straight ahead with our arms at the side. As like any prison, these lineups were a big part of our day from dawn to dusk, but being little brown prisoners, we quickly had to adapt to this degradation or receive a good beating."

Our dorm supervisor would accompany us on our march, taking every opportunity to remind us that she was in control, with shouts and sharp hand claps. Walking to chapel was not all that complicated, but she still felt the need to make her presence known especially when we passed by the area of confusion where there was construction going on at the time.

The loud bangs and yells from the construction workers were a welcome relief from the yells of our supervisor. It was a joy listening to her struggle to be heard, as if her authority was being challenged. I also noticed that the workers were not bothered by her yelling, which offered some insight that she might not be as powerful as she would like us to believe.

When we were all finally seated in chapel, we boys enjoyed a little reprieve from the scrutiny and wrath of our supervisor, who watched as we prayed for the forgiveness of our sins. Most of the prayers were said in Cree and English, with some Latin – but at the time, it sounded like just a whole bunch of mumbo jumbo to me. It left me wondering why it was so important to get up so early to participate in such a chore. In spite of my confusion, and in fear of being reprimanded, I tried to follow along with the rest of the kids in these languages I did not know. I still wasn't sure if I believed in God, but I hoped that he believed in me and would at least appreciate my efforts.

Concentrating on the business of praying, though, felt like a chore to me. Boredom would sneak up on me, and I would loose track of time until there was a stirring in the group as everyone began to stand up, indicating that the torture was finally over.

Tony:

"At 8:00 a.m., we would file out of the chapel to head to our mess hall for our daily gruel of porridge and tea."

On the way, we kids had to walk past thick, delicious smells hanging in the air like forbidden pleasures – hinting of bacon, eggs, and buttered toast. This came from the nuns' dining room, but their door was never open, so we could only imagine the good food we were missing. I tried not to notice, though, as a strategy for my emotional survival.

Sometimes, in an act of defiant anger, I even clamped my nose shut with my little fingers as I passed that cursed place that so clearly demonstrated the reality of our lives and reminded me of my past. I was not part of the land of plenty any longer; it was like an evil force had closed that door. It began to dawn on me that the nuns' dining room door was like our white picket fence back home; the social border between the "haves" and the "have nots."

That is not to say that I thought that all the nuns there were mean or bad; only that whoever was in charge was not allowing us such pleasures. Obviously, we kids were not entitled to any of that good food, so had no choice but to continue on our way. A little further down the hallway was the entrance to our dining room, where a nun stood guard making sure we kids were organized in two lines: boys on one side, girls on the other. Boys and girls were not allowed to sit together. The boys and girls each had their own area, with a divider in between. We sat on long benches with nuns standing guard in each section of the room.

Then they served the slop, or what was called "porridge" but was a very thin gruel, uninspired, and the most basic of nourishment. Our bowls were of various colours including blue, white, pink, and yellow melamine. A staff member would dump the watery slop into our bowls as if we were on an assembly line. I felt the indignity of the treatment. I now know we were just numbers, and each number meant more income for the Catholic Church in return for our care.

Occasionally we were fed a big cod-liver oil pill for our health. It sat on top of our slop like a little, brown, shiny egg. If one was not careful, one could gag on it, but the slimy porridge helped us swallow the thing.

The porridge was terrible. It tasted like snot, and sometimes you couldn't keep it down. We were provided brown sugar with the porridge though, which helped quite a bit to mask the putrid taste. The nuns that monitored us expected us to eat any food in our bowls. Some enforced this rule more than others. Our supervisor, Anna Wesley, was the worst when she was on duty.

Tony:

"Any child feeling sick and on the verge of throwing up, would have the beginning of a truly bad day, as we were expected to eat whatever was put in front of us. As often happened, the child would vomit, and for some perverse reason, Anna Wesley would go into a towering rage and force this unfortunate child to lick up his vomit. Of course, all of us children would be looking at this in great horror and were greatly terrified to say the least. But, after many years there, you begin to accept this as another normal day in hell."

I tried not to look up when the puking and gagging erupted around me. I feared that seeing another boy's vomit would make me throw up as well.

I would come to call the room where we ate by many names, as did the other students, depending on our mood and our experience with the meal. However, I never called that room a "dining room" ever again, after my first experience of seeing a kid having to lick up his vomit.

On rare occasions, we got to enjoy a change from the porridge with some kind of fried meat, which we kids enjoyed much more than the porridge.

Tony:

"Our morning slop fest would usually be porridge or fried spam. ... There was never enough food. If it was relatively desirable, there was not much of it at all, and it was handed out in small portions. No kid was fat; indeed, we must have all looked like skinny gulag inmates."

A Breath of Fresh Air

With the foul taste of snot in our mouths from the porridge, we boys would then file out to the play yard for a breath of fresh air. The girls likely experienced a similar routine on their side of the building.

Tony:

"After breakfast, we would be let out in the yard, where at least we were away from the staff and would be able to talk amongst ourselves. Prior to that, we had done everything in silence, so the first opportunity for us to talk was in the yard. I must mention that from the time we were awaken to the time we were let out in the yard, all was done with great military precision and no time wasted."

One might think that being in a Christian place, we boys would have seen ourselves as little soldiers of God, feeling empowered to speak and sing out, but it certainly did not feel like it. We felt more like prisoners being herded around by guards who, from their shouts and yells, considered us inconvenient, to say the least.

The yard was so uninspiring. I did not even try to use my imagination as I had done in my yard back home to figure out some playful activity to do. Here the grounds were dead; nothing grew, and our movements were now reduced to just kicking the odd stone back and forth. Like prisoners, we boys just shuffled back and forth mindlessly, but at least we were getting fresh air to start our day.

I usually kept to myself at those times, and rarely talked to anyone in depth, expressing solidarity among my little group with just nods and whispers. If we broke our silence, it was usually a hushed warning that we had seen a mean staff member or a bully roaming about, but usually we didn't talk much. There was never a conversation with anyone about anything of depth, to get to know each other, or even who I was; it was like it didn't matter. I was a prisoner like the rest, and being so young and small, I had no choice but to just assume my place with the others of my size and concentrate on breathing in some fresh air.

The barren and desolate boys' play yard at St. Anne's on the right side of the building. With no toys in sight, it was just a place for us little prisoners to get some fresh air. Extract. Source: Archives Deschâtelets-NDC, Fonds Deschâtelets, Fort Albany residential school.

The boys' play area on the left side of the building, (looking east) with the nursing station building and nuns' residence (with the barn shaped roof) in the background. Source: Archives Deschâtelets-NDC, Fonds Deschâtelets, Fort Albany residential school.

At 8:45 a.m., we were summoned by that hated handheld bell to stop talking, line up again, and stay in rigid formation until the command was given to march back into the building.

Going back inside was always a challenge because of the rotting stench that hit us like a punch – the signature of the hell hole that was our lives. We always made sure to take an extra breath of fresh air before we had to re-enter the building.

The Smell of the Boys' Wing

The smell that permeated the boys' wing of the building was so intense that we never could get used to it. We just had to accept the fact that it was there and brace ourselves against its nauseating impact. This odour caused discomfort and even concern in its aggressiveness. It oozed up through the floor, so intense that it stung one's nose at times; it was beyond just discomfort. I experienced an uneasiness bordering on fear, like something was alive in the depths below us, and in my young mind at the time, I worried that it might be hell and that the devil might be close by. After all, sometimes the staff would point toward the ground when referring to hell so I deduced that the smell was likely coming from that same place.

It was confusing for me at the time to have to face the fact that the devil might be living right below us in the basement of our Christian school. No wonder we had to pray so much.

Years later, I was to learn that the putrid smell that I feared might be hell was actually from the potatoes rotting in the basement.

Tony:

"Once these potatoes were harvested late in the fall, they were stored in large wooden bins in the basement, and these potatoes would do us till about March. However, as the months went by, the potatoes started to rot, and I remember we all had to eat these half-rotten potatoes till they were all gone. That awful stench would never go away."

Mixed with this smell was the scent of bleach. The bleach was from the cleanser on the floors, used in great quantities, likely in an attempt to mask the smell coming up through the floorboards. Although there were reasonable explanations, the combination of these smells suggested that we boys dwelled in the land of the damned.

After filing back in from our play yard, we boys went directly to our lockers to take off our outdoor clothes and boots and put on our indoor shoes. Then we lined up again as our dorm supervisor yelled out instructions, and we were marched to our classrooms for our daily scholastic activities. The constant controlling atmosphere of the place did not help to put one in a learning mood. It likely compromised my ability and desire to learn. Other students suffered in similar ways.

Since we were marched from one activity to the other, I did not really have to bother trying to remember where any place was located. The smells were usually enough to inform me about where I was at any given time. I did not want to be there, so I did not try to figure out where I was.

My focus was more on the immediate concern of following the rules such as: thou shalt not talk, or even question. I acted with a kind of tunnel vision and tried to anticipate the actions of the people around me. I took little notice of the physical layout of the buildings there, but I can remember smells, tastes, some faces, people's moods, and staying away from the bullies. Likely, I was experiencing psychological shock and post-traumatic stress disorder (PTSD), as were the other students to varying degrees.

CHAPTER FIVE:
DAILY LESSONS

SCHOOL STARTED AT 9:00 A.M. We attended six days a week, and Sunday was our day of rest. Our teacher was also a nun, and though scary looking, seemed more caring and interested in us kids than the enforcer nuns we were faced with in our dorm areas.

Although the school was segregated, the classrooms were co-ed. Once the boys were seated, the girls would be marched in to take their seats as well. Sometimes the seating order was the other way around but definitely one sex was seated before the other sex entered the room. Everything was synchronized so the boys and girls would not meet in the hallway or mingle physically in class if at all possible.

Maybe the seating arrangements were different in other classrooms with older kids, but that is what I remember in my classroom.

Such a strict division of the sexes sent a definite message to all of us; that our world was now divided. The natural interaction of the sexes on a day-to-day basis, that is so necessary to develop a healthy sense of social integration, was compromised. The message seemed to be that the girls were somehow alien and unknowable, instead of just people like we boys. Likely the girls had similar thoughts. In my young innocent mind at the time, I was not sure what the game was, but the strict rule of segregation was confusing, given that I had been used to interacting freely with my sisters back home.

Tony:

"Sad how the staff were always worried about the boys and girls ever mingling together. I realized that it was a sex thing, and they did all they could to keep us segregated. However, they didn't seem to have a problem with all the sexual abuse and pedophilia that went on in that institution. The staff certainly knew what was going on but chose to remain quiet about it."

These co-ed classrooms also provided an opportunity for some siblings to see each other, but as I mentioned earlier, interactions between siblings were not encouraged.

I was to learn that segregation in schools was common in Canada at the time, but what made it significantly different and especially hard to bear for us young kids at the residential school was that we did not get to go home and visit with our siblings after school; we only had the option of sneaking a peek at each other when the opportunity presented itself, such as during classes.

Tony:

"Our first lesson of the day would be learning a scripture from the Bible, and this was something that was never deviated from. The nuns who were our teachers, however well-meaning, were very unqualified because their main goal in life was one of prayer; subsequently, they saw no need for us to learn anything much other than prayers. ... Our daily lessons were a mixture of math, geography, history, and English. However, a lot of times we were given more Bible lessons."

Another lesson that made going to school at St. Anne's unique was having to learn to read and write some Cree words. Learning those Cree words was a challenge for me, and I did not take any pleasure in it because I did not consider the language novel or interesting. To me, it was just a collection of signs and symbols that were stitching me into something and someone I did not want to be. I also did not see the point of having to learn Cree at school because I did not speak Cree at home. My mind rebelled. But we had to because some of the religious material was written in Cree. Some of my fellow classmates also voiced an aversion to Cree, likely because they were starting to self-identify as being white. The school was having the desired effect of killing the "Indian" inside them. There were some, though, who still showed obvious interest in learning Cree. Likely they were the kids still trying to hold onto their past.

Tony:

"Unlike residential schools to the south, we learned how to write in our own language of Swampy Cree, and the main reason for this was that we would be able to read all the printed Cree prayers. ...As Fort Albany was very isolated and the local population was all Cree-speaking, the church had no choice but to learn the Cree language if they wanted to spread their religion. Also, the church staff were all French, and their command of the English language was minimal at best. So, a lot of our prayers and songs were in Cree. ...I know from talking to Natives from down south that they were punished for speaking their own language, but in Albany, the church had no choice but to use the local language. This must have rankled a few of them."

Of course, we were not learning the language; we were learning just enough words to understand the literature printed in Cree. We were not speaking Cree in conversation in class. We weren't learning the meanings of the words; we were just doing a translation to understand some religious literature. We were not having Native cultural lessons and learning these words in the context of traditions and actual Native tales. The genocide was still happening because learning those words in the context of English served to unlink the Native kids from their oral history and cultural traditions. Granted, the residential school system of assimilation had been going on for many years already, so there was likely not much "unlinking" left to do, but some of the Native culture still lingered.

Since there was still a lot of animosity and distrust between the Anglican world and the Catholic world up there at the time, and a history of the French and English crashing together still evident from the cannonballs found in the riverbanks, the Catholic Church may have felt that part of winning the territory was to ingratiate themselves with the local Native inhabitants, by printing the Good Book and some pamphlets in Cree. It might have been a hearts and mind campaign.

Although some of the literature may have been in Cree, a lot of their parents didn't speak English worth a damn, and their kids would eventually speak only English and very little Cree. So the link between tomorrow's Cree and their parents was gradually broken as well.

There are many ways of committing genocide and cultural genocide is just one of them. You don't need to kill people. You just have to wait awhile, and then they will all die off. If you want to destroy a culture without a war, I would think that's how you do it – and although I was not aware of it at the time, I was seeing it happen firsthand.

The schools were really conversion camps, with the ultimate goal of making everyone think and act like a white person in Canadian society; at St. Anne's, it was a white Roman Catholic person. So there I was, a northern Anglican boy, white in colour, with a slight understanding of white culture HBC-style, now experiencing the life of Roman Catholicism. Most of my Native classmates had two hurdles to face: becoming white and also Christian, Roman Catholic monastic-style. There was definitely no room for curiosity and debate in such an environment that was designed to make us all the same.

Learning some of the Native culture and heritage at school would have been beneficial to the Native kids, but of course that was not within the agenda of the school.

Instead, we kids had to memorize a lot of religious material. Each day in school was full of excruciating rote learning, repetition, and boredom in what passed as education.

I don't remember learning much of anything there, but maybe that is just as well because it somehow protected me from being sucked dry of individual thought and curiosity.

Although my brain was being filled with useless nonsense, and my voice was being silenced, my eyes still saw. A map of the world hanging on the wall would catch my attention at times. Its subtle message that my existence might not be limited to this classroom or situation was not lost on me. However, although it was a great distraction, it seemed out of place and out of bounds as I struggled against the mind-numbing effects of the lessons. Since curiosity was not encouraged, it did not occur to me to ask about the map, or the world it represented. My world consisted of a few-mile radius of where I was, and that was proving to be complicated enough to comprehend.

Mom recounts that the mother superior of St. Anne's said to her at the time, "Now don't judge the teachers by their Indianness, because they are in fact highly trained teachers." However, what was accepted as normal in the northern Native residential schools such as St. Anne's was not necessarily the norm in the South. This would become especially evident later on when comparing the schooling we were to receive in these two areas. The North would prove to be woefully inadequate when standing beside southern standards, which were designed by whites for whites.

Tony:

"When I first went to a normal school (down south), I was amazed at how smart and outgoing the white kids were compared to me. However, when it came to the Bible and prayer, I was way ahead of them. Hell of a lot of good that did."

(See concluding thoughts at the end of the book on the Quality of Education at St. Anne's.)

Lunch Time

Lunch at St. Anne's was at 12:00 p.m., and although it was a break in our studies, it was not much of a reprieve from the repetition. When we trouped out of the classroom to the mess hall for lunch, it was not with delighted anticipation, but rather with a sense of resignation and even dread of what awaited us there.

The girls would file out of the classroom first, under the watchful eye of our nun teacher, and then we boys would file out to face whatever was waiting for us. This was of course after another round of prayers.

Our usual lunch was some sort of leftover slop from previous meals, but sometimes it was fried spam or a soup with chunks of spam in it.

Tony:

"I am sure the mission must have brought in tons of this stuff as it lasts forever, and what better and easier way was there to feed two hundred boys and girls?"

Maybe these meals were meant well, and though the taste was not totally revolting at times, it was missing any home-cooked quality with love mixed in, which can be so soothing. Lunch was just another constant repetition.

There was one enjoyable food, though, that was served each day: the freshly baked bread, which smelled glorious. It smelled a bit like home. I never considered it on par with Mom's wonderful baking and sweet treats, but it tasted great. I have to admit that the bread was a welcome staple and somewhat of a treat.

It also represented a refreshing freedom in that you could put up your hand to indicate how many slices you wanted. However, if you were in trouble for breaking some rule or if the nun supervising the meal was a mean nun, you might not get as many slices as you ordered.

If a nun was not available, a well-fed-looking young white man in a white apron handed out the bread to us boys. I suspect that he was the person who had actually baked it because of his look of pride in handing it out. He would come out of the kitchen with a bread basket that was attached to a long pole and would deliver your bread request over the heads of the other boys. It was always white bread – never brown. We would put our fingers up – one, two, three – or however many pieces of bread we wanted. This man never looked at me with any recognition that we had the same colour of skin. He just seemed focussed on the delivery of the bread.

Sometimes, the older kids would show off by holding up all their fingers in order to get ten pieces of bread at a time, and these were hand-cut pieces about four by six inches in size. They would obviously do this to establish their place in the group's pecking order. I wanted to show the older, bigger boys that I was a force to be reckoned with too, so one time I ordered a whole handful of bread: five fingers for five pieces. There was a gasp from my mates of my own age when I dared to order so many. But I also noticed the look of acknowledgement and apparent respect from the bigger boys. Since no talking was allowed, they communicated with just smiles and nods. It felt good to be recognized – nothing to do with my skin colour, but because of all my bread.

It was a major chore to try to eat all those slices of bread myself, though, so I shared them with my friends by passing pieces under the table when the nun guarding us was not looking. Thank goodness, the boys came to my rescue. This was an example of solidarity among us boys and their acceptance of me. This defiant act of sharing food and not getting caught brought muted giggles between us and was a thankful reprieve from the constant scrutiny of our supervisors. But the threat of being smacked on the head if Anna Wesley caught us was ever present, even for such minor infractions.

Tony:

"Depending on Anna Wesley's mood, she took great pleasure in using the distribution of bread to antagonize the boys she didn't like. She would walk around with a great platter full of freshly sliced bread going from one row of boys to the next. But she would simply ignore the kids she didn't like or else give them a slap across the face. So you never knew if you were going to get bread or a slap, and after a while, it was much better to just ignore the bread; but you could still get a slap."

Although being able to handle more bread bought me status with some of the other boys, it did not seem to buy me any favourable looks from the bullies. There was no negotiation with the bullies – they were just to be avoided or eliminated, if possible. Although talking was not permitted, it was acceptable to cough, so sometimes when I had the flu, I would cough in the direction of the bullies as we were filing out of the room, hoping I could take them down with a few well-placed germs. I had to be careful, though, for fear of retribution. One time, I was almost caught when a bully glared at me in reaction to my coughs – as if I was threatening him and challenging his dominance. This was a close call and a lesson to me to be very careful as the bullies might fight back and even harm me if given the chance.

After lunch, if the weather was good, we would be let out in the yard to enjoy some fresh air. Otherwise, we would sit around in the common room waiting for afternoon classes to begin.

Our afternoon classes would go from 1:30 p.m. till 4:00 p.m., and it was much the same boring routine. The whole day was spent in great silence, listening to the teacher (unless spoken to), and any attempt by us to speak amongst ourselves would result in a verbal reprimand or a smack, strap, or even beating in some classes, according to some reports.

The backdrop of the residential school only magnifies the roughness of being strapped, but it was also being carried out in varying degrees in other schools and homes across the country. Mom even remembers that when she was a student, there were students in her grade-nine class that were being strapped and had things thrown at them for not paying attention. One significant difference, though, is that we kids at the residential school were never sure if a strapping might lead to a beating or worse. Regardless of how hard we were strapped, we did not get to go home for milk and cookies.

After Class

Our classes ended at four o'clock, when we would go out to the yard, or else go and sit around in the common room until suppertime, which was at five.

The only place we boys were allowed to talk openly was outside in the boys' yard or in the boys' common room.

Boys' common room, St. Anne's. Source: Archives Deschâtelets-NDC, Fonds Deschâtelets, Fort Albany residential school.

Usually when in the common room, we boys just talked in low voices amongst ourselves, as it was never a good idea to be noticed by the bullies. It is worth noting that the bullies never confronted me because of my white skin; they were more intent on indicating their dominance over all us younger kids through threatening looks, loud voices, and by controlling the toys. They made it known through their actions who was the boss in the absence of the bigger power – Anna Wesley.

Tony:

"Only a complete idiot or one of her favorites would at any time laugh aloud. Cardinal rule number one: never, ever attract attention from staff or bullies."

This was a concerning place for me because there was no agenda, so there was just a lot of sitting around trying not to be noticed.

I also worried that my original thoughts of the Natives as being inferior, my secret, as it were, might now spell my end. But I was never confronted at all. They either didn't see my skin colour or didn't consider me worth making an example of. So, I just faded into the background and tried to be invisible while being mixed in with the rest of the boys.

Even though I was withdrawn, I still monitored all the actions going on around me and learned many lessons through observation. The common room was a great place to learn. In fact, I think I learned more in the common room than in the classroom.

It was during these times in the stark light of the common room that a transformation in my mind also began to happen. Although lessons in our classrooms were meant to teach us our ABC's, it was in the common room where we gained insights into social relations.

It happened gradually for me, but I came to accept the fact that I was in prison with the rest of the boys, that I was eating the same slop as them, being treated the same, and feeling the same trauma and fear. And I began to think, *Wait a minute. I know that I am not supposed to be here, but I don't think this is right at all. Like, none of us should be here.* I began to understand that none of the boys belonged there.

I had to acknowledge that the little Native boys there took to me and befriended me and protected me. There was a lot of solidarity that I felt toward them that I had forgotten – till the writing of this book. I didn't talk very much, and not many talked to me in any great depth, but I was included.

I gradually realized that I was just like them in many ways – and my discomfort of being there was more to do with the monastic controlling environment that was being forced upon us. Maybe there is a time and a place for such authoritarian behaviour, but in my opinion, not when it comes to nurturing children to become the best they can be.

In response to the authoritarian environment, we boys played a role in protecting each other against the bullies and mean adults. On some level, we banded together. There was a pact. It might not have involved a lot of talking, but we all moved together. We all understood what was going on, and that self-defence force that I participated in could only work if they felt that I was with them, that I was one of them, and that I accepted that I was with them. Trying to figure out the rules and the survival tactics together gave us a sense of solidarity. I was frightened, and there were others around me at my age who were frightened too. We were protecting each other the best we could by presenting a common front.

There were some older boys who were protecting us younger ones as well, by just sitting in our area in silent solidarity. I didn't understand. I tried to understand the why of that. I had never seen that empathy. Why would any Native person protect me? After all, I came from a world (the HBC) that was exploiting them. Why were they protecting me? The truth of the situation could be observed in relative clarity in the common room. I eventually realized that these boys were becoming my friends, which was significant at the time, because they were my first friends ever. Before I had come to the residential school, my friends and constant companions had only been my two sisters.

In the common room (and occasionally in the play yard) was where one would experience the truth of the social relations between us. Everything else was staged. Every day, we boys were herded to the dorm room and had better behave. We were herded to the chapel where we'd better confess. We were herded to the mess hall where we were force-fed horrible food. We were herded to school to be force-fed religion, and so on.

We were told what to do, and we had no say or any other option. Even the bad boy bullies would be on their best behaviour at those times. It was only when we were released from the controlled agenda to play amongst ourselves that the power struggles and mental health of all the boys would be obvious. Thankfully, there was an evident social structure to respect and protect each other to the best of our ability from the bullies and dangerous adults.

I wonder now what would have happened if the boys were from a settler culture. How would they have treated me? Especially if I had a different skin colour from theirs? Would they have had any training in camaraderie and looking after the youngest, or would they have been taught from day one to respect the most predatory, the loudest, the most angry, the most powerful person in their group – the most authoritarian.

It would have made such a difference if the nuns and priests – the adults – had taken the time to teach us some life skills rather than us boys just sitting around. Even sharing stories of themselves would have been helpful to teach ethics and what it means to be an adult. Or they could have explained how they wound up in the Catholic Order in Northern Ontario and what happened to them in their lives that caused them to decide to unplug from society, to be a priest or a nun. These were giant, earth-shattering moments of their lives that were completely shut off from us kids.

To me, the staff were like cardboard cut-outs, offering little support or nutrients to us young, curious souls. They were like the rules of the Bible walking around: *thou shalt not, thou shalt not* ... It was like code. *If I just learn the Bible, then I can figure out everything.* But that is not the real world, or at least the whole world. Life was not black and white as they would have preferred it to be. Life, as we kids would learn, was complicated, and it would have been helpful if the staff had taught us skills to deal with it, showing us how to live in the larger world.

There was definitely a lot of tension in that room, and it was a relief when we were allowed outside. I was thankful to be let out regardless of how bad the weather was. There wasn't much to do for us younger kids outside, though, even if the weather was nice, because there was no recreation equipment to speak of, and the bigger boys controlled what little there was. For the life of me, I do not remember us boys just playing. Like, really playing!

If the weather was particularly dark and stormy, it would put many of us in a melancholic mood, and we would just stand around alone with our thoughts and look toward the horizon. I would turn to look in a north-easterly direction and imagine magically transporting myself across those five miles to home. Sometimes, I would also close my eyes and sniff the air, hoping to catch just a hint of home – trying to remember how it used to be. Other boys would do the same, looking in the direction of their homes. We would stand there with eyes closed, sniffing the air. This became one of the regular rituals for some of us who still dreamed of home. The freshness of the air helped clear our heads but also gave us hope. We would not share our thoughts with each other – these were our very private moments – but somehow, we knew that we were connecting with family and home the only way we could, by imagining and remembering.

I would sometimes stick my hand in my pocket and hold my rosary beads as I said a prayer, hoping I might conjure up some spell that would result in escaping this prison, but I never seemed to find any freedom. After a while, I just rubbed the beads like they were pet rocks or something that helped soothe the senses. Sometimes, especially if the weather was cold, we gathered together and huddled around in a circle, trying to keep warm. It was comforting to experience these impromptu group hugs after our personal reflections did not bring the relief that we so desired. These moments also helped me to come to realize that we weren't so different after all.

Tony:

"In the winter, when we were allowed outside in the boys' play yard, we huddled in small groups, wearing our threadbare canvas winter coats and felt winter boots. At this time of the year, we would have handed in our moosehide moccasins made by the staff in exchange for these winter-type boots as they were waterproof. We certainly must have looked like little convicts all gathered in small groups with our backs to the wind."

Eventually, the clanging of a handheld bell would snap us out of our frozen state of minds and signal that it was time to come back inside and get ready for supper.

CHAPTER SIX:

EVENINGS AT ST. ANNE'S

AFTER ENJOYING THE FRESH AIR in the yard, we were herded to our mess hall for our evening meal, which was more like a tortuous chore since once again we first had to file past the delicious smells oozing from behind the door of the nuns' private dining room.

> **Tony:**
>
> *"On only two occasions do I remember their dining room door being inadvertently open and seeing a smorgasbord of food piled on the table. Of course, the door would be slammed shut immediately as they didn't want us to see the good life they were leading. No wonder there were quite a few fat nuns."*

In contrast, our supper would often be the leftovers from previous meals, that resembled the swill fed to pigs, and was the worst meal of the day. If the meal was particularly putrid, I would try to make my mind go blank as I forced the slop down my throat.

Sometimes there was an attempt at something different such as a fish stew, but it was even worse than the usual slop. It was made with local white fish, which have a very strong smell. It must have been stored for some time because there was also a strong fermented aroma. The fish had been cut and ripped apart in what appeared to be an act of insanity, likely reflecting the frustration of some initiate in the kitchen who was working off their sins. The disjointed hunks of fish looked like a horrid living nightmare. Some pieces also seemed to be fish guts. The stench of the stew was revolting. We may as well have been dogs being fed on the trap line the way the food was prepared and dumped in our bowls. It was gut wrenching trying to eat those stinking fish parts, knowing we did not have much of a choice, and that we had better eat something just to keep our strength up.

I remember holding my breath and trying to navigate through those protruding fish bones, fat, skin, cartilage, and whatever else was sticking out of the concoction. The thick, grey-brown broth and rancid oil floating on top made one's eyes sting. My fellow Native schoolmates were used to eating a lot of fish at home, prior to attending the school, yet from the looks on their faces, this fish stew was a challenge for them as well.

The nuns served up this meal with such pride, like this was a new recipe. Now I am not sure whether it was pride in a unique but failed recipe or glee in seeing us kids trying to deal with such putrid fare.

The experience caused me so much inner turmoil that it set off loud alarm bells in my mind, a mental uproar barely contained by Rule #1: "Thou Shalt Not Talk." These two conflicting sensations emphasized the craziness of the situation, leaving me feeling more trapped than ever.

I could feel my sense of self, my identity, and my dignity, being pulled from me. It was as if there were an evil force digging, poking, one spoonful, one glance, one word at a time. I wondered in those moments if my parents knew what we were being fed, when food had meant such a positive family time at home. I eventually began to wonder if they even remembered me.

Although the fish stew was horrible, there was another meal that traumatized us inmates even more. One day, the silence at the school was shattered with the loud boom of a rifle shot. It was the only gun I was to ever hear at St. Anne's. There was no explanation, but we all heard it and wondered.

A few days later, the meat we were given for supper looked drastically different from any meat we had ever had before. Usually there was some fanfare if there was meat, but this time there was no excitement; just a sickening stew that was served up in heaping portions. That was also not normal, and it set off warning bells in our minds.

The vegetables in the stew were good, but the meat was fatty and had been hacked and boiled, offering up a rancid stench. The gristle and large clumps of fat clinging to the meat had varying colours from white to red to putrid yellow. My throat slammed shut when my tongue touched that fat. Our immediate concern, of course, was that we were expected to eat everything served to us. I cannot remember how I got through that bowl of putrid stew. I think I pretended it was Mom's cooked ham, but it was the most disgusting food I had ever eaten. Us kids wondered what kind of meat it was. What could be so bad? I prayed the meat wasn't what I thought it was.

When we were next let outside, we all looked for the old workhorse that was kept in a shed on the grounds, but we never saw it again.

I must have tried to block that memory because over the years I began to wonder if it had even happened. Many years later, my suspicions were confirmed when I saw a video online pertaining to the Truth and Reconciliation Commission in which another survivor who attended at the same time complained about having to eat that horse, so I know it was a valid memory.

I am not sure what was wrong with that horse meat, but it had not been butchered and stored properly. One would think that with so many hunters in the local community, they could have gotten the horse processed properly.

Tony:

> "I remember eating that old horse. Actually, it's one of my most traumatic experiences. As a sick joke, the Brothers, when they butchered the horse, also included the penis, which ended up in my younger brother's plate. I remember his pitiful look when he showed me what was on his plate, and upon holding it closer, you could smell the reekness of the thing. I shook my head at him to not try to eat it, and we both knew that he was going to get a good beating for not eating his meal."

In reaction to some of these gut-wrenching meals, I started to experience a recurring dream that I called the "spoon dream." I would dream of sitting at a table set just for me, with a white tablecloth and a big white bowl. In some dreams, a knife and fork would also be set on each side of the bowl. Then a big scary hand would place a large serving spoon beside my bowl. This action would cause me to wake up and gag. Sometimes I would even throw up, which resulted in puke on my pillow. Thank goodness my pillowcase was replaced without reprimand. Maybe the staff that cleaned our bed coverings did not have the same perverted need to reprimand, like Anna Wesley. I am certain that the dream was a subconscious reaction to the force-feeding we endured.

The Chapel

After our evening meal, and still trying not to throw up from the food we had been served, we were all marched back to the chapel, once more passing through the area of construction. With the workers gone for the day, and their tools and dust strewn everywhere, the sight beckoned to me as if holding a message – one that I could not fully fathom at the time. Our lives were so rigidly controlled there that we kids would have blown up the whole place, given the opportunity, so the construction gave us hope that something better was being created.

It was not till the writing of this memoir that the full message of that scene hit me ... that all things come to an end. Ideas and rules change, and physical manifestations of thoughts are altered. Walls get shattered, floors get dug up, because all are a construct – and therefore, prone to be destroyed and remade. I thought there was only one possibility at the time: being imprisoned there. But I was to learn that there are many possibilities in life, given the will and opportunity, and that I might even be able to make my own possibilities. But that realization was to come many years later. At the time, I just followed the rest of the boys as they plodded along in single file to evening prayers.

The red carpet at the entrance of the chapel was a welcoming sight and caused us each to feel ... special. Maybe the colour was just meant to highlight the importance of that place of worship, but it also felt like it was a way of welcoming all who entered. It was the only place where I felt that there was an attempt to acknowledge each of us as individual souls. But it was like icing on a rotten cake.

As we waited in line to enter, a few of the Native kids would run their fingers across the surface of the large wooden candle holders at the entrance, where the grains of the wood lay bare and vulnerable for all to see and appreciate. It was like they were acknowledging the beauty of nature and were maybe even remembering something of their past heritage of living off the land. Since no one can be forced to truly believe against their will, I wonder how many of the assembled were simply spectators, there in body but not in spirit.

I ran my little fingers across the face of that wood as well. That ritual of tracing a natural flow of nature seemed more comforting and engaging to me than trying to connect with the crucifix hanging at the front of the chapel, watching and waiting for us.

The general atmosphere of the chapel seemed to be threatening damnation to all who didn't follow the rules ... at least, according to the priest giving the sermon. However, I was experiencing all the fear I could handle already (as were most of the other inmates). Therefore, the priest's sermons had little meaning for most of us. Even though he tried to make his sermons come alive with action-packed examples of Satan and God having this eternal battle, he did not inspire or capture my imagination.

Tony:

"For many years I used to hear the priest in his sermons warning us to beware of wolves in sheepskin clothing, and I came to realize that he was basically talking about himself and the staff."

Although the chapel was meant to be the place where we prayed and visited with the Roman Catholic God, I was thankful for the safety it offered – safety from the bullies and sadistic staff. At least they were nicer in chapel, likely on their best behaviour while asking for forgiveness from the Almighty.

Being there in that disinfected place, the chapel felt confining and cut off from the world. I wondered what Jesus might be feeling about such living conditions if indeed he was alive in that room as Catholic belief suggested. He lived in that special place within our prison, locked away, even more secured than we kids – likely contained so he could not escape and witness the affairs and sins of the staff.

Possibly to pacify an angry God or to mask their guilt, the staff took great pains to look their best when coming to that holy place of business. They were clean and shaved, with their whiskers all clipped, wearing their freshly starched uniforms and ready to pray.

I wonder now what the prayers of both the abusers and the abused consisted of in that chapel when all were praying to the same God. I wonder how many prayed for the forgiveness of their sins, how many prayed for deliverance from this purgatory, and how many tried to justify their sins with well-worn excuses. I wonder what that God thought of it all – if he even heard all our prayers. Apparently, he was not listening to some, given what was to come to light so many years later.

Tony:

"Evening prayers were particularly depressing, as we endlessly repeated prayers over and over again for about an hour. Certainly to me, at least, this bordered on prayer torture, and I couldn't wait for this to be over."

Eventually the sermon would end, and we would all join together to sing hymns to conclude our worship for yet another day. The preaching was never inspiring – to me, at least – but the music helped to brighten our spirits. We all enjoyed singing together, including the hymn "Amazing Grace," and somehow, I hoped it could be about me too ... that I would be found, or even seen, or be seen as who I actually was.

I wondered if God even saw me. Judging from the blank, uninspired looks on the other kids' faces, they likely had similar thoughts – hoping to be found and rescued too.

After this last prayer session, we boys were all marched back to the common room to sit around, not doing much of anything, except maybe reflecting on our unfortunate circumstances or else participating in some sort of acceptable activity such as trading our religious cards with each other. I'm sure the girls would have experienced pretty much the same routine.

Then, at the ringing of a hand bell, we were marched to our dormitories to get ready for bed at around eight o'clock. Even though we had eaten our dinner and prayed and sang in chapel, the day always ended the same: going to bed feeling empty and hungry in mind, body, and spirit, and bracing for the visitors who snuck into our dorm at night – maybe the very ones who preached hellfire to us during the day. It was a horrendous feeling to carry to bed. In my child's mind, I did not understand why Jesus could not be allowed out of his cage, the chapel, so that he could come to our dorm to protect us from the late-night visitors.

The Boys' Dormitory

Although going to bed was a relief because we could escape through our dreams, the dorm was also a troubling place because it was the collection of all our pain. All of us boys plodded around in muted silence – going through our various learned tricks like putting on our pajamas and brushing our teeth.

Getting ready for bed did not conjure up any nurturing sense of home life. It was just the regimented routine of having to do our business in the washroom ... and it was important to do so, because going to the washroom after lights out was strongly discouraged. We would then lay down on our beds and be as quiet as possible for fear of being noticed by Anna Wesley. There we would wait for the call for evening prayers when we would all rise to our knees on our beds. However, boys being boys, it was hard to quiet down while waiting for prayer time, so sometimes we would whisper to each other and giggle over something trivial.

In contrast, other boys would lay completely quiet with their blanket pulled over their head, not interacting or making a sound. When we saw a boy hiding under his blanket, we knew that he wanted to be alone and not be bothered. This is where I spent a lot of my time while in the dorm: under my blanket. It was my safe place where I could disappear for silent contemplation in an effort to soothe my thoughts. I would remember my life back home at these times and feel somewhat comforted. However, we never felt completely safe because Anna Wesley could at any moment swoop over and pounce on us.

To be fair to her, with all the testosterone in that dorm room, she was one woman with her hands full, trying to handle about a hundred boys. Trying to get a whole bunch of boys to be quiet and do nothing was impossible. So, it must have been a challenge for her, especially since she was mean-spirited and spiteful in her attempts to control us. She was relatively young, about thirty, and probably chosen because she would understand the boys' Cree language and would know how to communicate with them. However, she was not the maternal type.

It would have been a great comfort to my fellow Native schoolmates to have had a few grandmothers from their own communities, with a caring nature, to provide solace and a sense of connection. However, the industrial scale of our lodgings, plus the controlling nature of the enforcers, left little room for individual nurturing.

Unfortunately, for some of us, our dorm supervisor did much more than yell at them. She was always looking for something wrong. She often yelled out commands in shrill, high-pitched sounds that hit you like a verbal attack. I swear the hair on the back of my head and even my ear hairs would stand up in terror when I heard that shrill shriek. She reminded me at the time of a big, agitated raven who was on the hunt – perched in the midst of us defenceless kids like a bird of prey waiting to pounce.

When she twitched her head, like a bird focussing on its prey, she appeared ready to strike at any moment.

While we got ready for bed, she watched us all intently from one of her vantage points. Sometimes she would swoop over to one of the boys (usually for a minor infraction like laughing), yank the blanket off him, and demand that he go stand in a corner. She would direct the boy by pointing, followed by a few stern words. The boy would submit to her command with obvious resignation. I was not sure whether it was a punishment or a game, initially. I hoped it might be a game for their sake – like hide-and-seek, but the rules were strangely strict. Anna Wesley would be very specific as to how the boy was to stand in the corner. She would direct him into a stress position (standing on one leg, or squatting) that did not look like much fun to my young and innocent mind.

It was strange that the boy in the corner stayed in the same position for extended periods of time, and sometimes even after the lights were turned out, with our supervisor continuing to shout out commands to him to not move.

I'm not sure how long his ordeal lasted because I would sometimes drift off to sleep before "the game" was over. I was to eventually learn more about the effects of this sick game (see "Physical Abuse and Punishments: Kneeling in the Corner" later in the book).

Tony:

"I know that your parents thought they were doing the right thing by sending you and your sisters to St. Anne's, little knowing that this place was one of great evil. Fortunately for your sisters, they had it fairly easy; however, you were not so lucky and ended up in a nightmare ruled by a psychopath who took great pleasure in subjecting most of us to her sadistic whims. As we were at her mercy, which she only knew too well, she could do anything without worrying about any consequences."

Everything and everyone were so public in the dorm, and all our pain was shared, strengthening bonds; but there was no place to hide, be alone with your thoughts, and feel invisible, until the lights went out. Eventually, sleep allowed us to escape through our dreams, but the process of falling asleep was slow, like waiting for water to boil.

As the peace of the night settled over us, with the occasional sound of snores breaking the silence, a strange smell or disturbance would sometimes awaken us.

Watching from under my pillow if I happened to be awake, I would see Anna Wesley's dark shape float by me if there was enough moonlight coming through the window. Sometimes, though, if it was particularly dark in the room, when I could not see her shape, the smell of the starch from her robes, along with the oily muskiness of whatever skin cream she was using, alerted me that she was close. The smell was terrifying, like being stalked by a wild, dangerous entity on the prowl. Trying to be as quiet as possible but still trying to sniff the air to see if she was close was like a deadly game. One did not want to be too loud for fear of being noticed, but my sense of self-preservation was so strong that I could not help but sniff the air, like the other boys who might be awake, trying to catch the scent of where "she" might be lurking.

Tony:

"Anna Wesley had always wanted to be white but was never accepted by her peers as nothing but Native. For the many years I was there, she used to put massive amounts of Noxzema on her face to try to whiten her skin. To this day I can't stand the smell of Noxzema."

Although Anna Wesley was a bully, she must also have protected us from perverted prowlers at night (at least while she was awake), since she would occasionally yell out to someone in the darkened dorm to "Get out of here!" I can only wonder who these intruders were. Maybe an ordained priest or one of the lay brothers (the workers) were making nightly visits, as there seemed to be another world that came alive there in the darkness.

I suspect it was white people who came to visit because Anna Wesley always screamed at them in English. Maybe it was the priest who had all the keys to the place. But after her initial yell, she would mutter something in another language, likely French, and then in Cree, so who knows? It could have been anybody. I was thankful that I was protected in the centre of that sea of boys when I heard those disturbances. However, I still braced myself and clenched at the bed frame each time I heard such noises, fearing I might feel a hand grab me.

Sometimes I froze in fear thinking that I had been singled out by one of these visitors because I felt something touching my hair. Thankfully it was always the boy ahead of me who would accidently touch my head with his feet as he sought comfort. We would occasionally tease each other in this way with our feet. This gesture helped dissolve some of the fear that kept us wrapped so tightly in its grip.

I remember a few times, though, when a disturbance would wake me up, in the deep of the night when Anna Wesley was sleeping and there was no protection between we boys and the nightly visitors. At those rare times, I would hear a muted sound and a slight struggle in the darkness as one of the boys was led from the dorm for some reason. I was never sure if he had done something wrong or was being chosen for yet another special game. And the visitor never said a word that I could hear – likely for fear of revealing their identity. I did not dare to sit up to get a better look for fear of the unknown, so I lay as flat and still as possible, with my little fingers curled around the bedframe. There was likely a lot of white knuckle fear in the dorm during such visits.

The boy must have been returned sometime during the night while the rest of us slept, because all of us were present in the morning, wondering which one of us had been led away during the night. Whatever happened, it was not talked about, and no boy came forward in the morning to say it was him. However, if one looked closely, there was usually a boy with his head bowed slightly lower than usual, who we suspected had been the one.

I remember wondering at the time if the girls experienced such strange games and visitors in their dorm as well.

In my innocence, even with all the drama going on at night, I looked forward to bedtime, when I could drift away under my blanket and dream of home. I went home each night in my dreams – so I always looked forward to bedtime even though I would sometimes be wakened up by noises when visitors who were not supposed to visit would arrive.

I did try to tell my parents of these strange night visits once, but it did not cause any alarm bells to go off in their minds. After all, I was being looked after by religious people they trusted, so what could be so wrong? They thought there was probably a good reason why strangers were visiting the boys' dorm room at night. Maybe a toilet was plugged and needed fixing, etc. Their response to the fear and concern I was trying to express was that I must be imagining things. It must be in my head, and I must be fantasizing as children did when they are afraid of the dark or what might be under their bed.

CHAPTER SEVEN:
DAY IN, DAY OUT

AND SO, LIFE WENT ON, one day following the next, and each one was pretty much like the one before. Because of the trauma and injustice there, a sense of disorientation clouded my thinking, to a point where daily experiences were disconnected and unfocussed.

My waking state was more like a dream. I just accepted and let myself be guided. It seemed easier that way. After a while, I became a sort of zombie, floating from one point to the next without any sense of orientation. Over time, like the rest of the students, I resigned myself to the daily routine and just concentrated on the rules of what not to do and who to look out for.

To add to our already stunned state of minds, we kids were forced to take part in the constant praying prior to each and every activity. With all the praying going on, our minds were so numbed that each day was just a blur, like we had been drugged. The frequency of praying was shocking. On any given normal day, we had to say prayers before each activity, and with two chapel visits as well, it amounted to about two hours of praying every day.

Tony:

"The whole day went by in great silence and prayer and never was this schedule deviated from except during the sacred holidays, where we had to pray more."

Meeting in the Hallways

Being so stunned from the constant praying and monotony of it all, we moved about in some sort of mind-altered state. To add to the challenge, there were staff on guard trying to keep the different sexes from interacting with each other if at all possible. The flow of students in the hallways was strictly regulated, especially for the boys. Of course, we boys and girls would glimpse each other when lining up at the entrance to our mess hall, or in the classroom, and in the chapel, but hallway movements were timed so we would never meet if at all possible.

There were rare occasions on Sundays after chapel, though, when we could move about with a little more freedom going to and from the yard. Although it was our "free time," we still could not just wander about. We boys especially had to display some purpose in our walks.

Stopping to talk to the girls was not allowed, even between siblings. Tokens of recognition such as secretive waves became less and less frequent, especially if a particular mean nun was on duty.

As a result, blood bonds gradually deteriorated. We were being "civilized" now in the image of something bigger than mere children. Or maybe it was just the easiest way for the staff there to control us – to not cater to the basic normal wants and needs of innocent children. It seemed like such a mean adult rule, though, not being allowed to talk to each other. Unfortunately, that authoritarian "rule" of "don't look, don't talk, just continue to walk" caused a lot of damage.

Tony:

"I had three sisters in that prison and I can't for the hell of me remember ever talking to them, thus by the time I was released my sisters had unfortunately become strangers to me".

The Final Report states that in other facilities in the residential school system older brothers were separated from their younger brothers, and older sisters separated from younger sisters. A nun would give a stern reminder by yanking a child's ear or slapping their head if they so much as looked in the direction of a sibling. Sometimes a "good pounding" followed, as one child described it (on page 41 of the report), when she just went to speak to her brother.

On the rare occasions when we kids had a little more freedom of movement, the staff still wandered the halls, looking for any one not following the rules. There were dangers to be concerned about at all times, including meeting mean staff and bullies. There were, of course, friendly staff, which was a relief, but it was rare. Usually, it was someone trying to exert authority over us.

When we were in an area where we were allowed to talk, like the common room or outside in the yard, we would warn each other of whom we had seen and who to be concerned about. However, since most of us did not know the names of the adults, we gave them nicknames. Hearing us whispering the names and giving each other warning of who was in the area, sounded like we were referring to mythical figures in some far-off land, but these figures were very real. For example, "Yellow legs was yelling at some boys," and "Big Nose was walking down the hall today. He looked angry."

When we kids were in the no-talking zones, like hallways, we resorted to other means of communicating with each other.

One way I used to test if a hallway was safe was to see if girls were standing around. The girls would usually be playing string games such as "Cat's Whiskers" and "Jacob's Ladder." Although not many girls stood around, the ones who did tended to group together. For some reason, girls were allowed to hang about in the halls, but not the boys (at least during my time there). There were also the muted giggles between the girls in the hallways, likely subconscious nervous signals to each other that they were okay or at least trying to feel safe. We boys attended to our own signals, such as: come, stop, and be quiet.

Tony:

"As we were never allowed to talk except when we were outside or in the common room, we resorted to using signals to warn each other of imminent danger by nodding or shaking our heads or surreptitiously pointing."

I recall one time that I missed a signal and came face to face with a scary priest – Mr. Belt, as I called him – the one who sometimes carried a rolled-up belt. Without even thinking, like a knee-jerk reaction, I began to cough as if I had a cold. Seeing me horking away with pretend coughs, he walked away in disgust. That was a close call, and I sure had something to talk about in the yard with my little friends after that experience.

It was a pathetic existence – just trying to survive and stay safe. The rule for us to keep quiet and obey was crystal clear. After all, the residential school was part of a monastic centre, and so, we kids were also expected to conduct ourselves appropriately.

We moved about like prisoners on some mind-altering drug of fear. It was as if there was a concern that excessive noise might invite the devil or something.

Occasionally, like a reprimand of some sort, maybe when we boys were exhibiting too much energy, we would be directed to our dorm room for an afternoon nap. I forget the frequency or reasons, but I do remember feeling like being caught in a net with no recourse, having to file back to the dorm for quiet time.

These afternoon naps were torture for us, as Anna Wesley our supervisor was watching. I remember laying on my bed, moving ever so slowly to just scratch at an itch, each time fearing that it might trigger a reprimand. Not even daring to move to scratch an itch is an example of how much we were controlled. And of course, talking was not allowed during nap time.

Being silenced was so destructive to little kids whose natural tendency is to want to express themselves by interacting and relating to one another.

The Sting of Identity Loss

The fear in some of the kids' eyes and the dazed looks in others was like a silent scream for help. The trauma of being silenced was like a disease, firmly destroying our sense of identity, until all that was left was the sting that one feels when their sense of self and self-worth is taken from them.

And here I was in the same situation, feeling the sting as well. I could see it in my schoolmates' eyes and even in my own eyes when I dared to look in the mirror in the washroom and the eyes of a stranger stared back at me.

I tended not to look at my eyes. I am not sure whether this was because of anger, fear, or sadness. I was losing my sense of self because there was no one around me who was from my culture at the school. I was being subjected to conditions that were designed to control and reprogram.

I tried to master my fear and my own loss of identity in this untenable situation. I was completely unprepared to handle it, and nobody gave me any tools or coping strategies. Maybe as a child this meant understanding that the hell I found myself in was not of my doing, and that I was not being punished by my parents. Being busy thinking is not productive if one does not have the right information, or enough information, to understand what is happening.

Native schools like St. Anne's were attempting to kill the "Indian in the child" and to assimilate them into the dominant white culture. But I was white and from the white culture. And here I was now, in the midst of this Native genocide and all by myself. Even though I was white and from the white culture, in that place I too felt something was being killed inside me, being sucked out of me, leaving me empty like a hollow "white" egg. I was at risk and was suffering too.

I had to create my own tools from scratch and borrow some caution from my little friends. I would stick close to the safety they offered, while holding onto hope for release and to the memory of who I used to be. After a while though, I presumed that I too was seen as a Native, as I moved about in fear and confusion.

There was nowhere for me to go, so I obeyed and kept silent and dealt with this situation. Assaulted with harsh and cruel conditions like the rest of the kids, I instinctively knew that the situation was not right. I had to learn to adapt. And so, I tried to be invisible like a lot of the other students. This included not expressing any point of view or raising anyone's attention. It was a confusing and frightening time for a child when children go through significant growth and change as they begin to identify their place in the world. However, thoughts of hope and joy now began to slip from my mind, and the world has looked different for me ever since.

As an adult now, I still catch my breath whenever I think back to that place and time: That horrid place where I didn't know how to be – with my feelings hidden so deep beneath the surface that I did not even want to breathe.

The Orphans' Area

Although the layout of St. Anne's always remained unclear to me, there was one place that stood out and was particularly troubling. Along one of the hallways, there was a room allocated for preschool orphans. This was a place to be hurried past and forgotten about, if possible. It was cold and smelled like infection. It had a sickly, dirty smell, and those little kids often had greenish-white mucus oozing from their noses. It was odd that they were all dressed neatly, but their noses ran constantly, always dripping with snot. They were looked after by a very old nun who seemed kindly enough.

This was one of the saddest places in St. Anne's. There was no other place for these unknown kids to go. This was the only place they knew. This was their home. This was as good as it ever was and likely ever would be for most of them.

Their courage and determination to survive was a reminder to count our blessings, what few we had, but it was still hard to walk down that hall and see their discomfort. It was also hard to see them because even though it was obvious that I had it better than them, it did magnify my feelings of abandonment when I was missing my own family. It was like looking at little copies of ourselves; like little chimps in a zoo who look back at you with faint understanding and recognition.

I tended to avoid this hallway if possible. In hindsight, this was probably where the religious order was providing a much-needed service to society and even humanity in the form of food, shelter, and comfort.

The church after all, was the original social welfare system. As stated in the Bible, "Pure and undefiled religion before God the Father is this: to visit orphans and widows in their troubles and to keep oneself unspoiled from the world" (James 1:27).

The Nuns

During my entire three-year enrolment at St. Anne's, I had no direct contact with the priests except during chapel or meeting them in the hallway. Others may have different experiences, but that was the situation during my enrolment there. My perspective, therefore, was that the nuns were the immediate authority figures for us kids, and their individual traits and descriptions were a constant concern.

There were different types of nuns, each with a specific role, including: education, public relations, nursing, childcare, discipline, and so on. Some nuns walked the halls with purpose, their heels on the hard floor threatening, clicking, and emphasizing their brutish attitude. Others swished along on their cushioned soles, as if walking on air. The ones lightest on their feet were the novitiates, in training to become nuns.

Sister Marie Albert was in charge of them, and they followed her around like little ducklings. These novitiates never went anywhere by themselves; they were always as a group. They were never involved in any of the day-to-day activities, as far as I could see. They just floated past it all in a state of bliss ... revelling in their faith and camaraderie. There was a freshness to them, a joyfulness that reminded me of the unbounded pleasure I had experienced back home.

Their group was made up of both Native and white girls. I wondered if the white girls were somehow related to the HBC culture. In my child's mind, I hoped that our similarities might be enough for me to be invited into their group. I so wished they would include me so as to rescue me from the hell of the boys' dorm. But they never did acknowledge me as one of their own. They just passed me in the hallway, sprinkling their looks of happiness over all us unfortunates as they walked by.

At the time, I had no idea where they came from or where they lived at St. Anne's. They were like a wonderful fresh wind that blew through the hallways at unexpected times. I was to learn that they lived with Sister Marie Albert in their own special quarters, on the top floor of the nursing station, which was a separate building adjacent to the school.

I wonder now about those initiates. Sure, they had found a place to hide from the world and wallow in their faith, but the church also had more workers as a result. I wonder about their responsibilities and workloads that would have gradually been heaped on them by the church. It must have been like the military, where becoming soldiers for God also meant they did not have a say in when and where they worked, when they rested, and what they were paid. According to their chosen faith, their rewards would be found in heaven – as the church got richer from their efforts.

The nuns in white uniforms (habits) were the nurses, and they seemed to be genuinely pleasant, not needing to be prodded by their religion in order to be nice. In contrast, most of the nuns wore grey and black habits, and though some were kind and meant well, this group also contained some mean ones, who took pleasure in reprimanding us, and who treated us like an inconvenience.

I was well aware that the controlling, oppressive tone of the nuns was not to be taken lightly or challenged in any way. The mean ones were to be avoided, if at all possible, but they were hard to spot at times, and there was really no place to hide anyway. It was so hard to know who you could trust. Some were nice, others were mean. Some were strict but nice, others were friendly with smiles, but dangerous

Some of the nuns' at St. Anne's including the girl's dorm supervisor (Sister Catherine) on the far left, and the boy's dorm supervisor (Anna Wesley) kneeling in the middle row. Source: Archives Deschâtelets-NDC, Fonds Deschâtelets, Fort Albany residential school.

Like the other kids, I had to learn as quickly as possible who was to be avoided and who meant me no harm. That was confusing to a young, sensitive child who did not understand this miserable, oppressive, dangerous environment after a childhood of relative freedom, joy, and safety at home.

Tony:

"All the staff were dangerous in one way or other, as many of us found out – some firsthand and others from whispered conversations amongst ourselves."

The confusing and sometimes conflicting signals coming from such a wide range of personalities caused us kids to live in a state of emotional uncertainty.

Also, since the staff were our caregivers while we were in residence, they had the added responsibility of not only keeping us all on the straight and narrow, but also of nurturing us as well. But their method of parenting was to control, not teach like good parents do. It is ironic that the very people whose vows by definition did not have room for kids were the very ones who were in control of us. It was like they believed that their strong sense of religious morality was enough to parent us. But at best, even though some were loving and empathetic, they could only act as guards in a monastic prison of their making, in my opinion anyway.

The Priests and the Lay Brothers

The priests (ordained brothers) seemed to be a solitary bunch, only appearing for church services and special occasions. There were about ten to fifteen of them, and there was usually one priest who was the big boss.

La communauté d'Albany.

Priests at St. Anne's. Source: Archives Deschâtelets-NDC, Fonds Deschâtelets, Fort Albany residential school.

RR.PP Loiselle, Langlois, Mgr Belleau.
RR. PP Nadeau , Parent.

Priests at St. Anne's. Source: Archives Deschâtelets-NDC, Fonds Deschâtelets,
Fort Albany residential school.

I do not remember seeing these priests interacting on a day-to-day basis with us boys. When they did appear, they seemed to be focussed on a task, and always with an air of authority. That is not to say that they were all bad, but it was hard to know just from looking at them who were the bad priests and who were the good ones.

The appearance of some of the priests also caused me some unease. With their over emphasized straight backs, piercing eyes, and large beards, they appeared to be bolted together into some form of humanness, that made them look somewhat manufactured and scary to a young child like myself.

The priests were likely responsible for administering the more severe corporal punishments. Occasionally, we would spot a priest in the hallway, red in the face and perspiring as if he had just finished some extreme physical activity. He would pass by in a hurry, carrying a coiled brown length of leather, maybe a belt. My little dorm mates and I would report such sightings to each other as a warning to be on the lookout for such priests.

Initially, I did not have a clear idea of the positions of all the adult males at St. Anne's. I was aware of what a priest was, but there were also lay brothers, the men dressed in rough, day-to-day work clothes as compared to the priests and their robes. They were expected to work at St. Anne's and were called "oblates." The dictionary describes them as people dedicated to a monastic or religious life or work. That is, they were not professed monks living in a cloister, but laymen living in general society, yet affiliated with a monastic community having made promises to follow the Rule of the Order. The Roman Catholic Church considered them part of their monastic community and often assigned them tasks as part of their vows. At St. Anne's, they were mostly on construction duty and contracted to stay for a set time.

From this lofty description, one would have thought these to be dedicated, spiritual people, attempting to live lives of service in the best possible way. However, Mom called them "slimy guys recruited from the wilds of Quebec," and my sister Ruth was to call them just plain "creepy."

Although the school was set in a monastic environment, all its rules and customs, however well-meaning, made the place feel like a barren, evil landscape that echoed the self-interests of the few who believed that might made right.

CHAPTER EIGHT:
MOM'S PROMISE

MY FIRST YEAR AT THE school was the hardest on me because I was there all by myself. My sisters had yet to be enrolled, and their absence only added to my sense of being alone and forgotten. I shuffled from one mindless activity to the other like the rest of the boys – just trying to deal with the monotony and stress of it all. One thought that gave me hope, though, was Mom's promise that she would come and visit me when she could. I held onto that promise like it was a lifeline.

In a way I felt somewhat guilty that I had the promise of family visits to look forward to because the boys in my dorm never expressed such thoughts or expectations. Likely for most of them there was no possibility of anyone coming to visit them, so what was the use of hoping for or complaining about it? What could they do, fighting against the reality of distance and poverty, anyway? Even though it was an unspoken pain, it was still obvious in their eyes and silence.

I was not aware of the bigger picture at the time, though, that without regular visits with their family and community, their family connections, their culture, and their past was also being taken away from them – in effect, evaporating and leaving them essentially with just their memories.

It seemed abnormal to me at the time that they did not voice their emotions, which caused me to try to be strong and not complain myself, but I did miss my mom desperately. Although I felt fortunate with my secret that my mom would eventually come to visit me, I thought it best to keep it to myself so as to not cause them any added pain.

It seemed like a long time before that first visit from Mom. She recalls that she was required to wait inside by the front door that day while a friendly nun came to get me. When I was told that Mom had come to see me, I became giddy with excitement. I can still remember that walk from the dorm to where she was waiting for me. It felt like I mattered again; like I was being rescued. I felt alive again in the blink of an eye. It was like flipping a switch.

When I got a visit from Mom, a "white," PR friendly nun would come and get me, essentially pulling me out of the grasp of the boys' dorm supervisor and delivering me to Mom. This is an important point to understand in terms of why my parents did not realize how bad some of the residential school staff were – because they were never given the opportunity to meet them.

On that first visit, Mom and I were allowed to be together for an hour or so in the same room where I had first been enrolled at the school. (I would like to call it a visitors' room, but since there were likely few if any other parents who ever got to come to visit their kids there, I just thought of it as a neutral room.)

There was already a marked change in me by that first visit. I was not the outgoing boy anymore. Even though I was happy at Mom's presence, I was subdued and almost lifeless, like the tired toys in the room. Mom tried to play with me by rolling a ball back and forth. However, playing with Mom there was not like it used to be at home – I just went through the motions. I had lost something inside and was filled with an intense feeling of resignation, without focus. Mom tried to cajole me to play, with a slight frustration in her voice, but I could not meet her where she wanted me to be emotionally. I had tried to stop all feeling entirely at that point in time, for the sake of survival, and it was evident in my lack of action. But at least I got hugs from her, which helped me to feel stronger and loved in the moment.

When Mom left, she tried to give me strength by pulling herself together as much as she could, but it only served to intensify my sadness. As the front door was opened to let her exit, the tantalizing whiffs of fresh air blowing in from the outside reminded me how confined I was. It felt that freedom and happiness was just outside that front door, but it was just beyond me.

As Mom left and the front door closed, the white PR nun led me back into the darkness and stench of the prison. She held my hand in a comforting but firm grip, as if she understood somehow. She left me at the foot of the stairs leading up to the boys' dorm – as if she were afraid of our supervisor, Anna Wesley. The touch of the nun's hand would be the last touch of caring until Mom's next visit.

One might say that by being "white" I had more status than the Native boys, because most of them did not get to enjoy family visits. For most of the students at the school, they were imprisoned for the entire school year, just getting to go home for summer holidays. That would be about ten months at a time between visits home. And students like Tony, I would learn, had been kidnapped by the church and shipped off to Albany for a total of eight years without a break from the place.

All I knew at the time, though, was that my mom's visits gave me hope and relief. I recognized how important they were and could not even fathom how the others were surviving without any visits. I was barely hanging on myself. Mom's visits helped me to survive just a little longer – though I wondered how long I could last.

Subsequent Visits with Mom

Mom tried to come once a week on Sundays, when there was no school and the weather allowed for safe travel. My usual routine on Sundays was to scan the sky for bad weather; bright skies usually meant she would be coming, and I would look in the direction of the river for any movement, anticipating her arrival. On days when the weather prevented her from coming, I would, of course, be filled with great sadness, to a point where feelings of abandonment began to surface. Even though my feelings were somewhat irrational and childish, I was a child after all. And so, although there was a high likelihood that she would appear, I never counted on it and was pleasantly surprised when she got to come to visit me.

If I was outside in the boys' yard when she arrived, she was allowed to join me there. Initially, I was concerned how to interact with her in public, fearing how the other boys might react. But thankfully, they acted as usual and just stood around looking at nothing and saying nothing. Mom recalls that there was a lot of coughing and sneezing, as all the boys seemed to be sick with colds on her visits, which seemed odd to her.

Although I had been emotionally numb and barely able to interact with Mom when I had been first enrolled, now many months later, and having accepted my fate, I found that I needed her emotional support more than ever in order to survive.

I would take her hand and lead her to an open space away from the others, where we had some relative privacy. I would then squeeze her hands as hard as I could while just looking at her. Maybe this was to make sure she was real or would not be taken away from me. At those special times I was so overcome with emotion that I would begin to whimper and cry, unable to say anything. She held my hand and shielded me so the other boys could not see me, and this is how we had our moment of alone time together. It was like a silent, lifesaving interaction.

We did not talk of home. I did not ask any questions about home. She just held my hands in silence as my whole body shook with uncontrollable weeping followed by a continuous flow of whimpers and tears. I tried to be strong like the other boys, but I could not hold back or mask such a flow of tears and emotion. It put Mom in a state too, as she could only say, "Ron, Ron, please, son," as she fought back tears as well. She was obviously in a state of alarm at my actions, but tried to be strong for my sake, feeling that she had no power to change the situation.

I would also look in the direction of home while holding her hands, and mark the place where we were standing in my mind in order to be able to revisit that exact spot – to sense or even smell her presence after she had gone, as a dog might sniff for something.

When the bell rang to signal that it was time to go back inside, Mom would begin to gently but firmly unpeel my hands from hers while propelling me toward the lineup that was forming. Unable to argue against the inevitable, but overcome with a desperate need to hold onto her, I clenched her hands as tightly as I could. As she unpeeled one hand, I would frantically grasp at the other. This obviously caused her pain, but she endured it as if she felt she deserved it. Finally, when she could not endure the pain any longer, she whispered, "Ow, you are hurting me." Her reaction would snap me out of my struggle and cause me to let go. It was so hard, though, for me to have to join that sad line of boys as they made their way back into that stinking prison once again.

Mom says that they were like robots, and when the bell rang, they just began to line up and troop inside, paying little attention to Mom and me, as if respecting our privacy. And then she would be gone, and I would join the others, lost in deep sadness. Interesting that not one of the boys ever teased or bullied me as a result of Mom's visits. It was like such occasions were sacred.

I never bragged afterwards to my dorm mates that it was my mom standing there with me, but I am sure the boys would have figured that out on their own. Some of my closer little friends just said, "That your mom?" And that was the end of it. We had to go on. We had to survive, so the less said the better.

Mom Recalls Her Teaching Experience

Mom later said that it was tragic to see all the boys standing around like robots. A few years earlier, before I was born, she had come from the South in 1949, at age eighteen, to accept a teaching job in God's Lake, Manitoba. Although she did not have a teaching certificate, she enjoyed motivating and inspiring the minds of her students with basic studies, as well as teaching them to play the piano, and even growing a garden together. Then one day, an airplane landed and rounded up her students and flew them off to a residential school. They did not even have a chance to say goodbye to her that day, and likely were not given a chance to see their parents one last time either – because some parents came to her to ask about their children.

Mom was left thinking that the kids were taken because she did not have her teaching certificate. They left her with just one student – or maybe that student hid during the roundup. That memory crossed her mind when she saw all my dorm mates standing and looking blankly at nothing, and she wondered why no adult was interacting and playing with them, inspiring them as she had tried to do with her students.

She reasoned that even though the sight of us in the yard was troubling, at least we were being taught by qualified teachers, so we kids must be receiving a good education at least. She and Dad felt this was still my very best choice at an education, given the location and the qualified teachers there.

Mom Makes Friends with the Nuns

Mom would sometimes be invited for tea by the nuns in the nursing station building, which she had to pass on her way home after visiting me. This building held a token two-bed nursing station, as well as a residence for some of the nuns and the novitiates.

If it was a particularly cold day, Mom would be invited to sleep over in a spare bed at Sister Marie Albert's residence on the top floor of the building. She might have even seen me standing outside with the other boys trying to be brave and strong, since the windows on the top floor provided a clear view of the school.

Mom would also be invited to join the staff for meals, where she got to experience their food and dining facilities. Unfortunately, she was not shown and so was not aware of the kind of food we children were being forced to eat as the nuns enjoyed a much better fare.

Some of the nuns at St. Anne's, in their dining room at the nursing station building, celebrating an occasion with a special cake, circa the late 1950s.

Nuns at St. Anne's in their dining room, circa the late 1950s.

She also recalls that during these visits, some of the priest and the lay brothers would give her stern and even sly looks that caused her to feel uncomfortable. But she thought, *Well, at least they are all Christians there, so how bad could it be?*

The young initiates, however, gave her peace of mind. They seemed happy, or at least high on their faith, as they concentrated on their training. They were like a walking endorsement to her that the place must be acceptable because they were a group of happy girls who had freely joined the Roman Catholic order and seemed content at St. Anne's.

After her visit, Mom would head out with her gun and make her way back home, crying but with no one to comfort her; the trip, as she recounts, was like a trail of tears. Her pain was from missing me and also seeing how homesick I was, but what could she do? She believed I was getting a better education than what she felt she could provide – so she reasoned that the sacrifice must be worth it, never fully realizing that I was stuck in a prison, and my individuality and sanity were being eroded one day at a time.

CHAPTER NINE:
MY SISTER RUTH ARRIVES

AFTER A YEAR ON MY own at St. Anne's, my sister Ruth was enrolled there as well, after attending school in the South for two years. Ruth arrived back home late in the summer, which allowed us a little time to enjoy reconnecting before going off to school. She was eight years old and seemed so different – she moved and talked with such confidence now. Although this change in her was unfamiliar to me, I was happy all the same that she was back home, and we were all a family again. She was my big sister, my protector, and my co-conspirator of the many adventures that we had enjoyed together in the past.

I was excited when school resumed again that Fall and experienced the same anticipation as some of the other kids – to catch sight of siblings. However, to my surprise, my furtive glances to catch a glimpse of Ruth went mostly unanswered. Sure, I would catch a flash of white in the girls' section in the chapel: the bright blonde hair and white skin were the clear signs that she was my sister, but I rarely got a glance of recognition from her. She now walked with such confidence and purpose, apparently enjoying her newfound dorm friends and never seeming to be looking for me.

I feared at times that she might have forgotten me, but at least I could see her even if it was from afar. It was like we had become emotionally unlinked by her absence and experience down south. And the segregation at school that prevented our interaction would only compound this division. I remember standing in that chapel, feeling so close yet so far away, looking over at the person who I hoped was still my sister. It seemed so unfair that I might have to wait till we were back home on holidays to be together with her again, which was still several months away.

Ruth was to say that in some ways she had forgotten about her siblings. She did not have the same need to reaffirm family bonds since she had been away from home already for two years and had, in a way, toughened up.

Her ability to remember more from that time, as compared to me, was also apparent and likely due to the relatively better conditions and treatment she experienced in the girls' area.

Ruth remembers that her dorm supervisor, Sister Catherine, was nice to the girls. She was strict – the dorms had to be clean and orderly – but she tried to bring some joy to the girls with games.

Sister Catherine, on the left, was a Native nun who was (according to Ruth) a rare and wonderful person at St. Anne's. Ruth is absent from the photo. Source: Archives Deschâtelets-NDC, Fonds Deschâtelets, Fort Albany residential school.

Ruth remembers being in the girls' playroom and wanting to play hide-and-seek with the other girls, but she couldn't hide because of her white skin, so Sister Catherine put a dark sweater on her head to cover her blonde hair so she would fit in. Ruth never forgot her act of kindness and empathy.

Ruth also recalls playing with other girls in the girls' play yard. One of her fondest memories was being tossed high in the air, bouncing up and down on a blanket held tightly by the girls standing in a circle. It was wonderful experiencing some of the games brought from the Native culture. She remembers not being afraid at all of putting her trust in the other girls, knowing they would catch her in time.

Another one of Ruth's happy memories with her dorm mates was enjoying what was called "collation," meaning a light meal. It was a treat only for the girls. Sometimes it was hot chocolate served out of gold-coloured pails (empty hard-candy containers from the priests), or if they were out on a hike, the nun in charge of the group would make tea for the girls in the same gold pails. They would stop and build a fire, and once the water was boiling in the can, they would mix in tea bags, sugar, and a big lump of lard. They would then pass the brew around in one common cup. That was an exciting outing for the girls, but we boys were never allowed to leave our play yard and enjoy such walks or treats. This was probably because we were more inclined to take such opportunities to run away. At least, that was the policy when I was there, and Anna Wesley was looking after the boys.

The food at St. Anne's also left an impression on Ruth. Although she found that most of the food was tolerable, she also recognized that it was quite putrid. Some of the Native girls would occasionally pass their remaining porridge to her to finish eating, thus saving them from being forced to eat it. She also remembers that we sometimes had dry cereal for a breakfast treat. For dinner, our extra special treat was a sausage sliced into one-half-inch rounds and fried. It was quite spicy and tasty, but it was rare that we had anything flavourful or as good as the sausage. One food that Ruth could not stomach though was the fish stew. She still cannot eat any kind of fish broth as a result.

There were girls she got to know who said they were happy to be there because at least they had food and a warm and dry place to live. A lot of Natives at this time were living in tents, and food was scarce, so this was seen initially as a far better place. As time went on, though, a number of the girls would experience abuse at the school, a terrible price to pay in order to have some of life's basics – food and lodging.

The girls were still homesick, and Ruth remembers hearing soft crying throughout the dorm room during the nights. She also remembers, late at night, hearing the sound of the security doors clicking shut very softly, and she knew someone was sneaking out, running away, trying to go home. To this day, the sound of that type of door closing brings back memories for Ruth.

Most of the girls there felt like prisoners. However, Ruth says that she felt safer in St. Anne's than she had felt down south with relatives, because she was closer to home now and also had her own bed.

Ruth later said that she did not think of the school so much as a prison but rather as a restrictive environment. After all, it was a monastic centre, as well as a school. The strictness of the place also found its way into the classroom. Ruth recalls, on one of her first days in class, trying to follow the rules to the letter. Filled with a fear of making a mistake, she forgot an important detail that resulted in an embarrassing moment for her.

She remembers Sister Hugette Marie, the teacher, telling the class to write their names at the top of the pages of their work. However, Ruth wrote the name "Louis" at the top of her paper, which was the name that the teacher had used as an example. When the student papers were handed back, the teacher asked who didn't have one, and Ruth raised her hand. Ruth says, "I was so concerned with doing exactly what I was told that I couldn't figure out that we were supposed to write our own name! We were also instructed to write 'J.M.J.' for Jesus, Mary, and Joseph, at the top of the left margin, which I dutifully did."

Ruth, second row on the right, with fellow classmates, circa 1959–1960.

Tony says he recognized himself in the picture with Ruth. He is the one in the picture wearing glasses and situated two rows behind her.

Tony:

"I don't much remember names or faces of fellow inmates so I was ... shocked to see that black-faced picture of myself, as I had written about this in my journal to my kids. Equally shocking was to see your white face in the pictures, as over the years we all assumed that only brown skins ever went to these prisons. However, I think we didn't see you as anything else but a fellow inmate and thus made no big deal of skin colour."

Ruth also recalls learning some Cree words in class and says she enjoyed the challenge of learning them, unlike my reaction to having to learn some Cree. Years later, Ruth could still recall some of the language, including counting to five and asking "what's your name" and "why did you come here?"

After school, unlike we boys, the girls were given cleaning duties, and Ruth remembers having fun helping clean the chapel with the wing of a Canada goose: that was her little dust broom. As she recounts, "It was also really fun to sit in the confessional, because when I sat down, the light went on and a chime went 'bing-bing.'" Her subtle act of rebellion against having to be as quiet as possible at all times helped to remind her of her unique individuality.

The confessional room was connected to the chapel, which she recalls was bright and cheerful. There was a large window located behind the altar. Imbedded within the glass of the window was the image of a large cross that caused the room to glow with the freshness of pure inspired light.

St. Anne's chapel: Source: Archives Deschâtelets-NDC, Fonds Deschâtelets, Fort Albany residential school.

She also recalls the seriousness of the chapel, with its symbols and the adornment of the priests. There were a number of statues (denoting saints) and twelve stations of the cross, depicted in pictures of bas relief carvings.

St. Anne's chapel: Source: Archives Deschâtelets-NDC, Fonds Deschâtelets, Fort Albany residential school.

Ruth also had concerns about the priest's message in the sermons. As she was to later recount, they were slanted more toward a religious ideal of the world as compared to the broader view of life and society as she had experienced in her first few years of schooling down south. As she would later recount as an adult:

Ruth:

"The Catholic Church is steeped in such symbolism, tradition, pomp, and ceremony. And that is part of the allure, that you feel very special after you've gone through all of this. But it does nothing to really address the question: what is evil? Like what is it? Like where does it reside? Where does it come from? You don't really get that talk so much in the Roman Catholic religion. You get all the symbolism. You get all the right answers, but have you really examined yourself to say, 'Yeah, I've fallen short.' Have you really examined what's on the inside of you? Or have you just followed the rules of the religious church?"

The Sound of Different Languages

Although Ruth and I were able to understand and speak a few Cree words, hearing Latin was also a challenge and a further reminder of the alien environment we found ourselves in.

Tony:

"In the first few years I was there, we did a lot of praying in Latin. Of course, we didn't know what the hell we were saying as we had to repeat the prayers as told us by the nuns till we got the pronunciations right. At times I wonder what somebody would have thought if they had somehow been magically transported into our chapel and heard two hundred boys and girls in the middle of nowhere reciting and singing away in Latin."

Hearing hymns sung in English or Latin sounded beautiful, especially when topped off with the highly practised tones of the nuns singing in unison. But it always seemed that we kids were more of an audience and not really key participants in such expressions of faith.

Although the residential school was meant to eliminate the Native culture, there was one surprising treat for the Native students: singing the closing song at the end of chapel service each evening in Cree. Ruth remembers that it sounded so beautiful. Even though I was not interested in learning the Cree language, hearing it sung with such passion by all the students was moving and inspirational. When the students sang in their Native language, there seemed to be a deeper and more enthusiastic connection. The language came alive and served to take us out of ourselves for a moment, filling us with a sense of strength and comfort.

Ruth's memory is that the tune was similar to the song "No Place like Home." The following picture shows the first two lines, but it's all she remembers now.

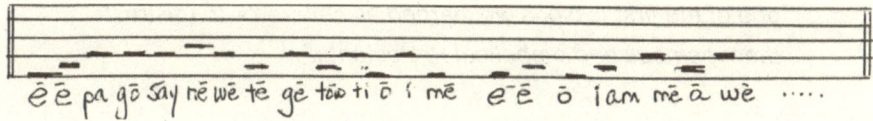

Drawing courtesy of Ruth.

It felt great to be able to lay our differences aside for those brief moments of song and to feel a connection during such heart felt moments.

Even though we HBC kids were struggling like the others to adapt to the strict Roman Catholic environment at the school, we still thought of ourselves as Anglicans. In fact, we were certified Anglicans having been baptized a number of times prior to attending St. Anne's.

As the family of a HBC manager, Ruth and I had been transferred a number of times throughout the North, before arriving at Fort Albany and attending St. Anne's. In each location, we were baptized to publicly reaffirm our faith. Ruth was baptized Anglican three times, whereas I recall being baptized twice. Maybe I got baptized more times in my travels, but I forget; I'm not sure if it is a sin to forget all one's baptisms! These multiple baptisms characterize the division of life in the North and the extent to which religious denominations competed for Native membership.

For us HBC kids at the time, we held onto the memory of being Anglican because it was a reminder of the relatively more relaxed family atmosphere of the Anglican Church back home, compared to this Roman Catholic environment with its strict rules and need for us all to believe and act the same.

We were never openly challenged or chastised for being Anglican while attending St. Anne's. However, what the staff thought behind our backs might have been another matter. Maybe we presumed that being white and from the HBC carried some weight as far as retaining our original faith, at least. But by having to follow the rules of St. Anne's, praying Roman Catholic style, maybe we were sliding toward a Roman Catholic way of worship while thinking we were still Anglican.

Tony:

"The Catholic Church had and probably still has a deep-seated hatred of all things Protestant. Actually, that was one of the first lessons we learned as children – to mistrust them heinous and diabolical Protestants."

Although some of the staff obviously had an agenda to control and convert, thankfully Ruth experienced unconditional caring from some of the nuns, including her beloved dorm supervisor.

Ruth Gets to See the Nuns' Private Quarters

Ruth remembers the kindness of her dorm supervisor once when she felt sick.

> *"I left the chapel and ran down the hall to the dorm. I believe I must have fainted, because when I came to, Sister Catherine had me in her arms and was carrying me to the girls' dorm. She must have allowed me into her inner sanctum because I remember lying on the bed and watching her ironing her headdress. I thought to myself, Why is she putting peanut butter on it? The starch for the headdress was the colour of peanut butter, but thinner. She applied it with a flat brush that looked to be one inch wide. The starch smelled a bit like varnish. She wore a white bonnet called a wimple that covered her entire head and tied under her chin so that her head would remain properly covered while she was doing the ironing."*

Ruth also remembers being in the nuns' dining room and seeing the silver-domed serving dishes on their table. Each nun had a small drawer in front of her at her place at the table. In the drawer were her cutlery and her cod liver oil pills. On the right side of the room, Ruth recalls a glass-door cupboard or sideboard.

It is interesting that Ruth got to see the nun's dining room because she can describe it in such detail, but I, and likely none of the other boys were ever allowed into this room.

Some of the nuns and nurses (in white habits) at their dining room table, circa 1959.

It was only during the writing of this book and viewing this picture that I was finally able to see behind the nun's dining room door, where all the aromas of the good food had come from.

Diapers or Kites

Ruth also got to go to the top floor of the nursing station building during one of Mom's visits, to see where she would sleep over at times. Ruth recalls walking up the creaky, old stairs to the top floor, where it was quite lovely.

On that same visit, Ruth found herself amid mountains of white cloth when she was shown where the laundry was done. These cloths were the perfect shape for making kites, but the workers were folding them in a very specific way. "What are they doing?" Ruth asked Sister Marie Albert.

The nun replied, "How old are you, dear?"

"Nine," Ruth told her.

"Pretty soon you'll know," was the only explanation Ruth got from the nun.

The piles of white material were, of course, menstrual cloths, which were still used at that time. They were folded with the points repeatedly turned in on top of each other until each was quite thick – in the shape of a triangular diaper. Ruth had no idea about any such thing. At that age, who knew that happened to women – even nuns, who aspired to be not quite of this world.

These cloths had to be washed, dried, and folded, week in and week out. There were about a hundred girls enrolled at the residential school then, although many were too young to be menstruating, and about ten to fifteen nuns, maybe about five other female staff including nurses, and of course a number of novitiates. This resulted in a constant laundry chore. A group of women from the local Native community beside St. Anne's were hired to do the job.

Tony:

"It really bothers me that people go on and on about how hard these nuns, brothers, and priests worked, when in reality it was the local people who did the heavy lifting.

98

When the local people worked for the church, they would be paid with some kind of a script that was only redeemable at the church-operated commissary..."

I never saw how or where the major bulk of the clothes were washed and dried but I do remember seeing a small clothesline outside at the back of the nurses' residence. When clothes were hung out to dry on that line, they could be seen dancing frantically like a flock of kites trying to escape. Watching them being yanked about in the wind did indeed look like they were trying to break free too. Their tortured movements and struggles somehow magnified the general feeling of wanting to escape the confines and dangers of the place if at all possible. They reminded me of how I was always feeling controlled there but unable to break free myself. Ruth, on the other hand, had more freedom of movement so may not have felt as confined or controlled.

As a result, she was also able to form an idea of the layout of the place, which she illustrated from memory several years later. It was not until seeing Ruth's illustrations during the writing of this book, that I got a better idea of where I had spent three years of my childhood.

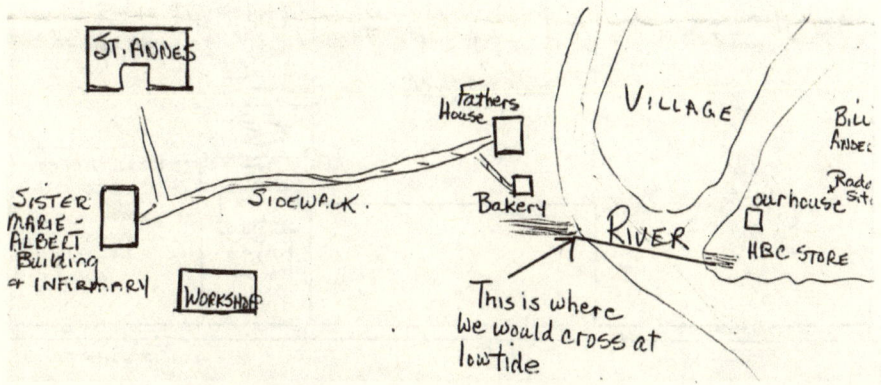

Map of the grounds and outlying buildings at St. Anne's, circa 1961.
Drawing courtesy of Ruth. Note: The church-run store (not shown) was located beside the bakery, and the sawmill (not shown in the foreground) was opposite the bakery. This drawing is not to scale and may not be accurate.

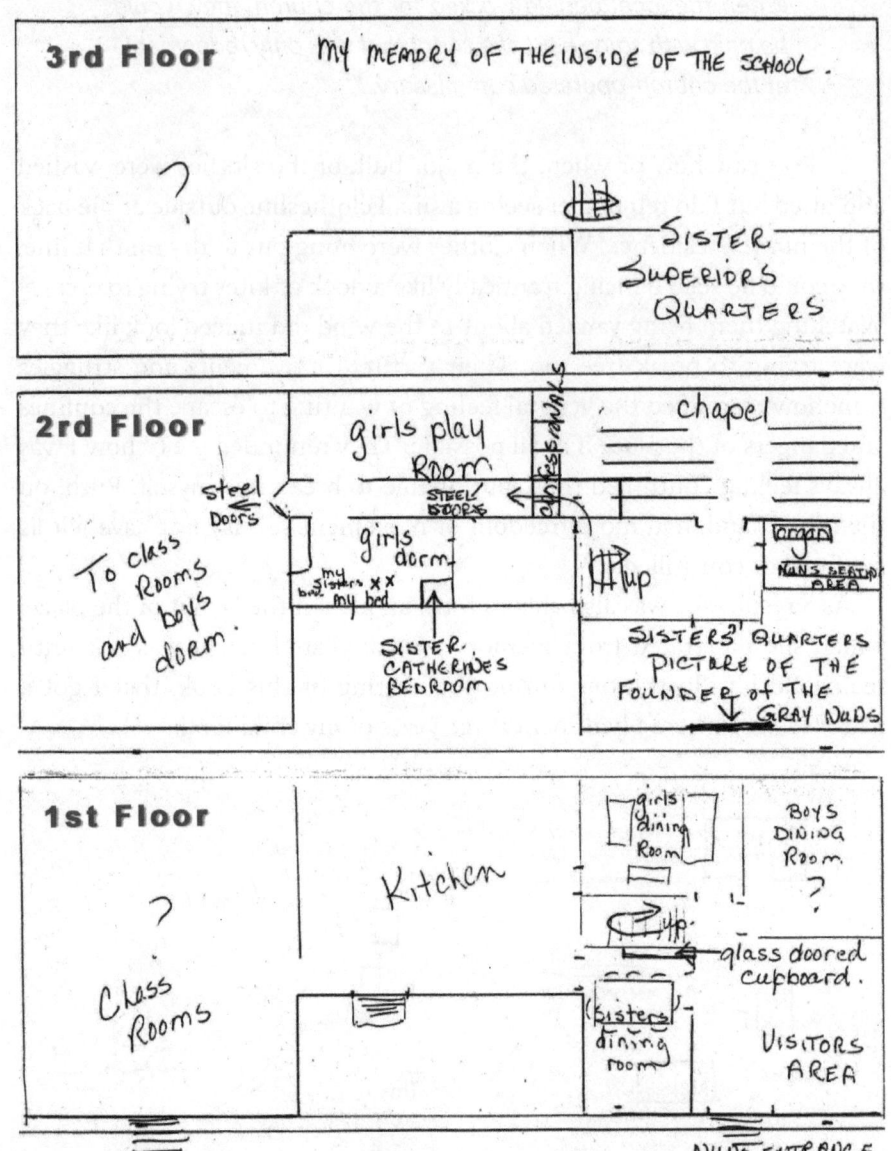

Memory of the layout of St. Anne's Residential School, circa 1961. Drawing courtesy of Ruth. Note: This drawing is not to scale and may not be accurate.

During all the years that I was at the school, I experienced such trauma that I could not even remember any of the names of teachers or students. However, Ruth retained some names. As she states:

> *"As well as Sister Catherine Ticaquetin, my dorm supervisor, Sister Hugette Marie, my teacher, I also remember Father Legarie, Sister Marie Albert, Sister Francois Pachelle, the Mother Superior, Anna Wesley, the boys' supervisor, and Sister Lea, who dressed in a white habit because she was a nurse."*

Ruth was also able to get a sense of the different natures of some of the staff and especially between the dorm supervisors. Her observations would eventually lead her to form an opinion that would help to shed light on why the boys' dorm supervisor might have been so mean:

"We have to remember that a lot of these women of the 1950s ... were nuns since the 1930s, so, if you think back to that time to what professions were available for women ... most if not all of those nuns must have thought, Oh well, I don't really want to get married, but I don't quite know how to support myself."

From that perspective, I can see how some of the nuns were not there because of a deep spiritual belief. I think for some it was just a question of survival. For those nuns who were there through necessity and not by choice, it must have been a living hell for them. No wonder some of them were mean and angry. For example, I don't think Anna Wesley was there by choice.

> *"Sister Catherine (the girls' dorm supervisor) was nurturing and loving, and she was very happy. Anna Wesley, the boy's dorm supervisor was anything but that. She was not a happy person. She didn't want to be there. But likely she was trapped. I'm sure she was trapped in a situation she didn't want to be in. Chances are after her parents put her in school at St. Anne's, she didn't want to go back to her village after graduating – so becoming a nun was her option to move forward. I feel very sad for the ones trapped like that.*

And to further add to their burden, in an authoritarian environment like St. Anne's, nuns would be expected to answer to the priests. If some of the nuns were trying to get away from men in society, well, they went right to the lion's den. Yes, the patriarchy was most definitely alive and well."

Sweet Treats from the Priests

Ruth remembers being in the priest's private house and him giving her hard rock candy from large, two-gallon, gold pails. I certainly did not experience any visits to the priests' quarters or enjoy any treats from either the priests or the nuns. I wonder why. Maybe these treats were reserved for just the girls.

Tony:

"Your sisters should consider themselves lucky that they weren't sexually abused by the priest when they were offered candy. Other girls were not so fortunate. Over the years, I have heard of how the priests and brothers sexually abused these girls, and my sisters among them."

CHAPTER TEN:
"FUN" AT ST. ANNE'S

The Maple Sugar Party

There was one event where we all got to enjoy a sweet treat together – and not behind closed doors. It was the maple sugar party, arranged one spring by some of the lay brothers.

On the day of the big event, we boys were instructed by our dorm supervisor to put on our outdoor clothes and line up to follow her. We younger boys were unsure as to what was happening, but as we scrambled to pull on our jackets and boots, the news that we were going somewhere to get a treat filtered down the ranks to us. Once we were all assembled, we set out, with our supervisor leading the way.

Like the rest of the boys in the line, I sloshed along across the field, through the melting snow, head down, following the boy in front of me, not paying much attention to anything. We had never seen a maple sugar event, so we were not sure what to expect and most were not all that excited. We just wanted the sweet treat. Going on a hike with our supervisor was not our idea of a fun time, but as she led us further away from our compound and toward the forest, I started to feel some excitement. After all, we were never allowed on a hike to the forest, so it was like an escape, which was a treat in itself.

As we marched along, we noticed girls marching in a separate line some distance ahead of us toward a column of smoke emanating out of the forest about a mile away. I realized at that point that I might get to see my sister Ruth and began to take much more of an interest in the event.

As we reached the forest, some of the boys broke away from our group and ran ahead on their own, likely excited that they might also get to see their sisters. Our supervisor yelled at them to stick together with the rest of us, which they disregarded.

Eventually, we all reached the centre point of the occasion, where two lay brothers were busy stirring the contents of a big caldron that hung over a roaring fire. Usually, we were not allowed to associate with such men, and yet here were two of them right in front of us. They looked downright scary, though, like large animals drenched in sweat from their efforts. Their roughness was accentuated by their work clothes; dark coats, and pants that had lost all colour years ago, and now, with the intense heat and steam from the bubbling syrup, looked more like heavy wet sacks. They moved about with obvious intention, conjuring up the tantalizing potion of sweetness that was being promised to us all.

At the time it was a mystery to me how these scary, colourless apparitions could produce such a tempting golden treat. Due to our concern of the fire and boiling pots, my little friends and I held back from getting too close, while some older boys and girls inched close enough to talk to these men and ask them questions. Although the men were very focused and busy with their task, they answered in hesitant but polite tones.

Other kids just stood around the caldron as it percolated over the fire or walked around in little groups of girls and boys. Some looked blankly into the forest as if they had lost something. One might say that the different actions of all the kids reflected their degree of the assimilation within the larger picture. Some were in the present asking questions, while others were in the past, still dragging memories of how it used to be as they stared into the forest or at the groups of kids as if looking for someone.

The uniqueness of the event was lost on me since the priority for me now was to get to see my sister. I looked toward all the kids filtering through the forest for the blonde hair of my sister Ruth.

Tony:

"I do remember the one and only maple syrup picnic organized by the lay brothers for the boys and girls. They took us all into the black spruce forest near Lac St. Anne,

which was close to the prison. Of course, not having any maple trees in the James Bay Lowlands, the brothers had imported gallons of maple syrup in metal containers. The syrup was poured into these huge vats, which were hung over an open fire, and once it reached its boiling point, the syrup would be scooped up by a dipper and poured out sparingly on the snow as so to allow a little portion for each child ... we had been given wooden spoons in order to scoop up this syrup before it completely hardened in the snow. As we very seldom got any sweets of any kind, we needless to say were very happy and excited to be given such an exotic treat. Also, as part of that picnic, the brothers had, before ladling the syrup out, boiled eggs in that liquid, and we all received one egg boiled in syrup.

"I always wondered after that where they got all them eggs but now am thinking they must have had chickens in that big barn across from the rectory. The lay brothers must have been feeling homesick and wanted us to experience the joys of maple syrup tradition as practised in La Belle Province. But of course, this was only done once, as I suspect the work and cost of such an event was just too much to be wasted on us inmates."

This event was one of the few occasions when the lines of segregation were blurred. Of course, the nuns watched us to make sure that we were not associating with the opposite sex too much, but I still held out hope that I would get to speak to my sister. I eventually spotted her and attempted a little wave. I felt she must have seen me since I was the only other kid with blond hair and white skin. But she did not seem to take notice of me and instead appeared preoccupied with her girlfriends.

Most of my little friends were laughing and running around, but I did not even try to join in. I just stood watching the sizzling hot syrup struggling for life, writhing and contorting as the lay brothers spread it out on its cold bed in the snow.

The maple syrup certainly did not seem like a treat to me now, but it still lay waiting for all to sample it. One of the lay brothers must have noticed my indecision and mistook it for inexperience. He extended a hand with one of the carved spoons toward me, gesturing to me to sample the natural pleasure, the fruit of his labour. It felt odd, though, to reach for the spoon to enjoy a treat, given my mood. But it felt good to be connecting with someone who seemed to care about helping me to enjoy the experience.

It was also interesting to see that even the staff were tempted by the nectar of the trees. Maybe it was all right to taste a little bit of happiness after all. I wished, though, that it was my dad showing me how to do this joyful thing, not these strangers.

To add to my lingering confusion that day, I noticed Mom standing with some of the nuns in the distance. They had obviously invited her, but for some reason, she had not taken the opportunity to visit with me. Now I realize why some of the nuns were congregated and laughing in the distance; they were entertaining the white lady. But she must have known I was there somewhere.

This is not to say that Mom was cold and unfeeling, but it is an example that shows most parents at the time, including ours, believed that we were getting a good education, were being looked after properly, and were enjoying the company of our school mates – kids our own age. And what's more, we were getting sweet treats that day. What could be wrong? Also, since Ruth was obviously enjoying a relatively happy time with her school mates, Mom likely presumed that I too must be enjoying the event and elected to leave me to play with my little friends.

Unfortunately, that was not the case. It felt like not only were the boys and girls segregated, but the nuns were also keeping my mom away from me as well. It felt like they were taking something away from me that did not belong to them – the freedom to visit my mom.

Tony:

"Everything possible was done by the staff to keep the girls and boys completely segregated, but when the Brothers had the syrup party, both girls and boys were allowed to be there together. Of course, being boys, we immediately

started teasing the girls and chased them around the forest throwing snowballs at them. This caused much controversy amongst the nuns and Brothers as they perceived this horsing around as sexual and for days after admonished us for being godless, deprived savages. It always puzzled me how teasing girls could be in any way turned into some kind of Sodom and Gomorrah biblical event. Years later, I realized that these people were so sexually deviant that they couldn't distinguish the innocent playing of children with that of their own moral corruption. So that was that for boys and girls being allowed to mingle together ever again."

You Will Have Fun Skating!

One evening, we kids were allowed to go skating on the little frozen pond in front of the school. Wow, just imagine the boys and girls getting to mingle together again! I was excited because it meant that I might get to say hi to my sister Ruth.

Doing something just for the fun of it and with siblings at the school was so very rare.

It caused me to remember how happy I had felt when going outside to play with my sisters back home, regardless of how cold it was.

I looked for my sister Ruth in anticipation that we could get to experience a happy time together again, even if it was in this prison, but she was nowhere to be seen.

I eventually joined the others as they assembled at the back of the nurse's residence, waiting for the skates to be distributed. A lay brother in the loft on the second floor then began throwing skates out onto the snow below where we were standing. He was just a shadow in the darkness because the sun had pretty much set by that time. His enthusiasm was evident though, as the skates began to fly from above and toward our heads. Maybe he was trying to get us skating as fast as possible, or else he was enjoying the fear he was causing by flinging those skates toward us so recklessly. The skates sounded like birds of prey attacking from above, like dark shadows with big claws; their blades striking and slicing at each other with frantic metallic blows until they thudded into the snow all around us. Click, clack, thunk!

I was still feeling sad that I might not get to see my sister, and driven by a desperate childish thought, I considered letting one of those skates hit me, in the hopes that it would injure me just enough so that my sister might be summoned, and I would get to see her after all. I stepped forward bracing for the inevitable whack on my head. Then the realization that I might get an eye gouged out from one of the skate blades caused me second thoughts. Getting an eye gouged out was probably too high a price to pay to get to see a sibling. But it speaks of how much I was missing my sister at the time. I stood there in deep thought and indecision until a nun shouted, "Get back," which brought me to my senses. I pushed back against the crowd until the rain of flying skates had ended.

Then the older kids shoved us younger kids aside to get their skates first. Anna Wesley assisted her favourite students to find the best skates. Then it was time for the rest of us to try to find a pair, but by that time, there were only the ancient skates that no one else wanted.

Tony:

"I remember rummaging around in the snow for leftover skates thrown out to the kids. Of course, it was a free-for-all, but the older kids fourteen or over would have first choice and us younger ones would be left with really old skates that I'm sure were made in the early 1900s.

"As she [Anna Wesley] knew that all the kids wanted to skate, she would use that against them just to further torment them."

Each pair was tied together, which saved some frustration as we struggled to force those skates on our feet, but they were so worn and dull that we couldn't even slide on them.

Standing on that frozen pond with the other kids on that cold night was pitiful. We just stood there shivering, wobbling back and forth, trying not to fall down. There were a few giggles from some of the kids, but they were mixed with the muted coughs, sniffles, and snorts from those with colds and dripping noses that underscored what a cold and dull experience it was for most of us. Within this sad gathering, a few brave kids and the favourite ones tried to actually skate. Even in this time of supposed play, we were still mindful of the rule not to get out of line or get in the way of Anna Wesley's favourites for fear of reprisals that would come once the fun was over, and we were back in the dark of the dorms once more.

As we tried to stand on those useless skates, some boys and girls, likely siblings, attempted to communicate with each other, but the staff – like referees enforcing the policy and morality of the place – reminded them that they were there to skate, or at least try to, and not to visit.

It was a sad indication to me that even if I had seen my sister, I likely would have not been allowed to visit with her. Maybe that would not be a big deal in the normal world, but in this environment, this prison, getting to enjoy the warmth of a loved one even for a second meant the world to us.

Standing there on that frozen pond, I found that without the company of my sister there, it was like having Christmas without any loved ones. It felt empty, hollow, and cold. Likely there were others there who were having a similar experience.

I had hoped to see my sister that evening, but no luck. Maybe there was a good reason, but it was a disappointment all the same.

If we siblings had been allowed to enjoy some organized time together, to reconnect, it would have gone a long way to helping us deal with some of the pain we felt from having to reside in that school, that god-forsaken place. But, of course, that was not allowed. It was beyond the interests of the staff.

With the event now over, the girls made their way back to their side of the building, while we boys were marched back to our dorm, cold and wet and still feeling the controlling grip of our dorm supervisor. Needless to say, there was no hot chocolate waiting for us, which would have at least given us a warm feeling.

Tony:

"The Catholic charities would ... send up boxes of used skates to be distributed to us inmates. Children would, for the most part, just end up sliding around the ice pretending to skate on our slippery moccasins. That's how close we ever came to skating. However, this one time there was a kid's exhibition game to which all the villagers had been invited and damned if Anna Wesley didn't give me an old, dull pair of skates and a broken hockey stick. As the villagers looked on, she made me go on the ice by myself, and I looked ridiculous as I couldn't skate, and it was all I could do just to stay on my feet.

"Of course, this brought great howls of laughter from the innocent villagers who thought that this was part of the entertainment. Once I had made my way to the centre of the ice, she sent out her favourite bully to come and give me a hard check. However, things didn't go as she planned, because when that bully got near me, I hit him hard over the head with my broken stick and damned near knocked him out. The villagers got really quiet, and all I could hear was Anna Wesley screaming at me to get off the ice, and I was subsequently hauled into the building and beaten up. However, this is one of my most cherished memories of Albany [St. Anne's] ... sad."

Anna Wesley standing rigid. Extract. Source: Archives Deschâtelets-NDC, Fonds Deschâtelets, Fort Albany residential school.

Movie Nights

Occasionally one of the priests or lay brothers brought up a few movies from the South for everyone to watch. Some of those brothers had a good side, since they brought us this unique entertainment. Of course, it was also for their benefit. They showed the movies in the basement where Christmas and Easter pageants were held. We were segregated, as usual, girls on one side of the room and boys on the other, but it was exciting all the same. Even the staff were segregated, with the nuns and novitiates on one side of the room and the priests and brothers on the other.

Despite all the controlled segregation, it was still one of the most enjoyable times that we ever experienced at St. Anne's. These movie nights reminded me of the fun time that Lou and I enjoyed seeing super 8 movies for the first time at our neighbour Mr. Anderson's home a few years earlier. It was a Walt Disney animated movie, which was more appropriate for the eyes of young kids.

The movies we watched at St. Anne's were more suited to grown-ups. For example, one was an African desert movie, and one was a fedora-hat-and-trench-coat movie with Humphrey Bogart that they liked, possibly, *Casablanca*. When the film got to a little romantic part, the Mother Superior stood up and clapped her hands sharply three times to communicate her displeasure and to get attention. All the novitiates and some of the nuns then stood up and left with her, like chicks following a mother duck. The movie kept going, and all us kids, plus the remaining nuns and all of the priests stayed to watch. I hunched down in my chair for fear that Anna Wesley would take the opportunity to reprimand us for finding pleasure in such entertainment and demand that we ask forgiveness next time we were in confession, but thankfully, she liked the movies too.

A year or so later, one of the brothers created another form of entertainment in the form of an electrified chair, which was to result in much more controversy than those movies.

CHAPTER ELEVEN:
CHRISTMAS CELEBRATIONS AT ST. ANNE'S

ONE OF THE MAIN ACTIVITIES at St. Anne's was practising for the Christmas celebrations held every December. Boys and girls got to mix together, but interactions were controlled and limited, so socializing with the opposite sex was minimized as much as possible. The basement where these practices occurred was usually divided into two separate areas for boys and girls. The wall separating the two areas was collapsed at this time, in effect removing the wall of segregation.

Since few parents were able to come to see their kids perform, these performances were really meant to entertain the staff. Most of the kids, therefore, did not feel much joy about these practices, but we were all expected to participate. Like pawns, we were moved around by the organizers, well aware of the contrived nature of the exercises. Kids moved their bodies as directed, concentrating on the task at hand, waiting to be animated with the added injustice of having no real sense of self to return to after the performances.

Tony:

"December 8 would signal the start of the Yuletide celebrations and end on the arrival of the Three Wise Men on January 6. This whole month would be one of endless singing, praying, and concert practices, which of course would culminate with the grand Christmas concert.... The

boys' exercise yard, especially around Christmas, was very depressing as, at that time of the year, we would file out to the yard in darkness and would have to mill around waiting to be let back in. I remember standing out there in the dark, bitter cold, looking at the brightly lit building and listening to nuns in the nice warm building practising their Latin Christmas songs."

During these times, we huddled together trying to stay warm, all the Native boys plus me, the little white boy, hidden in their ranks, shivering away and wondering when the hell we would be allowed back inside again.

I wonder whether the staff resented me attending St. Anne's, not only because I was Anglican, but also because as a white person I was witnessing the treatment of the Natives that I was never supposed to see. The contrast was highlighted when, in my first year of enrolment, during Christmas celebrations, I was not provided similar clothes to what the other boys were wearing for the performances. I only had my freshly washed corduroy brown pants and a plaid shirt to wear, whereas the others were wearing black dress pants with white shirts and ties. Whether the nuns wanted to single me out to acknowledge that I was special and unique, or unwanted, I am not sure. And so there I stood on the stage, sticking out from the others with graphic clarity, highlighting the clash of the two cultures and races. Shocked whispers, comments, snickers, and even laughter erupted from the audience, causing me to freeze like some frightened animal in the glare of a bright light.

No attempt had been made to minimize that difference, suggesting indifference or malice on the part of whoever was in charge that year. The decision to embarrass me may have come from Anna Wesley. But since the Mother Superior and the priests in charge sat not more than fifteen feet from the stage during these performances, one has to wonder about their presence of mind as well, and what they thought of the white boy standing out from the Natives on stage in front of them.

Photo of stern-faced audience with Mother Superior, plus some dignitaries, including Santa, at St. Anne's Christmas celebrations, circa late 1950s.

During these performances, Mom was also shocked to see me sticking out on stage for no good reason and asked her friend Sister Marie Albert if she would approach the Mother Superior to request that I be provided with clothes similar to my Native classmates. Her request was approved because a nun rushed me back to the boys' dorm to change into a pair of black pants, white shirt, and tie that were lying on my bed. I was relieved that I was able to blend in a bit more now, but I still felt indignant at being ordered around like the rest of the kids. My anger and frustration were overwhelming.

Me (front row) and my classmates at St. Anne's Christmas concert, circa 1958. Note my clenched fist. I remember consciously trying to send a message to my parents, who were taking this picture, of the stress and trauma I was feeling at the time.

I resented being ordered around by the nuns, my skin colour and social standing counting for nothing, while other white people, including my parents, enjoyed respect. My Grandma Gosbee, who was visiting at the time, noticed my clenched fist and alerted my parents of my anger – but they thought it was just stage fright. Just because they cared does not mean they could see through my eyes to understand what I was experiencing.

Me on the left, at St. Anne's Christmas concert, circa 1959.

These creative exercises with Christmas themes provided diversions, but they also played a role in the process of cultural annihilation for Native children. In one of the performances, my sister Ruth was chosen to act as Mother Mary in the nativity play. Clearly the nuns were aware of their choice in the blonde-haired, pale-skinned girl in this central role – even though the real, historical Mary had brown skin.

Ruth playing Mother Mary, with her classmates, circa 1959.

I remember feeling angry at the time that I had no such role in the focal point of power to reflect my HBC status. I feared that I might be truly like the rest of the Natives, expected to act like a Native but with white skin. I was no longer at the level of my sister, who was being worshipped and idolized as Mother Mary.

Ruth in centre of photo, Christmas concert, circa 1959.

Most of the kids were all smiles, behaving as expected, because it was supposed to be a joyous occasion. However, it was not so joyous once the celebrations were over.

Tony:

"Your pictures certainly brought back a lot of very bad memories especially the Xmas concert one. I am sure that the black-face kid in that picture is me, as after the concert I was severely beaten up by Anna Wesley for somehow having stained that white shirt with shoe polish. The next day, which was New Year's Day, I was forced to clean toilets all day as added punishment."

Students performing at St. Anne's Christmas concert, circa 1959.

Tony:

"I swear that boy with the top hat is my younger brother, Tom, and my wife agrees with me. This concert was probably one in which the sanctity of marriage was the main theme in order to educate us to stay chaste and pure. Funny how these people had such a fixation on the future sex lives of the little children. But, in the meantime, they all knew of the sexual assaults going on in that prison."

Students performing at the Christmas concert, circa 1959.

It is sad that the environment at St. Anne's was so focussed on stripping the identity from the kids that there was little to no effort in recording their images, dooming them to obscurity even in their lifetimes. As a result, most of the kids of that time are essentially just faceless prisoners of the past; what they looked like erased from time. Hopefully, the few pictures Mom and Dad took of these activities will help to illustrate that this was a real place. Some might even find in these few pictures a precious image of someone they recognize, now frozen in time and staring back at them.

Students performing at St. Anne's Christmas concert,
wearing angel wings and halos, circa 1959.

Tony:

"I swear these pictures really brought back so many memories of how Xmas celebrations turned into an orgy of singing and prayer. In that one picture of the boys choir all dressed in white gowns and wearing angel wings and crazy looking halos sure reminded me of how these nuns had an obsession with organizing all manner of Xmas concerts. Am sure they must of wasted a whole month just trying to outdo each other on these extravagant Xmas concerts and decorations. It seemed to me at least that the more joyous they tried to make Xmas the more depressing it was for us inmates. However in hindsight I believe they were doing all this for themselves and not for us."

Students in Choir at St. Anne's Christmas concert, circa 1959.

Students with one of the nurses' at St. Anne's Christmas concert, circa 1959.

Students with nun standing by the nativity scene, circa 1959.

The central focus of the celebrations was the nativity scene erected in the chapel for all to see. It was shaped in the form of a mountain, complete with the figure of baby Jesus in a manger. It was also lit by tiny lights that brought the display to life in a supernatural way, making the manger appear to be blessed by a higher power. Although the lights were a distraction to the message of the display (the birth of Jesus), it resonated in my young mind that Jesus was getting to be with his parents. I wished I could be at home with mine, as did the other kids who milled around the display, looking for some tangible hope and happiness to hang onto.

Experiencing the loss of home and family and being expected to forget and adopt this land of make believe instead was infuriating, and I was not sure who I was more upset with – the staff or my parents for forcing me into such a place of control. Why were these nuns and priests who exhibited such authority seen as the normal ones? Why did I now feel like an unseen child whose thoughts didn't seem to matter anymore? As a young child, I could not understand my parents' decision to trade the wonderful home life I had for this cold, controlling environment with all its rules, customs, and beliefs.

As we kids wrestled with our own thoughts, the nun guarding the display focussed her intense look of anticipation upon us. This suggested that she not only wanted us to appreciate her effort and craftsmanship of the display, but that she also wanted us to believe, not only for our benefit, but to validate her faith as well. I could feel the pressure from her stare to submit and believe with an urgency, like our very lives depended on it.

It caused me, and likely the other kids, to question not only our circumstances but our sanity. We all wrestled with our sanity to varying degrees. For me, it was like a war between being told who you are and what to think, and knowing who you are. I was in constant anxiety about who would win.

The saving grace of all these Christmas celebrations was the live music performed by a group of girls who were also students there. They helped to create a festive atmosphere not otherwise evident in our daily life at St. Anne's.

A group of musicians, who were also students, at St. Anne's Christmas concert, circa 1959. The girl standing behind the girl with the guitar is Tony's cousin Anastasia.

They were really talented musicians and singers, who could sing country and western songs like Patsy Cline so beautifully. Ruth remembers seeing them in the girls' dorm and watching how they learned their songs listening to a little 45-rpm record player. It was allowed, I suspect, because Sister Catherine was a gentle and caring person as compared to Anna Wesley, who was a whole different kind of person.

It is so hard to put one's finger exactly on where the evil was at St. Anne's, because there were freedoms allowed, such as those students practising their music in an environment where we were all essentially prisoners. However, allowing pockets of happiness within a larger context does not make the context right.

Although the music was a happy diversion during the festivities at the school, it too was controlled. A nun clapped officiously to signal that it was time for the musicians to perform another song, as one would turn on a radio.

The Arrival of Santa

Tony:

"In the evening on Christmas Day, the folding doors separating the boys' and girls' common rooms were opened and chairs were set up with the girls on one side and the boys on the other, and we excitedly awaited the arrival of Santa. I remember always trying to catch a glimpse of my sisters and maybe at least get a smile from them, but for most years was never able to. This was one of the few times that we boys and girls were in the same room in celebration as opposed to one of constant prayer."

Tony says that he and his brothers hardly got to visit their sisters during the entire eight years they were at St. Anne's.

As a token of the Christmas celebrations, we were each given a small bag of goodies as a present. These bags usually contained some apples and candies. It was not much, but at least it was something to look forward to.

Nuns giving out Christmas presents at St. Anne's Christmas celebrations, circa 1959.

One year, though, Santa must have thought that I was extra special, because I was handed a big package, wrapped with actual paper, and with my name written on it. This was obviously a special gift and just for me! I returned to my seat proudly and unwrapped it for all the boys around me to see.

But what a traumatic shock I experienced. What did I get for a present but a doll – and a girly "white" doll with curly eyelashes at that! And it was not a small doll. It was about a foot high, with an oversized head, so it was hard to hide. It looked back at me as if waiting for a response, maybe waiting to be accepted. I could hear the sounds of shock and snickers erupt around me as the boys looked at me and my new friend.

I sat frozen in shock and embarrassment, at a loss as to what to do or even how to interpret such a gift. But the reaction of the boys around me left little doubt about the intent of the gift. They laughed and pointed at me, the closest ones even squirming away in their chairs, obviously concerned at being so close to such a sight. We kids usually just got the small bag of fruit and candy, and here I was with this damn doll. It was unbearable holding that cursed thing as my dorm mates snickered at me, crushing my identity even more. Who could I tell that would make it right? Mother Superior? Dad? Mom? Santa? I just left the doll on my seat when it was time to go.

After the formal performances, everyone mingled around to visit and participate in the various activities held as part of the celebrations, both at the school as well as in the nursing station building.

Nuns and priests during Christmas celebrations at St. Anne's. Photo of tickets being sold for the opportunity to throw a hook over the curtain. There was someone on the other side of the curtain to ensure that the hook would always snag a present, circa 1959.

Although there was some prejudice toward us "white" English Anglicans, some of the priests singled out Dad for conversation, while Mom took the opportunity to chat with the few nuns she was friends with.

Mom with the nurse at St. Anne's celebrations, circa late 1950s.

As the celebrations concluded, I took the opportunity to run upstairs to the boys' dorm to change my clothes to get ready for the trip home. One year, as I entered the dorm, there was Anna Wesley yelling at some unfortunate boy who was still dressed in his black and white concert clothes. Whatever his infraction was, it was a shock to witness her aggression. Her high-pitched shrieks were startling and frightening, even though I was not the one being attacked.

Her long, dark robes flowed to the floor, and she loomed over the helpless boy, about to strike with all her fury. In that instance, I turned away but still heard the dull thud as the boy was struck with something hard. Oddly, he did not cry out, likely in fear of receiving any more attacks. When she was angry, it was like something took control of her, like an entity from the underworld, maybe even the devil. We kids had learned that the devil could appear in many forms, but the idea that he could even inhabit our dorm supervisor meant that no place was safe. How could something so horrible enter the inner sanctum of Christian safety such as our school?

How could I protect myself against such power that seemed to defy the laws of nature?

Having to make my way past that evil apparition to my locker was an act of courage, as it continued to lash out with a barrage of shrieks and yells. The hair on the back of my head prickled and stood up. I could almost feel her devil-charged breath on my exposed skin as I changed my clothes, trying not to pee my pants from fear.

I left the dorm as fast as possible, not even bothering to close my locker door. In fact, I hoped that the few religious cards that were lying in my locker might serve to burn the eyes out of the demon if it happened to look at such images.

Reflecting on that scary situation for a moment, during the writing of this memoire, I now wonder who I witnessed being struck that night in the boy's dorm – maybe it was Tony.

Upon exiting the dorm, I grabbed my parka and mukluks hanging in the hallway and rushed as fast as my little legs would carry me back downstairs to the safety of Dad. I wanted to tell him what I had just witnessed, but I knew that telling him there was an evil creature, possibly a shape-shifting vampire or even the devil himself, in the boys' dorm in the form of our dorm supervisor would be too unbelievable for him to accept. Since he thought I was such a daydreamer, I already knew he would not believe me or be understanding of my fear. So, I just stayed as close to him as possible, sweating away in my parka.

At that young age, if your little friends are scared or in pain, so are you. If you get to see your parents, you are happy. Emotions were compartmentalized. That's the only way I can explain the range of my emotions – from intense feelings of fear to feelings of happiness and entitlement.

Eventually, all my family assembled to get ready for our trip home. It was great to see Mom and Dad and my two sisters together again, although there was always a hesitation to our initial interactions because it would have been months since the last time that we had all been together. But within a few minutes, we began to loosen up and interact like a family again.

I took the opportunity to announce that Santa had given me a doll present earlier that evening, and they all looked at me oddly as if I was being weird as usual. Since no one chimed in that the doll was meant for my sisters or could shed any light on the origins of the gift, the matter was dropped.

As we prepared to leave for home, shouts and sharp handclaps could be heard echoing down the hall toward us. These claps were the signal that the enforcer nuns had been given orders to take charge once again. This meant that the wall of segregation had returned, and any chance of visiting between the boys and girls in the school was lost until the next celebrations.

In stark contrast, there I was with my family, all bundled up and ready to walk out the front door to freedom. There were a few other kids from the local Roman Catholic community who were allowed to leave with their parents as well. For us fortunate ones, Christmas was just beginning. For the kids being marched back to their dorm rooms, Christmas was over. We made our exit into the fresh night air as the school tightened its control once again around the unfortunate kids still trapped there.

CHAPTER TWELVE:
CHRISTMAS AT HOME

ENJOYING THE HOLIDAYS AT HOME with my sisters and parents was such a contrast to the strict, choreographed celebrations we had endured at school.

Photo of Margaret Gosbee at Fort Albany, checking to make sure all is ready for Christmas, circa 1959.

Mom and Dad really tried to make the occasion beautiful and memorable. Gifts arrived from the South on schedule, chosen to match each of our whims and sensibilities. These presents would have been ordered by Mom and Dad from the Eaton's catalogue months before and delivered by bush plane – Santa's sleigh of the North. A priceless addition to the Christmas decorations were the Christmas cards received from friends and relatives. Cards and messages meant so much, especially to Mom and Dad, who were so isolated from loved ones down south.

Mom with Christmas tree at Fort Albany, circa 1959.
Notice the HBC clerk in the picture as well.

These Christmas cards reminded us that we belonged to a larger extended family who cared about us. The Native people had their tribes, and I guess in a way, the people from down south were our tribe. Even though we three kids had never met all of our relatives due to our isolation in the North, we still felt special to be part of a clan, a tribe, as it were, that was something bigger than just ourselves.

I was too young at the time to understand the full effect that the residential school was having on the Natives. It seemed odd to me even at the time, though, that I was enjoying the benefits of belonging to my extended family without even trying, and yet my Native friends at school were having to struggle to preserve their family bonds. It didn't seem fair.

I also realized that aside from the glitter of the decorations, I had really been missing the unconditional love and good food of home.

We soaked up the warmth of home during these holidays, the best gift of all. Even with a clerk living in the house, it was still better to have one person living with us, who we got along with, as opposed to the number of mean staff and bullies we had to contend with when residing at the residential school.

It was also great seeing Mom and Dad wearing normal clothes, such a relief from the uniforms worn by the nuns and the priests. Mom and Dad's clothing was certainly influenced by the HBC's business expectations, but it also reflected the style of the day, which was a breath of fresh air compared to the prevailing look of suppression and control at St. Anne's.

The relaxed loving atmosphere of home was so healing. It felt wonderful to drift off to sleep, feeling safe, with our hearts and minds and tummies full and content.

I was always slow to open my eyes in the mornings. I knew that if I were still at the school, I would see the stark white pillars of the dormitory standing rigid, tall, and cold in front of me. So, I would brace myself and open my eyes just a crack. If I saw a warm brown glow, I knew it was from the wood panelling of my bedroom at home, and I was filled with such joy and relief.

Mom really concentrated on making a happy home, and she made every effort to create the best time for us with the resources available. She packed as much love and caring as she could into our brief holidays, breathing life back into us and readying us for our next stint at that residential school. Dad, of course, cared as well, but the demands of running the HBC post and store took most of his attention.

If the clerk had some free time, he would play with us instead. There were a number of clerks who boarded in our home over the years, and each one had their unique appeal, but I especially enjoyed playing with the clerk, Hew McCallum. Although Dad played with me when he had the time, there was always a sense of having to do things right, whereas Hew allowed me to follow my imagination to see where it would lead. That was such a growing experience.

Prior to me attending St. Anne's, Hew's sincere interest and patience in my questions had helped me feel that I could create and achieve anything I put my mind to. But something had happened. Something had broken inside my mind from the trauma at the residential school. I did not have questions any longer, and my thinking was sort of mixed up. Hew noticed the change and tried to rescue me from whatever had taken hold of me, but his questions and enthusiastic tones were no use. It was too late. I had retreated so much into my head that not even he could help me.

It was troubling to me that Lou, who was still not enrolled at school, was able to interact with Hew and keep up with the creative process. Ruth was also able to easily interact, even though she had been away at school down south, and was sort of a stranger. I on the other hand was now so withdrawn and frozen, unable to imagine or even interact, without fearing a reprimand.

I felt ashamed, frustrated, anxious, sad, and angry, that I could not keep up with the conversation.

My thinking was somehow mixed up and my words were unavailable to me, and what I was able to say was uninspired and more monotonous than usual.

As mentioned earlier, fellow schoolmates were loosing their ability to communicate with their families in their Native language. Likely some of them were also loosing the ability to find the words, any words in any language to communicate, given the trauma we were experiencing at the residential school.

Photo of the HBC clerk Hew with me and Ruth (home from school),
Fort Albany, circa 1959.

Visiting the Anglican Community during Christmas holidays

While at home for the holidays, our family also attended the celebrations
held in the little Anglican hall and classroom close by the church. Seeing
this classroom again brought back memories of when Ruth and I had
enjoyed some lessons there before being sent to St. Anne's. It was certainly
a more relaxed learning environment, but since the classes there were
not consistent, it had not been considered to be a viable alternative for
our education.

Ruth and me and local musicians during Christmas celebrations in the Anglican school, Fort Albany, circa 1959.

The fact that I got to have a picture taken with my sister and to visit with my family and the community over the holidays is indicative of our good fortune. Most of the other children residing at residential schools (both Roman Catholic and Anglican) did not get to enjoy visit home over the holidays. Here we were, the white HBC kids, included in the community celebrations, unlikely representatives for the other missing children still stuck at residential school. I could feel the loving looks from the Native parents, obviously missing their own children, sensing an unexpected weight far beyond my years.

The spontaneous music coming from the musicians during these celebrations and the ready smiles and hugs added to the relaxed family atmosphere. Certainly, the controlling Roman Catholic staff at St. Anne's would have had something to say about those heinous Anglican musicians for daring to be so loose and relaxed with their creativity. I was not sure anymore whether I was still an Anglican or a Roman Catholic, but I enjoyed the relatively light atmosphere compared to the crushing rules at St. Anne's.

Going Back to School

When Christmas holidays were over, I hated having to go back to St. Anne's. Mom would always seek to keep our spirits up as we made the trek through the bush. One year, I was allowed to carry my new Christmas present, a plastic machine gun, held at the ready in case some bad person or animal might attack us. Mom, of course, also made sure to have her gun with her on these walks. It was usually her Remington shotgun, but sometimes she carried the .22 caliber instead because it was lighter. In my child-like mind, I thought my gun was the best gun because it was the lightest, being made out of plastic.

Sometimes we would enjoy a picnic together on our walk. Usually, it would be sandwiches and tea cooked over a little fire along the way. Mom would sometimes surprise us with little boxes of raisins.

Mom, Ruth, and I between St. Anne's Residential School and home at Fort Albany, circa 1959.

Those walks were bittersweet. As we set out, I was full of playful expression, but as we got closer to the school, I started to retreat into my head. I could feel the claws of St. Anne's reaching out to grab me the closer we got to the school. My carefree behaviour changed along the way, and I became more introverted and troubled.

Even at my young age and with my relative lack of experience, I knew very clearly that the school represented something abnormal and unhealthy. Unfortunately, Mom did not equate my behaviour with cries for help, but rather the disappointment of a child not wanting the holidays to end. Ruth, who was having a relatively better time in residence, did not seem as troubled, so Mom (as well as Dad) did not think there was any deeper reason for my behaviour. And Mom was also distracted by her own pain, suffering from the fact that she would be without her kids at home until the next holidays.

Arriving at the school, I had to hand my gun over to Mom and enter that prison again, unarmed. With parting hugs, Mom bid us farewell at the door. Ruth was immediately whisked away to the girls' dormitory. She just seemed to evaporate, with hardly enough time to say "bye" to me, and I found myself all alone, with no choice but to enter into that living hell once again.

I had to brace myself as I made my way down that dark, stinking hall to the boys' dorm. To re-enter that stench and become ensnared in that controlling atmosphere of monastic life once more, with no power or say so, was torture. It affected me so much that I shrivelled, walking down the hallway with hunched shoulders like a pained and broken old man.

As I walked deeper into the darkness, I tried to become invisible as fast as possible in order to avoid any dangers that might be lurking in the depths of the place.

Some people might feel safe cloistered within such an authoritarian environment, people who need a hierarchical structure in their life to have a sense of place, but for me it was a controlling, soul-sucking, scary place, which only heightened my sense of abandonment.

Walking into the darkness and up the stairs to the boys' dorm was an act of courage – like walking back into hell. But what is hell to a small child? To me, it was like having to walk undefended into a dense forest at night, with the sound of snarling wild animals lurking in the shadows, ready to rip me to pieces and reduce me to nothingness. This challenge transformed me from the carefree little Hudson's Bay Company child back into a tormented soul, just another inconvenient number to be forgotten, regardless of skin colour or class.

Upon reaching the boys' dorm, I felt another emptiness. Who was I to connect with now? My family did not seem to understand me anymore. My new family of Native boys in the dorm were traumatized like myself, likely more so. All we could do was try to stay sane, try to avoid harm, and try to help each other survive.

A lot of me as a child is still trapped there, as it is with the other kids. I was likely showing the signs and symptoms of PTSD from abandonment. And even if I was not being physically abused myself, observing it was a source of trauma and a form of abuse as well.

CHAPTER THIRTEEN:
PHYSICAL ABUSE AND PUNISHMENTS

AS TIME WENT ON, I started to notice more abuse taking place. I learned to match up what I was seeing with what I was feeling but became numb to it in a way. Who was I now, and what did it matter anyway? What was real? I began to feel like those preschool orphan kids in that special area in the complex, who stared out at a confusing and threatening world.

And there were certainly threats to be concerned about for us all. If you didn't follow the strict rules, there were forms of corporal punishment, even though some were more symbolic than others, when performed in public. For example, I remember seeing an awkward whipping once in the boys' dorm. One of the older boys was singled out for some infraction, and Anna Wesley took it upon herself to give out corporal punishment. She did not seem to know what she was doing, and there was laughter from the other boys as to how to handle the whip. Even the boy getting whipped seemed to react with embellished reactions to the touch of the whip (what looked like a few stiff reeds tied together). Listening to the laughing and taunting from his peer group standing in the crowd was confusing. It made me wonder if it was indeed a punishment or just an act, like a practice demonstration of what might happen if we did indeed deserve punishment.

We younger boys were always at the edge of the crowd, and I did not really know the extent of the boy's apparent wrongdoings. Probably pretty minor, I would think. This lack of explanation also created the fear that maybe I might unintentionally do something wrong and be the next one to suffer the indignity and feel the lash.

I do not clearly remember the severity of this incident, but I suspect the more severe corporal punishments were carried out in private with the priests involved. In those times of being forced to watch these spectacles of abuse, I wondered whether I was part of this group of Natives that was being punished or whether I was a visitor, possibly immune from danger. I was never really sure. I was seeing two worlds and living two identities at the same time. So, I lived in fear. My white skin/brown skin dilemma and my warm home/cold school confusion were troubling and all-prevailing at such an early age. I lived both identities in both places, but in those times of abuse where it was boy versus authority, I sided with the immediate concerns of my survival and the safety of my dorm mates.

I also remember that by standing there watching, I thought I might be considered part of the process and therefore be held accountable by the person being whipped, and that there would be an accounting for my association if and when we met in some dark hallway. That thought sent terror through my veins – and so I dared not look at him while he was being whipped for fear that our eyes might meet and he might remember me.

I just wanted to hide under my blanket during these times and disappear, but I knew it was not allowed. I quaked in fear sometimes, worried that my name would be called, and that some of the older boys would come to drag me to the pillar because my time to be whipped had arrived.

Getting Hit and Punched

Tony:

"I was an inmate from the late summer of '54 to '61, and all the traumatic experiences I endured in that hellhole have haunted me for life. It was my and my brothers' great misfortune to fall under the reign of terror by that psycho nun Anna Wesley, and as year-round inmates, we had no respite from her viciousness. Although we were terrified of her, we at the same time didn't trust any of the other nuns, brothers, and priests, so we had no one to turn to.

"Anna Wesley was a fully consecrated nun, and she was known as Sister of the Immaculate Conception, with her feast day being December 8 in the Catholic calendar.... Anna Wesley was always in close proximity to us and even had her own room in the boys' dormitory. So as you can imagine, we never had a moment of respite from her cruelty, as at any moment she would explode in great fury and lash out at any boy unfortunate enough to break any of the countless rules she had in place.... When Anna Wesley went into her rages, she would use anything at hand to beat you with, and I've been on the receiving end of a soup ladle to a leather shoe. You don't realize how hard an Oxford shoe is till you get beaten by the heel of one!! However, her main weapon was her fists, and many a time I was left stumbling around seeing stars after she took a round out of me."

Kneeling in the Corner

Sometimes Anna Wesley would direct a boy to kneel, sitting back on his lower legs, in a corner of the dorm room. Seeing boys kneeling in this position, they looked to me as if they might be doing extra prayer duty, or maybe even playing hide-and-seek, but they did not move – which I thought was odd. They just stayed there in the same position for very long periods of time. I had learned to keep to myself, so I never questioned this strange game. Eventually, I learned that there was something a lot more serious and sinister going on, and it was not a game. The dorm nun was making them suffer. I would pull my blanket over my head, trying to be invisible at times like that.

Tony:

"Anna Wesley was also very inventive in finding diverse ways to torture kids, such as standing at attention for hours outside in the dead of winter or kneeling in a corner on your back legs in order to cut off all circulation. She would find

it greatly entertaining to watch you try to stand up after this ordeal. She was completely psycho. The daily brutality inflicted on the boys by Anna Wesley was traumatizing to all who witnessed her cruelty. Today I understand that you don't necessarily have to be the victim being brutalized to be traumatized, but witnessing it is just as bad. With upwards of a hundred boys, there weren't too many days where some poor kid wasn't being slapped around."

More Beatings

Another classmate who reached out to me during the writing of this book further illustrates the conditions in the boys' dormitory. His name is Mike Gull, and his account is as follows:

"My first year there was 1960. I used to get beaten up by a nun who was Native. The nun was from Attawapiskat and her name was Anna Wesley; she used some other name for being some former saint, and she wasn't much of a saint. She used to beat me for unknown reasons. One time she hit (me) with both hands to my both eyes, and that hurt.... She used to beat my brother Luke, and the beating [continued] onto me ... I came back when Brother Lauzon was in charge, and everything was good with him ... at least he was good to me. He used to ask me to look after young ones on weekend camping trips, so I did."

Hidden Abuses

I was old enough at the time to understand what being spanked and whipped meant but anything more than that, like torture or sexual abuse, was foreign to me, and I would likely not even have recognized it if it was right in front of me. But certainly, there was more abuse going on that I was unaware of.

Tony:

"There's nothing scarier for a child than to see a nun in a towering rage. For eight long years, I witnessed so many little children being abused, and we amongst ourselves would somehow know that one of us was being sexually abused by a staff member. As we were always together, if a child was gone for no good reason, we would suspect something happened, and sure enough the absent child would reappear ... looking very sad and quiet."

The Effect of Such Abuses

Such physical abuse would live on in the lives of many of the victims, and they sometimes went on to abuse others, as noted on page 136 in the *Final Report of the Truth and Reconciliation Commission:* "Many students who spoke to the Commission said they developed addictions as a means of coping. Students who were treated and punished like prisoners in schools often graduated to real prisons" in adult life. Many students grew up to become parents who were cold and withholding from their own children because they did not learn compassion or receive positive reinforcement in the residential school life.

Tony:

"I was just talking to a former inmate who I haven't seen in years and years, and he became very emotional when talking about Albany. He told me that he could never hug his kids when they were growing up, which makes sense because any display of love or kindness in that hellhole was looked at as a sign of weakness. The Catholic staff, having sworn themselves to a life of celibacy, didn't of course see much use in children and probably just looked down on us as just a nuisance."

The Electric Chair and Other Punishments

As I think about these torturous times, I recall not only leather straps and other whipping tools, but another device known as "the electric chair." I remember us boys crowding around the apparatus. The older boys were in the closest circles around the device, with us younger boys on the periphery trying to catch sight of it as best we could.

Apparently, one of the more inventive brothers at St. Anne's had devised this contraption, which was a chair hooked up to a battery of sorts. He would instruct a student to sit in the chair, hold onto the handles (which were either metal or had metal wires on it to conduct the charge), and then he would crank a box, bringing an electrical charge to life.

Tony:

"The brothers were a poorly educated bunch and probably bored with their station in life and would come up with what they thought was amusing entertainment, like the electric chair."

The chair was located in the basement where we performed our Christmas concerts and watched movies. Staff would gather to watch and enjoy the spectacle of kids being electrocuted. At the time, it was not thought of as being electrocuted so much as being shocked or even surprised. I do not remember seeing a student forcibly strapped in to receive punishment. Maybe when it was punishment it was done in private, or else I have been able to bury the memory. I also do not remember hearing any crying, just brief vocalizations from yelps to snickers of bravado.

Some of the boys would volunteer to feel its effects as a way of indicating their status and bravery within the group. I was tempted to show my bravery as well by letting the brother sit me down in the chair and zap me with that thing, hoping it would raise my status within the boys' group, but I did not have the courage. I was not sure what I was more afraid of: the shock or breaking rank and moving from the back of the crowd to the centre of attraction.

I can only recall a few memories of that chair, including a metal arm and wires leading to a box with a handle on it like a crank. I remember inching my way closer to it with my little friends after it was turned off and touching it gently, pulling my little finger away as quickly as possible as if it was a flame that might burn me.

In my memory, it did not fit in the same place as boys being hit on the head with the heel of a shoe, or getting strapped or whipped, so I likely did not see it as a tool used for punishment at that time, but it was something to be cautious of.

During the writing of this book, accounts have come to light that students were forced to endure the pain of being shocked by the chair. Apparently, by their report, the chair was used as a torture device. But it must have been after my time there – or else, I was unaware of its full use. After all, I was in such a stunned state, as I have mentioned before, so I might have just been oblivious of what was in front of me. Evil can be banal at times; it can be right in front of one and yet is unseen.

I believe now that if I had viewed the electric chair as a punishment device, then it would have seemed frightening, but when I viewed it as a curiosity, a novelty, or a gimmick, like some of the other students, then it had less fear attached to it even though the physical shock would be the same.

Regarding what happened to the electric chair, Mike Gull had this to say:

> *"Mathieu Nakogee did mention it was destroyed or thrown away in the dump by Mr. John Kataquapit, the janitor at the time."*

Interesting how "intent" plays such a significant role in determining perceived torture – regardless of the degree of pain involved. For example, what could be a simple science experiment to one person can change with context into an instrument of terror and torture, and it can be exactly the same instrument. Because of this dynamic, people might be doing things to others even now and might not even realize that they are unknowingly administering torture.

The Quality of Care

Some of the ailments at St. Anne's were hard to identify, and other diseases were more obvious, although the treatment was still questionable. These devastating "white man" diseases would visit our dorm on a few occasions and strike with a vengeance. Thankfully, Mom had made sure that I (and my two sisters) were inoculated against such diseases a few years earlier, so I was pretty much immune to them. My dorm mates were not so fortunate.

> **Tony:**
>
> *"You know, we had all manner of illnesses: measles, chicken pox, mumps, and the usual flu, which was on a yearly basis. Of course, once one kid got sick, everybody else would get sick as it would spread like wildfire. We would be all confined to our dormitories and made to stay in bed till the pestilence was over. Certainly, there was no caring person checking up on you, and we all just toughed it out. Funny thing is that on the onset of any illness, the nun would take out her thermometer and check each kid's temperature, which of course only helped in the spread of any illness, as this non-sterilized thermometer was inserted in each kid's mouth, spreading the illness faster."*

This was one more example of the inept, indifferent, and in some respects intentional abuse by our caregivers – some well-meaning and highly trained, who went through the motions of care, but apparently only with half-hearted measures.

CHAPTER FOURTEEN:
ESCAPING FROM ST. ANNE'S RESIDENTIAL SCHOOL

AFTER ABOUT TWO YEARS AT St. Anne's, I reached a point when I could not take it any longer. It was not one event, but a combination of everything that compelled me to hatch a plan to escape. I hated the atmosphere of that prison and also still held the vision of my happy home life firmly in my mind. Thankfully, the school had not shattered that memory of home, a shining beacon of hope. This demanded action. I wasn't sure whether I had the nerve to escape by myself, but I knew that if my sister Ruth went with me, we would have the courage together.

It was difficult for boys and girls to talk to each other, but eventually I was able to exchange a few words with Ruth when we were filing out of chapel one day. This opportunity was not just a happy coincidence, though. I had to time my movements perfectly so I was beside her when we exited. Although I was not sure how she would respond, I whispered a hello to her.

To my relief, Ruth whispered a "hi" back to me. Although we only had a few seconds to talk, while we were mixed in with the others exiting the chapel, I was able to communicate my intensions to her. Thankfully, she agreed to escape as well. I wonder now whether her motivation to escape was more of a need to protect me than a need to leave the place. After all, the girls were enjoying more freedom of movement, like going for collation and walks in the woods with their dorm supervisor, as compared to the lack of freedom we boys were experiencing.

On the evening of our escape, I went to bed and waited till the lights were out and my dorm mates were all settled in their beds. I had wanted to keep my outdoor clothes on, given the winter conditions that I would be facing outside. But since we boys had to change into our pajamas before kneeling on our beds to say evening prayers, there was no opportunity afterwards to change back into my clothes that were now hanging in my locker and separated by many beds and prying eyes. Like any prisoner, I had no choice but to attempt an escape with just the clothes (my cotton pajamas) on my back.

Ruth and I had agreed to meet at the base of the stairs leading to the boys' dorm, and even though it was uncertain whether she would be waiting for me, it was now or never. I summoned all my courage in an act of faith and began to slide out of my bed, trying not to disturb any of my dorm mates. I moved as quietly as possible in the darkness and made my way through the tight maze of beds, pretending to go to the washroom. Concern that I might be noticed prompted me to be as quick as possible before anyone might wonder and question my movements.

The security door to the hallway was on the way to the washroom, and I eased it open as quietly as possible and exited. The latch clicked shut with a cold, deadening "thunk" as I made my escape.

I was now in the quiet hallway and moving quickly to where my coat and boots were hung. I put them on and began to sneak down the stairs. Thankfully my parka was long enough and my boots high enough to cover most of my pajamas. The desire to just get out of that place had overshadowed any concern of not being dressed appropriately for the long, cold, and uncertain journey that lay ahead.

The stairway was unusually dark and lifeless since I had never been there during the night when most of the lights were turned off. It was also surprisingly peaceful, but the fear of running into a nun or priest made me choke on my breath and my hair stand on end. (Imagine what it might be like to run into a symbol of fear like Darth Vader or Dracula in the dark hallway – likely it would be scary at any age.) Thank goodness, it was Ruth waiting for me in the shadows at the bottom of the stairs. After whispering a hurried greeting and an expressed concern over my pajama-clad knees, we began making our way down the hallway. I forget if Ruth was just wearing her pajamas under her big parka as well.

Reaching the front door, we looked at each other, took a big breath, and stepped outside. A cold blast of fresh winter air met us as the front door closed with a firm "thunk" behind us. In our heightened state of fear, it seemed that the building was alive and aware of our movements. With the rush of adrenaline still pumping through our systems from the last few stressful minutes, we started out, not sure whether to run or walk quickly. I think we did a bit of both.

As we passed by the little log building situated away from the main complex, we noticed that a window was slightly open, and there were loaves of bread within our reach. So, we reached in and pulled out two round loaves of bread, one for each of us. This was, if I recall, the little store that supplied the staff and surrounding community with various goods and supplies. We had not planned to take the bread, but it came in handy through the night, as we began to make our way home.

It felt like the first night of the rest of our lives, and also like it might be our last. Ruth was about nine years old, and I about seven – but I felt much older at that moment. With the sound of dogs or maybe wolves howling in the distance, we set out. It was about 9:00 p.m. The realization that there was danger both in front of and behind us started to sink in, but we were now too afraid to turn back. We began moving with purpose and dreaming of the comforts of home. No turning back now.

Thankfully, we had a clear idea of the direction we had to take because of our outings with Mom: through the field, down to the frozen river about a mile away, then across the river and into the bush beyond, along the trail for another few miles on Anderson Island, then out onto the ice again of the Albany River headed toward James Bay.

Even during the day, the trail over Anderson Island felt confining with the trees so close on each side of the trail. But at night it was an act of courage to walk into the unknown and through that thick stretch of forest.

The trail over Anderson Island during daylight, circa 1960.

The trail was dark and frightening. Add the howling animals – dogs or wolves, both dangerous – and you get a sense of how intimidating it was for two little kids walking on that frozen path through the dark. Every branch seemed ready to grab us. It was like walking through a haunted forest where anything might come alive at any moment, reach out, and grab us with its tentacles. The sense of fear was so thick for me, it was like walking through molasses.

I also remember the horrific realization, as we moved through the bush, that the howling dogs were likely the same ones that had attacked me when Mr. Anderson had once parked his dogs outside our home. Now we were walking right past them a few hundred feet away, in the dark of the night. The sound of them lunging against their chains and their howls, growls, and snarls was terrifying. I tried to numb my thoughts to the possibility of pain and death, fearing that they would suddenly attack from the shadows. I listened for any sudden panting or breaking branches that might be coming toward us, and I remember thinking that at least we had moonlight.

Hopefully, it was light enough for God to see us and protect us. In times of need, praying seems to come so readily, almost naturally to one, regardless of their degree of faith. Our whispered prayers, mixed with the crunch of the snow, added dimension to the fear we were moving through. There was a sense of urgency, as if we were in a race against time, as we searched for the right prayer, the right spell to say, that might keep us safe. Finally, we were past the dogs and still alive.

As we walked, we snacked on the bread, which kept us busy and more importantly, distracted us from the dangers we were walking through. We eventually ate out the centre of the loaves, and then made two openings for our eyes out of the remaining bread crusts and tried to put them on our heads, thinking that this tactic would scare off any wild animals. They did not quite fit over our heads though, so we just kept eating the bread and headed out of the bush, down the riverbank, and onto the ice of the river. That is when it hit me: *Oh God, this is where the polar bears roamed.* My fear almost got the best of me, and I took hold of Ruth's hand, hoping I could depend on her bravery as mine had about run out. So out onto the ice we walked, hand in hand, two little morsels of meat covered with bread.

About halfway across the river, we came upon big, uplifted chunks of ice many feet high and many feet thick that glowed in the moonlight. This must have been a pressure ridge in the channel of the river to have caused sheets of ice to be pushed up. Spring break-up might have been coming soon to cause such upheavals.

Frozen pressure point on Albany River, where a polar bear might be hiding, circa 1960.

In such surreal surroundings, fear was normal. Some sort of big animal, maybe a polar bear with the stink of hunger on its breath, might lunge out from behind one of those sheets of ice, and then what? Best not to think of it. We continued on and crossed the river and then followed the northern shoreline for about another mile. Making our way through fresh snowdrifts on the river ice that covered any hint of a trail, we tried to stay composed and calm as we kept an eye out for the break in the cliff that led up to our home.

We only had the moonlight to guide us. There were no electric lights on any of the buildings in those days. If we missed this break, we could have walked forever out onto the ice of James Bay. Luckily, we saw the way and walked up the river bank, past the Anglican Church, finally reaching our picket fence – the mark of colonialism, the HBC protected area, and our quintessential symbol of home. We felt elated. We were home! We had escaped! We were still alive! Even at our young age, we were both very aware that we were lucky to have made it home safely. What a feeling of relief and accomplishment. It was an amazing feat that could have gone so wrong!

Our home at Fort Albany looking toward the Anglican Native community, with St. Anne's over the horizon on the left, and our picket fence buried in snow, circa 1960.

Rather than go bursting into the house, we decided to surprise our parents by knocking at the door. No strangers ever visited, so knocks on the front door were very rare indeed. I am struck by the symbolism of us knocking now. Our life at the residential school had changed us. We were to some degree different – so maybe it was appropriate to knock. I remember Mom's shock as she gasped and called out our names first before asking any questions. Dad appeared from the bedroom, certainly surprised, but also concerned and even perturbed and agitated at our actions. He then went back to bed, grumbling under his breath, although Mom made us some porridge for breakfast. It tasted so wonderful as we recounted our adventure to Mom.

Despite our successful effort to escape, our joy was short-lived. Representatives from the school found us later that morning. I remember enjoying looking at the pristine white of the snowbank surrounding our yard and feeling safe, when suddenly a vehicle with ugly steel cleats (similar to what a military tank uses), broke through the white stillness of the yard, crushing the beautiful blanket of snow and my happiness. It was a swamp buggy of sorts that could travel over the snow.

When I see war movies now as an adult, where the tanks come crashing through the fences, it reminds me of that morning when they came to get us at home. I knew we had been found and that there was now nowhere to hide. It felt like life had ended for me and that I would never escape the confines of the school ever again.

The vehicle carried two men who were part of the search effort. One was a serious-mannered priest wearing starched robes and a cross, and the other (the driver) was an unshaven lay brother in stained work clothes, a hat, and a roll-your-own cigarette dangling from his lips.

Then Mr. Anderson's Bombardier arrived. Two nuns, accompanied by Mr. Anderson, got out in all their finery: crisp, smartly designed uniforms with sparkles and beads and crucifixes. Likely the nuns had stopped at the home of Mr. Anderson (the justice of the peace), to ask for his assistance in finding Ruth and me. The establishment had come all decked out in formal clothes to represent their concern and authority. It felt like the guards had come to round up us defenceless kids, and we might never be seen again.

A number of our schoolmates who had come with the nuns, also exited the Bombardier. Rather than walking through our front gate though, the kids jumped over top of the big snow bank that was covering our white picket fence instead. Their mitts, connected through their parkas with red and white string, flapped excitedly from their movements. It was a surprise to see them enter our yard so boldly since it had been off limits to the community in the past. Maybe with the nuns leading them, the Native kids felt brave enough to enter HBC territory. Who knows, but it was still a shock to me and felt like an invasion even if it was a friendly one. It was like their actions were piercing the HBC bubble of protection that I had hid behind for so long, which also added to the drama of the morning.

Bringing those kids was likely an attempt by the nuns to put the school in a good light. I remember being unsure how I felt, though. Seeing them in the HBC yard, and a few even entering our house with the nuns, left me with the uneasy realization that my home was not separate from the residential school any longer, that it was part of the larger world whether I liked it or not.

I remember that those Native kids did not show any interest in the interior of our house, but rather just looked excitedly at Ruth and me as if they were happy to see us and that they cared about our welfare regardless of our class and privilege. I have to admit that seeing them in our home felt strange at first, but their smiles helped to disarm the situation. Their heartfelt concern for us, their fellow students, also taught me a lesson in that moment. Friendship can find its way through many barriers including class, race, even our white picket fence.

The nuns, on the other hand, did not offer me any comfort. I was surprised at their laughter and the smiles pasted on their faces, like animals baring their teeth, a threatening gesture in the wild animal kingdom, although my parents just saw the smiles. The hint of whiskers sticking out from the exposed skin of the nun in charge also seemed odd. It was like some sort of manliness was oozing out of her face. Obviously, she had not taken the time to shave earlier that morning in order to start the search to find Ruth and me.

I hoped against hope that my parents would defend us now that we had risked our lives to escape. There was lots of talking, almost as if it was a social occasion, until I heard Mom give out a gasp. I caught the words "polar bear tracks." The nuns said they had seen tracks over top of our little footprints in the snow. This of course reminded Mom of the polar bear she had seen on the other side of the river on her way home from a previous visit to the school. I just heard exasperated sighs coming from Dad. There was that look again – yes, that one. He was looking at me like I was the little hellion – out of control and likely the cause of this momentous escape. Well, maybe I was. I shudder to think now what horrible feelings of guilt it would have been for me if the bear had eaten Ruth.

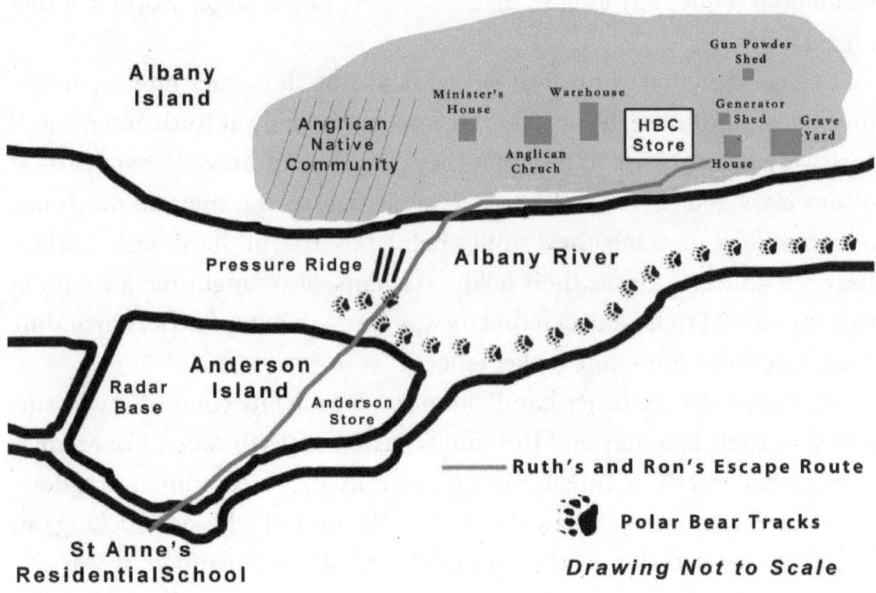

Drawing of Ruth's and Ron's route home and the polar bear tracks.

Unfortunately, our courage was still not enough to win our freedom and get our parents' understanding. There was no question about whether we were being sent back, but I do recall that I was given the option of riding in the swamp buggy or in the Bombardier with Ruth, the nuns, and the rest of the kids. I decided to travel back in the swamp buggy. I think I made my choice based on my experience with tanks from my days driving my pretend snow tank at home just a few years before. Since the swamp buggy looked like it might be a real tank to my young eyes, I thought I may as well experience it – even if it was an enemy tank.

I hugged my mother. I forget if I got a hug from Dad, but I waved to my sisters, and with sadness and tears welling up inside me, trying to be brave, I climbed aboard; the seven-year-old survivor being sent back to the trenches. The priest just acted officious – your typical ignorant authoritarian, like an SS officer commanding the troops.

The swamp buggy that took me back to school, Fort Albany, circa 1960.

Riding in the swamp buggy was loud, with the smothering smell of oil and gas filling the cab. I was surprised at how jarring it was inside the vehicle, because its outer appearance looked so sleek. The atmosphere was friendly – likely the men were enjoying a break in the monotony of yet another day – but it was a sad ride for me knowing that we were going back. I just stared at the floor, trying not to feel anything.

At some point while crossing the frozen river, the vehicle slowed down and stopped. Were we turning around? Maybe they had a change of heart and were taking me back home – but no. The driver began backing the vehicle up as if looking for something. Then he slammed on the brakes and pointed to the snow saying, "There, and there."

The two men were talking. I did not even bother to look up, I was so sad. The driver then raised the canopy of the vehicle and gently shook my shoulder and said, "Look there," as he pointed downwards. And there they were – Ruth's and my little footprints in the snow from our walk the night before, but now there were also tracks of a big animal with claws over top of ours. Polar bear tracks. Although the men insisted on showing me the tracks, I did not want to acknowledge them, because they served no purpose to me except to compel me not to run away from school anymore.

I knew that they were showing me the tracks as a warning. But it also felt like they were trying to show me that St. Anne's Residential School had won, and that Ruth's and my courage counted for nothing. The image of the claw marks over our footprints may as well have been a symbol of the school's control over us: it had its claws in us, and we could not escape its clutches.

We resumed our journey, and I retreated into my thoughts, anticipating that horrid environment of St. Anne's so fast approaching. Ruth rode back in the Bombardier, so I was not aware if she had any apprehension of being taken back to school. I do not remember seeing her for some time after that.

The swamp buggy delivered me right to the front door of St. Anne's, where a nun gave me a token greeting and then pointed into the depths of the place, directing me back into the dark and toward the stairs leading to the boys' dorm. When Anna Wesley saw me, she was all business, and dismissive, as if I was not even worth talking to. She did not even express any relief that I had survived my daring dash home. She just treated me with a cold indifference. Likely she had received a reprimand for allowing one of her charges to escape during her shift.

I did receive a silent but very public punishment though for running away. For a few weeks, no matter how many fingers I held up for bread at mealtime, I only got one slice when Anna Wesley was serving the bread. The wide-eyed looks of concern from my schoolmates around me was noticeable as I suffered through the silent but public form of punishment. It may not seem like a big deal, but to a young child who cherished this one liberty, it was significant. My voice and now even my hand signals had been silenced. I became concerned that she might even have one of her favourites make her displeasure more known to me in the privacy of the bathroom or some such place. I moved around in fear and terror – painfully aware that Mom and Dad were nowhere close to protect me.

I came to realize though, that having risked my life to escape that prison, I possessed the courage, even at my very young age, to take action to deal with anything destructive to me. This experience helped me to learn what I was made of. This was a liberating revelation even though I was still trapped.

CHAPTER FIFTEEN:
NO WAY OUT – I CAN'T ESCAPE

OUR DASH HOME WAS SUCCESSFUL because we did not die. Others were not so lucky. Many fellow students that made the break from time to time were found frozen to death. Some were never found. That is how desperate we were to escape and return to the comfort of home that we missed so badly.

Some of these kids came from hundreds of miles away, and they might not have known what direction their home was. They were doomed before they even set foot out the door. Others might have had an idea what direction to go but still never made it home. One former student from St. Anne's, Pauline Veenstra, says this:

> "(My) late uncle John Kioke was one of the three boys that disappeared in 1941. And his dad was the one that used to take his brother John back to St. Anne's each time he ran away. He told the priest, 'If my brother runs away again, I'm not bringing him back,' and that was the last time he saw John. He was seventeen at the time and carried that guilt with him until he died."

Self-serving interests of both Church and State had brought these children to this foreign hell, but they knew they still had kin out there who loved them.

Aerial photo of terrain around St. Anne's and Fort Albany.

What would cause "students" to try to escape, even at risk of death? They knew that as well as the unforgiving terrain, they would also face the possibility of animal attacks, the lethal cold of the North, and having neither food nor shelter to keep them going. They had only the roughest idea where they were heading, but at least they were going HOME.

How many students knew it was hopeless, and feeling abandoned and abused, were just happy to die free? I wonder how many students were never found. I wonder how and whether their parents were informed of their child's death. I wonder where the kids that were found are buried, and what their grave markers say, if anything. I wonder how many parents will never be able to visit the graves of their children. I wonder how many of my fellow students, my little friends that did not care about the colour of my skin, but just whether there was solidarity between us, are lost there, the ones who banded together with me as we tried to protect and comfort one another.

Even with the dangers associated with escaping, many students still attempted it. On certain nights we could still hear the dorm room door slowly open and then the hollow click of the latch, the squeak of hinges, the pounding of feet down the hallway and then down the stairs. Next, there was the sound of another door closing with a BANG, followed by the dull thud of the outside door. Another successful escape. At least, a successful escape into the night and into the darkened forest.

I tried to fall asleep when these escapes happened ... on the one hand wanting to dream that I was running away with them, but also not wanting to feel the pain of being left behind. I also feared that Anna Wesley might be hovering over me and any indication that I was awake might make me complicit in the escape and invite her wrath. So, I lay still, with my head under the pillow, not daring to move. In the morning, it was as if nothing had happened and life went on. No questions were asked ... we were just expected to be quiet, pray, and follow the rules as usual.

Native children attending residential schools died at a higher rate than school-aged children in the general population and were often buried in unmarked graves, according to the *Final Report of the Truth and Reconciliation Commission*.

Trying to End it All

After my failed escape, and realizing that there was truly no way out, I tried to kill myself a number of times. As a child, I didn't think of my actions so much as trying to kill myself, but rather of wanting to make the isolation, the frustration, the trauma stop, which of course when followed through might have resulted in killing myself.

Once, I tried to freeze myself to death in the frigid school yard by taking off my parka. I sat in the snow crying and staring in the direction of home until a nun bundled me inside.

Another time, I tried to stuff strips of cloth up my nose in an effort to stop breathing.

I also made numerous attempts to bash my head to a pulp against the cement wall in a stairwell. The response of the nuns' was not to ask why. They merely wrapped my head in a towel to cushion my blows.

I was not old enough to have developed any mental tools to figure out what was happening to me. In retrospect, suicide was quite rational: I was banging my head against the wall for a reason. Insanity is a very rational response to insane conditions, and St. Anne's was an insane condition!

I don't even think it's fair to say I wasn't given the tools. I would say that every time I picked up a tool or tried to create a tool to try to develop an understanding of the situation, it was torn out of my hands. One was expected to go through the motions of the day-to-day agenda and not ask questions, and "be quiet!" I was feeling something was wrong, but to even express that I was feeling that something was wrong, was wrong. That just destroys a child. How do they function?

So I snapped. With my head wrapped in a big cloth bandage, I was now "turban boy": a white-skinned child, imprisoned in a deeply conservative Christian-run residential "school" built to remove generations of indigenous opponents. Bizarre!

I certainly wasn't the only inmate under stress. We were all traumatized to varying degrees and in many ways. I made my own suicide attempts because I'd become convinced that I would be at St. Anne's forever; a life of endless terror, with no hope for anything better.

What was the reason for the strict code of silence? Why could we not show emotion? Why could we not say we were scared? Why could we not play with the girls at recess? And why were the girls allowed to go on picnics, yet we boys were kept locked up? There were no explanations.

The closest attempt by any of the staff to address my actions was when I felt my shoulder gripped by the same nun who had originally dragged me into St. Anne's. Squeezing my shoulder, she sighed with a tiredness that suggested to me that my behaviour was exhausting. Perhaps she wanted to be "motherly" but had no idea how this was done.

Mom Is Allowed to Visit Me in the Boys' Dorm

When I had fully given up on life, I was allowed to stay in bed. I now suspect this was privileged treatment granted because I was white. I did not have any life-threatening disease: I just gave up and refused to get out of bed. A Native boy would likely face being slapped or whipped, but I did not know or care anymore whether I was special. At that point, I must have been broken: the possibility of a beating did not scare me anymore. It did not matter, and even if it had happened, I would not have cared.

During the day, I lay alone in the darkened dorm room, surrounded by a hundred beds. In retrospect, the blinds were probably drawn to allow me to rest in the shadows. One afternoon, like an angel of light, my mother appeared by my bedside and whispered quietly to me. She had been allowed to visit me during the day, when the other boys were away.

Was it coincidence that she happened to visit that day? Or had she somehow been notified of my state? Years later, Mom forgets what caused her to arrive at that crucial moment.

It was the one and only time mom was allowed into the boys' dorm: letting parents visit the sleeping quarters of their kids, regardless of gender, was unheard of. Yet, I suspect the rules that applied to the families of my darker-skinned friends could be bent by my own family. This privilege aside, there was no doubt that I was emotionally sick and in a deep depression. I had given up: by this point, I had heard quite a lot about the Christian "afterlife"... a destination clearly happier than St. Anne's.

Mom sat on my bed. To her credit, she tried to comfort me, but since she didn't understand why I was broken, she obviously had no idea how I could be fixed. And if no one else on the outside knew how to fix me, and since I didn't have the words to communicate what I was experiencing, broken I would remain.

Years later, as the horrors of St. Anne's eventually became public, Mom would express feelings of guilt for enrolling me at the school. Her words are quite poignant:

> *"Forgive me, Son, where I failed. My purgatory will not come at death. I am experiencing it now."* (See the Afterword to read her full note to me).

The Man in the Light Green Suit

The head-bashing incident must have gotten the attention of higher ups, possibly Mother Superior, because I was informed by a white-uniformed nun (a nurse) that it was okay to continue to stay by myself in the boys' dorm. Although I was concerned what being "quarantined" might lead to, I was also relieved to have some time for myself without having to worry about being quiet, standing in some lineup, confessing my sins, etc.

As I wandered back and forth between the rows of empty beds, enjoying the sunshine streaming through the window, a tall, slim, middle-aged man with light hair came into the dormitory and just stood and looked at me from the other side of the room for an unusually long time. He was not wearing a uniform, but rather a light green suit. The thought that he might be a medical doctor worried me, so I picked up a broom and began sweeping the floor: a demonstration of productivity in case he might be planning to "disappear" me. Odd that I thought of that word — "disappeared" — as a child: I wouldn't think of it again until decades later in relation to concentration camps and the actions of dictators.

I was curious why this man in the light green suit didn't walk over to me, instead standing across the room as if he just wanted to observe. Taking the initiative, I walked over to him and introduced myself. He did not show any recognition when hearing my name, which just added to my uneasiness.

I wanted to express my fear and trauma to him, but I was not sure whose side he was on. But given his gentle demeanour, I decided to trust him a little. He asked me questions I do not remember now. I believe I did tell him some things, but I was uncertain of his intentions, so I remained cautious and said I was okay. My answers must have satisfied him, though, because once the questioning was over, he nodded to me and left, and I never saw him again.

I remember the feeling that I was missing an opportunity to say more. Here was someone obviously in authority, someone who might be able to rescue me from my circumstances. But my uncertainty about who he was, my inability as a child to articulate, and the school's policy of intimidation led me to keep silent about my feelings and emotions and the reasons for my suicidal actions.

My state of mind was confused, as though I was crazy on the outside but sane on the inside, wondering whether I had gone crazy or whether I was just acting crazy, trying to survive in a crazy situation. I knew that something was wrong, but because I could not articulate it to the right people who might have been able to help, I was at a loss as to what to do.

I felt so trapped and confused and just wanted to escape what I was feeling. With no option to fight back, rather than trying suicide again, I just went to live in my head, hoping to find some happy lost memories of home that I could hold onto.

But I could not shut off the outside world completely. I still had to get through each day and deal with any injustices that I saw or experienced. It was a struggle to weather the cruelties of the place that came at me like a sandstorm – each tiny particle stinging, each barbed word or threat ripping at my peace of mind, each thunderous clap of authority robbing me of my voice. It was pure survival, one day to the next.

I had lost the few words I ever had to reconcile my experience. My emotions and feelings chased each other round and round, making me so dizzy that I was not able to think or even speak. I felt abandoned, like an orphan, my identity and freedom lost. The only glimmer of hope was to hang on until summer holidays. Only then might the storm of abuse cease and the grip of control lighten.

Although I felt like an abandoned child at the time, there were actual orphans who had it a lot harder than me and my two sisters.

It was not until the writing of this book that I realized why Mom and Dad did not come for long periods of time to visit us in the spring. It was simply too dangerous. Just as we had experienced at the HBC post, the Albany River would rise over its banks and flood the surrounding countryside, including St. Anne's. During those times, we were trapped from venturing outside, marooned with our persecutors.

Spring flooding. Source: Archives Deschâtelets-NDC, Fonds Deschâtelets, Fort Albany residential school.

Tony:

"We used to pray like hell that the school would flood during break-up, but my prayers were never answered. Every break-up I was there we would have to pray that there wouldn't be a major flood; however, a few times the water came close to the building but never high enough to do any major damage. When this happened, we were kept in the prison till the water had gone down. Alas, my prayers were never answered."

CHAPTER SIXTEEN:
EASTER – KISSING THE RING OF AUTHORITY

SOON AFTER SPRING BREAK-UP, THE week of Easter celebrations would begin. I was used to the excitement of Easter back home when we got to enjoy the chocolate treats brought by the Easter Bunny, a more tangible highlight to a child than the symbolic religious meaning of Easter. The lack of treats at St. Anne's was disappointing, and the stressful orgy of praying, sacrifice, and self-denial there was painful, to say the least.

Tony:

"I don't know which one I hated more, Christmas or Easter. Talk about a gloomy week, what with constantly praying and having to fast on Good Friday ... as if we didn't fast enough as it was. (We were) told we had to give up something we liked eating or doing for Lent. Seeing as how we never got candies, fruits, or desserts, what the hell were we supposed to give up? I remember when being asked I would say bread but very rarely would I get bread, so it wasn't a big sacrifice. I sometimes wondered what the other kids would say."

To highlight Easter celebrations, a bishop would come to visit us at our remote location each year. Among the many times, we were expected to bow to symbols of authority at St. Anne's, I think the visit of the Roman Catholic Bishop with his precious ring demanded the most attention.

Tony:

"Anytime the Bishop came to Albany, the staff would go all out to celebrate his arrival with much pomp and ceremony. One would think that Jesus H. Christ himself had miraculously appeared at this desolate institution ... Usually a week before the arrival of His Eminence, as the staff would call him, the nuns would busy themselves making all manner of paper flower bouquets, which they placed all over the damn place, while supervising a major clean-up by the local servant staff. These servants were an indispensable part in ensuring the prison operated properly, as they did all the heavy lifting required such as cleaning, cooking, laundry, and sewing. Oftentimes, I hear of all the sacrifices and hard work these nuns did on behalf of us inmates, and to this I say bullshit, as they had these servants.... For their part, the brothers would busy themselves in making sure the exterior would look welcoming by installing rows of coniferous trees strategically located where His Eminence would walk."

On one of the Bishop's visits, the nuns assembled us two hundred or so kids on the boardwalk in a line-up that stretched between the priests' residence and the nursing station building. They patrolled this line with loud hand claps and shouts in an attempt to keep us traumatized little prisoners in order. The barking of the stray dogs there could have been taken for guard dogs in an internment camp.

As a child, the game of power being played out with the Bishop's visit was lost on me. When I first saw him, I thought he might be a section manager of sorts, like the HBC section manager who flew in to check on Dad and our family at the HBC post. At those times at home, we had to snap to attention and hope like hell that he did not find fault with us, as

Dad's job depended on it. I thought, therefore, that this bishop visiting St. Anne's might be the section manager for God.

However, as the Bishop inched his way toward me, he did not look like a manager in his frilly dress uniform. He may as well have been Santa Claus and, in truth, I hoped he was Santa and that gifts might be somehow involved. Others in the line-up may not have had such childish, fanciful thoughts, but all could be boiled down to one desperate wish. We hoped that this special person could validate our efforts and existence at St. Anne's – or else deliver us from it.

Tony:
"When the big day came, all of us kids would have to line up and kiss his goddamn ring while he stood there all high and mighty. I always found this practice to be unsettling and for some reason ... humiliating."

The Bishop would walk along the boardwalk with one of his fingers outstretched with a big ring that we were to take hold of and kiss as we bowed. Being expected to participate in such a ritual seemed silly. The ring and erect finger glided below the noses of some like a butterfly too fast for them to catch. So they just responded with near-blown kisses of submission toward an unattainable prize. And yet for some, including Ruth, the bishop showed signs of interest and even affection by smiling and pausing long enough for her to catch and kiss the ring. It was curious to me how he stopped in front of some kids if they caught his eye and moved past others with little regard.

This kissing of the man's ring was seen as a special social event at the time, but when I look back now, its symbolism was huge. Imagine that an alien presence has arrived on Earth (in a bush plane), with all of God's Glory shining behind him. Then every adult, all the nuns and brothers, and the leaders, as well as the meanest and scariest ones there, bowed in reverent submission to this apparent Friend-of-God. This deference from the adults appeared somewhat spooky, and I wondered at the power he and his special ring commanded. I paid close attention as he plodded along, presenting his presence to us all, jabbing his finger in our faces, one at a time in a constant motion, like it was a job to do, a role to play, and he had a very tight schedule to keep.

I remember thinking that for someone like him to have so much power he must know of us HBC people – so he must know my parents. I became very hopeful and excited that he would recognize me as special and unique. The possibility of being saved and taken back home made me almost giddy with anticipation. I could scarcely contain my excitement imagining how surprised my schoolmates would be when the Bishop confirmed how special I was, being from the powerful HBC Post.

What would I say to him? How could I tell him that I did not belong in this place? How could I tell him that I felt abandoned? Through my child's mind – and doubtless through the minds of the other children – these questions raced. As I was lost in my thoughts, his finger suddenly slid under my nose with its all-powerful ring. It was my turn. This was my opportunity to call out to him, but I was suddenly at a loss for words. There was just a ring and finger to focus on as it dangled briefly before me. I felt speechless, now faced with his condescending action. With a loss of words, I just bowed and blew his ring a kiss as it flew by, mimicking the actions of my friends and classmates. Then it was gone. But he did not show any indication or recognition that I was different. Was I just another soul in the crowd to him? Why did he not see that I did not belong here?

Our acts of submission appeared to comfort the nuns and brothers, as seen from their smiles, as if each of our kisses represented another score for Jesus. With the deed done, my little friends and I took the opportunity to enjoy fresh air on that bright and beautiful day. We stepped out of line to chase each other around in the field, experiencing a renewed wave of solidarity that helped us forget the emptiness we all felt. Thank goodness for my little friends who overlooked all divisions in favour of play and solidarity, which helped to raise my spirits. One definite benefit of that all-powerful bishop visiting us was that it gave us kids the freedom to run about without fear of the bullies.

In other years, and during other visits by the Bishop, kissing his ring was just a prelude to more intense acts of submission that went beyond good taste and bordered on abuse.

Tony:

"When kissing that ring we would have to genuflect while he extended his ring finger down. Genuflecting would be the practice of quickly kneeling on your right knee while doing the sign of the cross, at times while quickly kissing the Bishop's ring on his outstretched right hand. However, to kiss his goddamn feet, we would have to kneel down on both knees or when in deep prayer in the prison chapel ... the worst of the worst was when we had to kiss his feet. Thankfully, he always had his shoes on. Some of the priests over the years also had us kiss their damn feet, but thankfully not on a regular basis. I guess according to their religion it had something to do with humility, but whatever you call it, it was very demeaning."

I am glad my perspective remained that of a child, as it shielded me from the larger implications of this slavish obedience to authority. Imagine forcing little children to kiss the symbol of a foreign religious power held by a grown man who expected this act of humility as a sign of respect. Some might say that such a symbolic act of submission, in the form of that dangling ring finger, was a profoundly public foreshadowing of the sexual abuse endemic to Catholic organizations like ours.

CHAPTER SEVENTEEN:
SUMMER HOLIDAYS

AS THE LAND DRIED OUT toward the end of spring, we all began to look forward to summer holidays. I was in such a state of withdrawal, though, that I did not even try to figure out exactly how many more days it would be until holidays arrived. I just knew that with spring break-up, they would arrive soon after. A calendar might have helped, but the thought did not even occur to me. I don't remember ever seeing a calendar at St. Anne's, come to think of it. Why would we need one, anyway, since all our movements were planned and controlled on a daily, even hourly, basis? To question anything carried a risk of reprimand, so I did not even bother to wonder. I just plodded along watching the land dry out, hoping that the days of freedom would come soon. When the holidays finally arrived, they were such a welcome relief to me.

The hopeless trapped days of midwinter, when some of us would risk our lives to run away, were behind us now. The holidays of June and July were approaching. Most kids were excited about going home, but some were also concerned. A lot of Native families struggled to get by with few resources, and a lot of kids were going home to where there was a shortage of food. Ruth remembers some of her dorm mates voicing their concern. Since the Church kept a close watch on the bottom line, it was unlikely that the students had the option of staying for the summer, if they had homes to go to.

And so, they would leave with trepidation as to what was waiting for them at home; on the one hand happy to be leaving such a strict place as St. Anne's, but also knowing this might result in going hungry, not to mention the ever-widening social and psychological distances with each year they were separated from their families.

Mom remembers seeing a number of airplanes and a boat arriving to transport students back to their homes at this time of year.

St. Anne's students on boat. Source: Archives Deschâtelets-NDC, Fonds Deschâtelets, Fort Albany residential school.

Although most of the kids were getting ready to leave, there were others who hung back from the preparations as if out of step with the excitement. These kids were the orphans and others who had no place to go. They were the "year-round" students who were in effect stranded at St. Anne's. Tony and his siblings were among them.

The look of these year-round students troubled me. They seemed disengaged, and I was to learn that they were just put to work at St. Anne's, doing various chores for the summer. I was glad to be going home. The idea of having to stay and suffer the controlling atmosphere of the place, and to work there as well for the summer, was unimaginable to me.

Leaving those dorm mates who obviously were not going anywhere was something I tried to ignore. But I could not help but notice them. They seemed troubled, as if they had a life-threatening disease that they were ashamed of. They looked away, resigned to their fate, pinned against the reality of their situation with no hope or magic words to save them.

Tony:

"Of course, us kids who had to remain behind would be in a deep funk. Some of the kids going home would feel sorry for us and would give us their collection of rosary beads, little statues, and holy pictures. To this day, every time I see these things, I think back to them sad days."

Even though I was one of the lucky ones, this is one time when I felt somewhat embarrassed at my fortune. Mom says it was heart-wrenching to witness the pain and suffering of some of those kids who stood around in the hallways looking at her as she and Dad waited for Ruth and me to appear. Their blank looks informed her that they had no sense of family anymore. They had no place to go. But what could be done for these unfortunates, except maybe to say a prayer for them while she waited for her children to appear?

There was a nun positioned at the front door who visited with Mom and Dad while they waited for us kids. When we finally appeared, the nun, with a big enthusiastic smile, gave our parents heartfelt handshakes and hugs. Dad got the handshake, and Mom got the hug. Mom somehow knew how to hug the nun without crumpling her starched bonnet – which I knew from experience was very fragile and precious to them.

The nun then rested her hand on our shoulders and heads with what I presume were well-meaning blessings. Even Lou got a little token hand squeeze from the nun as she sat safely in Dad's arms. I'm not sure what the blessing was. Was it just a goodbye, a go with God, be good, or permission to have fun? I took it as permission to have fun.

Feeling blessed, we exited into the fresh air and walked across the field, past the screeching sound of the sawmill blade, and down to our big trusted freighter canoe waiting at the shore. As we took our places in the canoe, our movements caused it to rock back and forth, which gave us a wonderful feeling of connection.

Dad then revved the motor and guided us out into the river toward home. His confidence reassured me. I felt rescued, safe, and free again! Even with the euphoria of going home, though, we all had to get used to each other again. After all, it had been a number of months since we had all been together as a family. That included Ruth and me who, because of the segregation at the school, were now like familiar strangers, each with a different response to the same situation.

Ruth says now that she did not feel that she was escaping the school residence, she was just happy to be going home. I on the other hand felt like I had been imprisoned and was being rescued. I felt somewhat troubled, and Ruth seemed happy.

Re-integration into home life was a struggle for me. It felt that I was carrying a strange flu, but in the form of trauma. But was I too sensitive? Or was the boys' residence just so destructive? I just didn't know why I felt so alienated and alone, like a child who did not understand.

Had I changed or had the rest of my family changed? Their laughter and conversation informed me that they were happy and therefore feeling normal. I, on the other hand, was losing my ability to even speak. It was becoming harder and harder for me to find the words, any words, to express myself.

I began to feel an increasing emotional distance, as if I were being left out of the party and not understood as I once was. I did not even understand myself. I felt like I did not belong anywhere anymore, not even in the family pecking order, and I felt unseen.

Recuperating

Mom usually had some special baking ready to welcome us. Dad would go back to the store to keep working for a while if it was not too late, and we kids would settle in to the joys of being at home. Although it felt great to be at home again, I would seek out the comfort and solitude of my bed and just lie there quietly, as if recovering from an illness. Sometimes Mom would come into the bedroom with a cup of hot cocoa and sit quietly on my bed and check for signs of a fever on my forehead and rub my back.

But it was not your standard variety of flu. I was in recovery – and it was in the safety of those quiet moments with Mom that I began to thaw. It was as if whatever was bothering me was an inconvenient illness that could only be expressed in the quiet and safety of one's room.

The reason for this trauma was almost invisible to our parents since they could only see from the perspective of home. They also had their own daily struggles and chores to attend to.

Eventually I would begin to take stock of my own space. I adjusted to home in quiet contemplation, appreciating what was important to me. I began to look at my toys and then began touching them with some caution. It was as if I had to remember how to play again. I had to introduce myself to my toys, maybe even to myself again. Had they forgotten me, or had I forgotten them?

After enjoying a wonderful "welcome back home" dinner, including yummy desserts made with motherly love, we all felt better. There's nothing like a good meal with dessert to take a child's mind off the bad things for a while. We then all went off to bed for a much-needed sleep at home again.

As if to underscore the extremes of our existence, Ruth and I, along with our younger sister Lou (who did not go to school yet), shared the same bedroom. Why was it okay to sleep in the same room at home, but not at school? Somehow my young mind made adjustments for this, but the glaring contrast still existed.

In the morning, it was so wonderful to wake up and see the warm, golden glow of the sunshine on the wood panelling by "my" bed. I would dream about this glow when away at school, seeing the comfort of its memory in my mind's eye whenever I longed for home. And now here it was, and it was real. I was home! It was time to enjoy the summer holidays.

With the smell of breakfast in the air, and the sound of Ruth and Lou also starting their day, I wandered into the kitchen to find Mom busy trying to make it perfect for us all. Whatever Mom cooked was great – even the porridge.

It was not the big things but the small things that made it feel like home. It was relating to my family again, where love and caring came naturally, in just the right quantities and at just the right time, rather than the industrial caring that was in place at school. Here at home, our interactions were natural, and I felt safe again.

However, there was also a definite shift in the pecking order now that affected my sense of self. Our sister Lou had had Mom and Dad all to herself during our absence at school, and it was apparent how she was now coming into her own.

Lou enjoying life at home in front of the HBC store, Fort Albany.

Ruth and I were visitors, to some degree, and it was obvious Lou was experiencing Mom and Dad's undivided attention in our absence. I felt somewhat jealous, of course, but was happy for her. I had more pressing concerns now to try to survive the residential school experience. Gone were my hopes and interest of learning any skills from Dad that would have helped me imagine and aspire to what life as an adult might look like.

Revisiting the Anglican Church

While on holidays, Ruth and I also attended Sunday services at the local Anglican church. Going to church just once a week was such a relief, compared to the daily grind and prayer torture we were subjected to at the residential school. It was also somewhat enjoyable to be at the Anglican church with its relaxed atmosphere – and especially with our whole family in attendance.

The church was also a good place for connecting with the rest of the community and getting to see the other kids who were home from school.

Sunday congregation at the Anglican Church on Albany Island, late 1950s.

Although the kids in the congregation jostled and fidgeted about, as most kids do when in church, when it came time to pray, we residential school kids immediately assumed the correct prayer position; with straight backs, heads bowed, and clearly clasped hands for all to see – like little soldiers of God. As Ruth and I assumed the position, Lou looked on in her usual detached but curious way. I guess we made an impression on her because she began clasping her hands in prayer, mimicking what Ruth and I were doing. I hoped that Mom and Dad would also notice our progress.

With my new prayer skills, I was not the same little boy, who just a few years earlier, had sat in a huff, not understanding the reason for quiet contemplation and communal worship. Before being enrolled at school, I had been very timid, and tried to tuck myself into a ball when associating with the Native kids at church.

Ron with fellow Anglican kids, Fort Albany.

Now that I had the experience of attending a residential school, though, and feeling like I had something in common with the other kids, I was motivated to reach out and ask them what they thought of attending the Anglican residential school down south in Moosonee. The answers were short, with shrugs of their shoulders, looking down at the ground, big sighs, and short words like, "Okay," "rough," and "no good." There were also quizzical looks at me as if I did not have the right to pry into their thoughts like that and ask such direct questions. I tried to be respectful but was also excited at hearing their answers, which were a validation of some of my own experiences at school.

I also wanted to find out what they thought of the world down south, the white man's world, where my dad and mom came from.

Although my family and I had travelled to southern Ontario a few years earlier, prior to my enrolment at St. Anne's, I could not recall much of anything from that visit because I was so young at the time. So, I had lots of questions and blanks to fill in as to what it might be like in the South.

Their answers were clipped and eloquent in their simplicity, with silent shrugs. But there was also a willingness to share experiences in order to enhance status. They talked like little explorers comparing what they had seen with questions such as: "Did you see what they call cars, trains, roads, stop signs?" One little friend asked me if I had ever seen places where you could just go in and eat all kinds of food, saying, "I think that they were called restaurants." He said he had actually gone into one with his uncle.

Fellow Anglican Survivors

Even though we shared a common experience of attending a residential school, it wasn't easy at first to be accepted by those Native Anglican kids. They were wary of us. After all, we were white HBC people, and now probably Roman Catholic as well because we went to school at St. Anne's. Eventually our curiosities got the better of us, though, and we started to meet on the steps of the church – the halfway point between our home and the Native community.

We played games that we were used to playing behind the safety of our fence at home, such as hide-and-seek and hopscotch, etc. It felt great to be actually playing rather than just standing around, as we did at school. The Native kids also opened our minds to other forms of play that were more daring, such as building forts, fishing, and venturing along the river bank looking for movement in the water. Once we saw three or four beluga whales on their way back out to James Bay. That fired our imaginations and made us wonder what other monsters were swimming in the river, and if we could possibly catch one.

The Native kids taught us how to cast out fish hooks attached to long lines of twine that we would whip around our head and then let go of, sending the hook far out into the water. I shudder to think now what might have happened if we had hooked one of those monsters of the river, not to mention somebody's eye.

Can you imagine hooking one of those huge beluga whales, the twine getting snagged around our feet, getting yanked off the big dock into the frigid water, and pulled into its depths and out to sea? It would have taken only a few moments for that horror show to happen.

We kids liked to tell each other scary stories like this as we dangled our legs over the big dock. Our stories were a welcome change from all the religious doom and gloom we had to listen to at school. It was so refreshing finding common ground through play, daring and adventure.

On one occasion, meeting a group of Anglican kids also resulted in a connection and a unique bonding experience that would transcend time and place.

Blood Brother Ceremony

One spring day, Ruth and I set out to explore along the riverbank, not far from our house. Eventually we came upon a dense stand of tall, dry reeds. We paused when hearing Native voices emanating from it. Fighting against the thought that it might be spirits or something, I froze in my tracks, trying to figure out if there was an earthly reason for voices coming from a bush, before jumping to any conclusions. To my relief, it became apparent that it was a group of Native kids hidden in the reeds.

Curiosity getting the best of us, we peered deeper into the reeds as one of the kids confronted us, saying, "Hey, are you from that big house?" It was not so much a question as a statement; where else would we have come from as the only white kids for many miles around?

"Yes," we whispered.

"Come in here, join us," was the response. I had been used to playing with Native children by that time, but not in a bed of dried-out reeds, so I felt somewhat cautious.

As we crawled deeper into their hiding place, the group of kids materialized. There were about six of them, both boys and girls, ranging in age from about eight to twelve. They all seemed to be bound together by the oldest boy, whose assertive attitude, served to reinforce his stature within the group.

As we talked and began to mingle with each other, the boy took out a knife and began hacking at the reeds. I froze, hoping that someone would stop him. I was used to knives being handled by grown-ups. But he was obviously the one in control – after all, he had the knife. It was not huge like the kitchen knives Mom used; it was a neat-looking thing called a jack knife, and it was bright red. Obviously it was from civilization far to the south of us. Likely he had acquired it while in Moosonee.

I had never seen a jack knife before, let alone a bright-red knife, which in my mind, added to his stature within the group. He must have accepted me, as eventually the conversation moved to blood brothers. I said I did not know what that was. He explained, and I was intrigued. He asked if I wanted to become a blood brother, and offered to become one with me. I said okay – after all, if I was to have a blood brother, what better person was there to be related to than the leader?

With great fanfare, he then pulled out a cigarette lighter from his shirt pocket. With a flick of his thumb against the starter, a flame appeared, over which he began to heat up the blade. He then nicked his finger with it, reheated the blade, and passed the heated blade to me. His need to kill the germs was a surprise to me but felt reassuring as well.

I had never tried to intentionally cut myself before but the group kept on pressuring me, so I pressed a little harder on the knife till my finger felt the pain. It was just a token nick, but apparently adequate when I said, "Ow!" He then reached over to me and clasped my hand. I could feel the warmth of our few blood drops combining. It felt strange, like a bit of warm, watery glue, yet somehow powerful.

It was clear to me that through this ceremony I would attain acceptance and status in the group. I felt elated. Heck, I felt invincible! I was part of a brotherhood now and, hopefully, maybe even the community. This ceremony felt as powerful to me as my baptism had felt in the local church that had made me an Anglican – maybe even more powerful.

What now? My new blood brother calmly cut a piece of reed and lit it with his lighter. It took a few flicks but finally it was burning! He was experienced, I could see. No wonder he was the leader. He inhaled the putrid smoke of the dried reed as if it was the best tobacco ever. He flicked his lighter again, lighting my piece of reed. Soon we were all puffing away and choking. Thinking back at that incident, I can't help but see the symbolism of a peace pipe ceremony in play as well. I don't know if any of us thought of it at the time – probably we were just feeling powerful smoking something, like some of our parents did.

I never told Mom or Dad of this incident; fraternizing with the local Natives when not at school was still frowned upon, but I knew even at my young age that these kids were more my people than any nuns or HBC people, because I shared common residential experiences with them. Adult society had not been gentle with any of us. We were surviving terrors that we would have to face again when summer holidays were over and school resumed.

Even though I enjoyed some commonality and friendship, I also sensed that the culture of my Native friends was not my world; not totally. I suspect that they felt the same about us three "white" kids – that they did not quite belong in our world either. We three HBC kids were a minority in numbers but represented the powerful white culture. The Native kids were more numerous there but were losing their old way of life. Somehow, we met in the middle in the uncharted overlap between the two worlds. Even though we were so young, we were able to function in our in-between place, lumped together by circumstance, perfect little witnesses to the collision of the two cultures at the time.

It was obvious, though, that the Anglican Native community wanted to preserve some of its culture. Over time, there were fewer kids in the

Anglican community to play with because they were moving north to the new community of Kashechewan.

As they moved away, the Anglican church beside our home was faced with closing. The HBC was also faced with the dilemma of not having enough customers to support its store.

Although we kids did not realize it at the time, plans were also in play to move the post, including our home, closer to the Roman Catholic community and St. Anne's where there was more economic potential.

Summer Fun with Family

Even with all the social changes going on, one of the hallmarks of summer holidays at home was taking a dip in the Albany River. But, because the water was so cold, we kids usually just got our toes wet. Despite the shock of the cold water, it was one of those rare moments when the three of us kids experienced something fun together, a very special memory.

Ruth, Ron, and Lou drying off by Albany River, and Ron with his radical haircut.

Sometimes the local Anglican minister would also brave the cold of the Albany River when he and Dad raced each other by swimming to the end of the big dock and back. It was fun cheering them on as they passed with big breaths of air and happy sounds of freezing agony. Surprising how pain can be so much fun when experienced in the context of play.

It was also refreshing to see our Anglican minister enjoying nature compared to how uptight and controlled the Roman Catholic priests seemed to be, at least to me at the time. I remember wishing that he could be our dorm supervisor at St. Anne's, but of course that was not possible. Eventually he moved back down south, but continued to come up with his family to help at the Anglican residential school in Moosonee for a number of years after that, so at least the Anglican kids there continued to enjoy his presence.

The HBC staff would also join us on our summer activities, and I especially recall my favourite HBC clerk Hew. He was always interested in playing with us kids and encouraged our creativity whenever possible – such as teaching us how to build sand castles. It was so much fun to imagine even if we froze our fingers and toes while playing in the sand.

Hew the HBC clerk, with Ron and Lou making sandcastles, Fort Albany River.

Dad, Hew, and Ruth, Fort Albany River.

Dad, Hew, Ruth, and Ron, Fort Albany River.

Someone like Hew would have been a good mentor at our school. He was able to fire our imaginations and motivate us kids to want to learn, as opposed to the authoritative teaching style we were being subjected to at the school.

Little did I realize that it would be the last summer we saw Hew. He quit the HBC shortly afterwards and returned to Scotland. Maybe it was just as well, because my sense of identity was so squashed by that time that I was losing my curiosity and playful attitude, and beginning to act somewhat belligerent as well.

Summer Fun at Lac Ste. Anne

The Albany River was not that great for swimming, but there were some freshwater lakes in the area that offered relatively warmer waters. One of these lakes was Lac Ste. Anne, located in Roman Catholic territory and close to St. Anne's. Our family would sometimes make the journey over for an afternoon summer adventure. Most times, Dad would stay home to mind the store, so the clerk would join us instead. To get to the lake, we travelled in our freighter canoe to the landing on the river by St. Anne's. Then, we would walk past the school and a further mile or so to the lake.

Although school was out for the summer, some students were still there, working at various chores. These, of course, were the students who had no home to go to, so they were stuck at St. Anne's all year long. One of the students working in the fields was likely Tony, who I would have passed by with my family on our way to enjoy some time at the lake.

Tony:

"Do you remember the big fields around the place? Well, the mission used to plant enough potatoes to last us for most of the winter. I remember working in these fields during the summer months, weeding, hoeing, and spreading a white powder substance that I now believe to be DDT. It certainly wasn't a fun job what with the zillions of flies and no bug spray."

Students working in the fields, St. Anne's. Source: Archives Deschâtelets-NDC, Fonds Deschâtelets, Fort Albany residential school.

Sad to admit it now, but I found myself not wanting to catch sight of those students if at all possible. In my selfish, childish mind at the time, I wanted to stay far away from any sights that might remind me of the school – as it was such a troubled place. And so, I continued on, focusing on the fun that awaited me, as those fellow students struggled under the weight of their summer chores.

Because we had not yet learned to swim, Mom made us three kids wear life jackets while at Lac Ste. Anne. Odd that we were not required to wear them when travelling in our canoe on the river, but they were a must when swimming in the lake – even though we just splashed around in a couple of feet of water. On one occasion, the silence was broken by Ruth, who screamed at seeing a snake swimming with us. This put a damper on our carefree fun, and left us with a worry of what other dangers might be lurking at the lake.

Although I was not aware of it at the time, Lac Ste. Anne was also where others from St. Anne's came to enjoy some fun. Unfortunately, there were still strings attached for the unfortunate year round students, even when they had a break from all the work they were expected to do.

Tony:

"I remember that during the summer holidays, I and other year-round prisoners spent dreadful Sunday afternoons paddling Anna Wesley around so she could fish at Lac Ste. Anne. I don't remember [enjoying nature], as we were too busy keeping the canoe from rocking or making any noise whatsoever as we would be hit over the head with a paddle if we were not concentrating. No wonder I don't really like fishing."

Students with nun in boat on Lac Ste. Anne. Source: Archives Deschâtelets-NDC, Fonds Deschâtelets, Fort Albany residential school.

Although we never saw it on our visits at the lake, there was a cabin further along the shore from where we were swimming. Maybe it was just for the older kids and staff to enjoy, since I was not aware of its existence till years later.

Cabin on Lac Ste. Anne. Source: Archives Deschâtelets-NDC, Fonds Deschâtelets, Fort Albany residential school.

After a day of splashing around in the warm water and enjoying a picnic, my family and I would make our way back home, with another happy memory to add to our summer holidays.

Unfortunately for students like Tony, their summer holidays were filled with constant chores. And as if he didn't have enough to do working in the fields, Tony was given other chores including one very memorable one.

Tony's Memorable Chore

Unlike a lot of schools, St. Anne's also had its own cemetery. It was likely the resting place for the local Catholic community as well as for kids who had attended the school. Maybe the cost of sending bodies back to loved

193

ones was too expensive, and it was more expedient and practical to just bury the departed there. It was one place, at least, where there was some attempt to show respect for the dead. But even the bodies in that graveyard were at risk of losing their identity.

Tony:

"I remember working in that graveyard behind the school one summer when I was about nine. My assignment was to replace the old wooden and rotten crosses with new ones that had their names on them. As I was being tormented by great swarms of black flies and mosquitoes and not having any fly dope, I pulled all the old crosses out as fast as I could. But when it came time to put in the new ones, I didn't know which name went where, so I just stuck them wherever. Needless to say, when they had the summer memorial service the local people were somewhat puzzled that their loved ones seemed to be in a different location. I think that's the only funny thing that happened to me."

This is a disturbing story, but it is also illustrative of one of the themes of the book, notably, hypocrisy within a religious institution. This school was run by a religious order. Of all possible organizations, you would think that these people would not screw up their main product: life after death and commemorating the lives of "God's children." Instead, they sent one little boy.

The Nuns at St. Anne's Create a Happy Memory

In contrast, some of the staff at the school performed tasks that helped to improve the lives of the students. For example, some of the nuns sewed clothing for the children.

During summer holidays while we three kids enjoyed our time at home, Mom would pack her heavy sewing machine into our freighter canoe and travel the few miles upriver to St. Anne's, where she would join her nun friends in their sewing tasks. She enjoyed her time with them because they were at least from the South, even if they were from a different denomination and the Francophone culture.

The nuns sewed clothing for the children and offered to help Mom sew pants for us kids for the coming school year. It was a comforting feeling the following year to know that my pants had been made with love by my mother. The wonderful charity of these "nice" nuns and their expertise in designing and sewing clothing is a lasting memory, and a testament that not all the nuns were mean – some were quite loving and caring, at least to my mom.

Mom also recalls that these nuns sewed a dress for her once to cheer her up. She was trying to make the dress herself, but it was proving too complicated for her, and with frustrations mounting, she told the Mother Superior of her struggles. The Mother Superior asked how long she had been working on the dress. Mom said, "About two weeks."

Mother Superior said, "It should only take about one day. Our nuns will make one for you."

By the end of the day, they presented her with the dress. They made it out of material meant to be used for robes for the church.

Our beautiful mother, Margaret, in a new dress made for her by nuns at St. Anne's.

The nuns also made a coat for Mom from the same material as their capes and lined it with a shimmery green satin cloth. Mom loved it and told the nuns it was beautiful. She wore it even when she flew south; in other words, it was acceptable to the southern sensibilities of fashion.

Nuns, Priests, and Brothers in Our Home

Mom's nun friends would also come to visit her at our home, on occasion. Although we were raw from the weirdness and strictness of that school, we kids did not mind those nuns visiting because they were the nice ones.

They came just to visit Mom, not to check up on us. I recall that they were quite friendly and polite, and I would acknowledge them with a polite greeting in return, before wandering off to play. I wonder now if my happy demeanour might have informed them what a different boy I was at home, and how my family's love and caring made such a significant difference in my behaviour.

Mom recalls that some of the staff from St. Anne's including priests, lay brothers and nuns would also appear at our home, either departing or arriving by airplane, which would land and tie up at our dock on the river. She never had a bad experience with the nuns but she particularly remembers some of those "slimy" guys coming over to our house while they waited for the airplane. They would cause some of her warning bells to go off, but at the same time Mom did not connect them with any trauma that her children might be experiencing at the school. The priests and lay brothers were just the workers, and so, in her mind, they did not figure into the day-to-day environment that we kids found ourselves in at the school.

Nuns Visit Grandma Gosbee in the South

Some of the nuns of St. Anne's who travelled south on holidays would stop off in Sioux Lookout, Ontario, to visit with our Grandma Gosbee, who lived there at the time. Grandma would have met them on her visits up North when she came to watch us perform in the Christmas pageants at St. Anne's. Being a teacher herself, as well as being Mom's mother-in-law, helped her to form friendships with the nuns. She extended an invitation for them to visit her on their travels down south.

The nuns' friendships with Grandma helped to strengthen Mom's conviction that the nuns of St. Anne's were okay. She presumed that all the nuns were as loving and caring as Sister Marie Albert, which was not the case.

Sister Marie Albert (called sunken eyes and far/deep eyes by the students), visiting Grandma Gosbee in Sioux Lookout, Ontario.

Sister Jean Henri (who taught Cree in grade one and two), visiting Grandma Gosbee in Sioux Lookout, Ontario.

This nun looked so normal to me while I attended St. Anne's, but now she looks downright scary in the picture. She might have been a good, caring teacher, I forget, but the picture suggests the stark difference in appearance between the teachers of St. Anne's and teachers we would encounter years later down south.

The End of Summer Holidays

It was always a traumatic time when summer holidays were over and school loomed on the horizon once again for us kids. There was a lot of crying at this time, not just the tears of departure, but also tears of terror of what might be facing us at the school. Mom says that our tears were the biggest sign to her that something was just not right. She says our crying weighed heavily on her as she so desperately did not want to subject us to the confines of St. Anne's, but what other choice did she have at that time?

It was confusing for Mom, as well, that the nuns who came to visit her at home were so pleasant and loving, and yet I was pleading through sobbing tears not to be sent back. It was hard for her to make informed decisions when the signals were so conflicting.

Our parents were doing the best they knew how. But they had no clear overview and could not connect the dots. And so, they were unable to make informed decisions regardless of how well meaning they were.

In order to prepare myself for my return to school, I envisioned a safe place in my mind where I could escape if necessary. Escape to me meant imagining who I used to be: the little white boy with fun memories of life at home. Somehow, I had the wisdom to pack these memories quickly into a safe place deep inside where they could not be erased and where I could retreat. Now holding tightly to the fun memories, I was ready to be taken back to that controlling hellhole called school. Dad would always get upset with me at these times because he thought I was just daydreaming.

We envied our sister Lou, who got to stay home and enjoy the freedom it offered. Ironically, life for her would change forever in one horrifying moment while Ruth and I were at school.

CHAPTER EIGHTEEN:
LOU'S ORDEAL

IN 1960, WHILE RUTH AND I were away attending school, Lou was seriously burned in a home accident that changed her life forever. Dad had lit the kerosene camp stove in the kitchen to start the day, and Lou had gotten out of bed as well. The stove was positioned on the floor so it was more stable, but it was also more accessible to a curious child interested in fire. She still calls herself a "fire bug." She says, "I carry that burden because Dad told me, 'Stop and go back to bed,' but I remained sitting there playing away, getting closer and closer to the fire with this little gun that shot out little sparks when you pulled the trigger. When those sparks hit the flame on the stove, they gave off a puff of smoke, which was exciting to watch." Then, in one horrific moment, larger kerosene sparks erupted out of the flame and spattered all over her, causing her to burst into flames.

Lou has only limited memories, other than the sudden intense burning pain, but our mother remembers seeing her little five-year-old daughter turned into a fireball and running down the hallway to her. Mom had a nylon house coat, and she picked it up and wrapped it around Lou to smother the flames; however, the nylon melted into Lou's skin. Her hair, skin, everything was burning. Dad ran to the store and radioed the nursing station at St. Anne's for help, and two nurses travelled incredibly fast by boat to our house. However, they plastered Lou with Vaseline, which is now known to be the worst thing you can do for a burn victim.

Mom then got on the short-wave radio and called Austin Airways and told them, "My baby has been burnt. Please send a plane." However, since there was no such thing as 911 in those days, the plane did not take off till Dad convinced the dispatcher that he would pay for the flight. The plane finally arrived late in the afternoon to fly Lou and Mom down to Moosonee – about an hour's flight south of Fort Albany.

Photo of plane taking off from Fort Albany, circa 1960.

Mom was petrified by the thought that Lou was going to die that day. All she could do was hold her in the back of the bush plane as Lou vomited repeatedly during the flight. Lou recalls that even though she was in shock, she was very clear in her mind about what she had done and the state she was in. When they arrived at the hospital, a nurse gave Lou some medication to help her relax.

Mom was offered lodgings at Bishop Clark's house and visited Lou over the next few days. Lou was now all bundled up in bandages, but Mom worried because Lou was getting worse and worse. Eventually one of the nurses whispered to Mom to get Lou out of that hospital if she wanted her daughter to live.

Since Lou wasn't receiving adequate care, Mom decided to transfer her to Toronto's Sick Kid's hospital. Thankfully, Mom was in a position to demand action, and although she had no idea if she was doing the right thing, in response to her request, Lou was released into her care that night.

There was no airlifting medical service available, so Mom had to arrange for transportation by train instead. But when the conductor saw the state Lou was in, he directed them to the caboose where they laid her on his bed for the journey south.

Our mother was relieved when she finally carried Lou into Sick Kids' Hospital, expecting to find competent medical help. But the admitting staff callously said, "Oh, just put her over there." They were very rude and condescending. The staff was likely of the opinion that because she was from way up north that she was on welfare, and they treated her with curtness and disrespect.

Then a doctor arrived and said, "You know, the Moosonee Hospital was really looking after your little girl very well. We're just cleaning up the wounds now."

The nurses furthered the doctor's claims and said, "You have no right to blame Moosonee for anything. They did the best they could."

This perspective seemed out of place since this specialized burn unit at Sick Kids had to reverse some of the previous treatment. So, it begs the question: did the hospital at Moosonee who "did the best they could" give Lou the proper treatment? (In years to come, there would be lawsuits from others claiming that the Canadian government was negligent in "Indian hospitals.")

When Lou was first admitted at Sick Kids, Mom indicated that Lou had medical coverage through the Hudson's Bay Company. The hospital staff didn't believe her at first, but when they eventually confirmed that Lou did indeed have coverage, their whole tone suddenly changed. The hospital staff finally realized that they were not dealing with a family on welfare, but with the family of an HBC employee that might demand accountability. Their attitude and their treatment of our mother and Lou became conciliatory and noticeably changed from indifference to attentiveness. Mom was now considered part of the community, but it had taken a day or two to be properly acknowledged.

Yet we still have lobby groups, including drug companies, who push these days to re-configure or even dismantle our health care system for the sake of profit – thus resulting in classes of "have and have-nots" with all the stigma that comes with it.

Eventually Lou was stabilized and treatment began. During that time, Mom stayed in the city and was in touch with Dad through letters. This really speaks of the remoteness of Fort Albany at the time. It is hard to imagine in this day and age that back then, letters were the only option for them to communicate and that there would be a delay of a few weeks between communications.

Because Ruth and I were at school, we had no idea of the pain and suffering that our sister Lou was enduring down south. In fact, there was a further delay in finding out anything because Dad had to mind the store, and until he was finally able to visit us, we were not quite sure why Mom was not coming to visit us at school.

Lou's Absence

Ruth and I did not really have a clear insight or understanding of the full extent of what had happened to Lou. Mom was usually the one who came to visit us, but then she was gone because she flew out with Lou the same day of the accident, leaving no time for her to come to the school first to explain what was happening. The next visit was from Dad, which was a surprise to us and gave us a sense of how significant Lou's injuries must be.

Dad did try to explain what had happened, but not seeing Lou's burns for ourselves, his explanation was inadequate. He simply stated that Lou was hurt from being burned and that she had to go south and that Mom had gone with her to help her to get better.

Because of the segregation at the school, it was only when Mom or Dad visited us that Ruth and I got some time together as well. However, because Dad did not visit as often as Mom had, there were periods that Ruth and I did not get to associate with each other for months at a time. I tried to be brave, but I didn't understand why I was left alone, and I felt abandoned. Ruth says she did not fully understand the relative lack of visits either.

Once, I saw Dad walking across the field from the river to enter the nursing station, which was a separate building from the school, likely attending to business relating to Lou's accident. I waited for him to exit the building, ready to wave and catch his attention so he would come over and visit me.

When he came out of the building, I waved frantically, and he waved back, but inexplicably did not come over to me. The distance between us was about 250 feet. Instead, he just continued on his way across the field and toward the river where our freighter canoe would be waiting for him. I tried to console myself by thinking that he must be very busy, but it still hurt, and I felt the sting of tears in my eyes. I felt like a prisoner. Interesting that I was so conditioned to not leave the yard that I dared not run to him for fear of being reprimanded by the nuns or the guards, who were always watching.

Visiting with a Lay Brother

In desperation, during this time of feeling so alone and cut off from family, one time I was able to sneak out of the boys' play yard to try to catch sight of Ruth, whom I presumed was playing in the girls' play yard. On my way, I had to pass by some of the lay brothers who were standing by the nursing station building, across from the front entrance to the school. As I got closer, they motioned to me to come over to them. This was a radical move on my part because it was well out of my play yard area. It was also rather daring because I knew we were not supposed to go near these men, but I was used to playing with grown men (the HBC clerks) back home, so I felt compelled to take a chance. I was not sure what to expect, but I began to make my way over to them.

One of the men, who was leaning against the building, gave himself a little push as if to get enough momentum in order to move in my direction. He wore a pair of pants that were too big for him, with the biggest belt I had ever seen, cinched up so tight that the front of his pants was folded in half in front of him. There was a slight smell of urine coming from him, and his hair was close cropped in tufts, as if someone had snipped away at it to keep it short. Maybe he had done it himself. He looked almost mouldy, but gentle and frail, with a trace of class that suggested he had experienced a higher status sometime in the past. He moved slowly, with an uncertainty that one can only attain from being beaten down by life. I felt an affinity with him for some reason.

He stopped a few yards away from me, as if running out of steam, and then raised a very clean white finger pointing toward the side of the building. It was hard to know what he was pointing at because of the tremors in his hand, but I looked in the general direction of his shaking finger and noticed a ball lying in the weeds beside the building. I was afraid to move and just stood and watched him with caution. He might have been sixty years old, but looked and acted more like eighty. He shuffled over to the ball and kicked it awkwardly toward me. One thing that attracted me was that this brother seemed gentle and friendly, and so I presumed he was likely harmless.

We kicked the ball back and forth to each other a few times. I was aware that associating with these men was not allowed, but I was also hopeful about the possibility of play. I had the presence of mind to keep our play in plain view, in order to stay safe, but a nun spotted us and shouted at me, "You! Get back there," pointing toward the boys' yard.

I hesitated and she quickly walked over and escorted me back to the other boys. Her level of concern indicated I was not in a safe place in the company of this man, even doing something as innocent as kicking a ball. The nuns were aware that men of potentially nefarious intent could lure children away so easily, even in broad daylight. I am grateful that some of the nuns were well meaning and caring, helping us kids survive yet another day.

The Construction of the Fence at St. Anne's

Eventually the boys' yard was relocated to the same side of the building as the girls, possibly to prevent us kids from wandering around the grounds unnecessarily and visiting with the lay brothers. This would have been such a great solution for kids such as myself who had siblings at the school. However, a fence was created to keep us boys and girls segregated.

Tony:

"There was some kind of chain-link fence located there, and it was strictly verboten to approach that fence and talk to the girls on the other side. With the fence, I could at least see my sisters and wave at them, but once the solid structure was built, there was no other means of seeing them. It was very cruel to have siblings in the same building and at the same time not being able to talk to them. I suspect that it was just another attempt by the Church to destroy the family bond of the inmates. In a way, they did succeed as over the years our family became splintered, and we rarely if ever got together and talked and laughed as a family should."

A Letter from Mom

During this lonely time, I received a letter – my very first letter ever – from Mom. Even though St. Anne's was attempting to keep siblings separated and was not supportive of family bonds, a letter from Mom somehow got through all the distance between her and myself, and arrived at the school with my name on it. It was given to me by one of the friendly PR nuns. Mom must have mailed it directly to the school rather than mailing it to Dad to give to me. The nun caught up with me in a hallway and simply said, "From your mom," and presented the envelope to me with a smile, as if giving me a gift. It was a big, brown sturdy envelope decorated with many stamps, and for a moment I was not sure what to do with it as I had never received such a thing before. I looked at the envelope like it was a fancy food, unsure of whether to eat it or just look at it. The nun offered to help me open it up to see what was inside, but I felt it was just between me and Mom, so I thanked her and clutched it as she walked away.

Unsure what to do next, I went out into the boys' yard holding the envelope gently, as if fearing it might melt on me. There weren't many boys around me at that time, which allowed me a private moment to open the envelope just enough to peek inside. I'm not sure what I was hoping for, maybe a treat or something, but I caught a faint whiff of familiar perfume, so I knew the words written on the letter were from Mom. However, I could not read all the words, regardless of how precious they were to me. The few words I had learned at school were not enough to make sense of what was written in the letter.

Then I noticed an older boy standing by himself. I had never seen him before so thought that he was likely a new student. He was kicking at one of the newly erected posts on the edge of the yard as if questioning its purpose while getting to know his surroundings.

I had presumed that the posts were part of a fence being erected to imprison us even more. Only later did I find out that the posts were part of an ice rink.

Interrupting his pensive concentration, I asked in a timid voice if he could read, and if so, would he be willing to try to read my mom's letter. I was relieved when he agreed. He was quite decent about it, perhaps having compassion for the meaning of contact with home. Interesting that even though he was a few years older than me, he still struggled with each word, but slowly Mom's message emerged one word at a time. It was such a powerful experience to feel Mom's presence while savouring each of the words as if they were rare candies. I asked if he would read it again to make sure I had not missed anything, which he did without complaint.

Even though the need to control us at St. Anne's was ever present, Mom's letter somehow served to give me a sense of freedom that no amount of control could contain. Mom asked me to be strong and patient, telling me she would be just a little longer than expected down south. I was happy to receive the acknowledgment of my existence and felt an emotional maturing, as I wanted to comply with her request for me to be "strong" while I waited for her and Lou to arrive back home.

I held the letter tightly in my hands, looking first toward home and then toward the South where I imagined Mom and Lou might be, feeling a faint but certain connection to love and affection.

The Treatment of the Nuns

During Mom's absence down south, there seemed to be a marked difference in some of the nuns' behaviors toward me. I cannot remember being molested, but there are glimmers in my memory of some questionable things that happened to me during this time. On a few occasions, I was invited into the bedroom of Anna Wesley, our dorm supervisor, which was connected to the boys' dorm.

I remember her comforting me and talking to me like a friend, and I enjoyed the attention. I was starving for it. But I was also confused and on my guard. I was well aware of how mean she could be and yet here she was being friendly to me. I had to try to normalize her mean behaviour in order to experience her now friendly treatment. It was like wanting to play with something unfamiliar with soft fur, but sharp teeth.

I forget how many times these visits happened, but it was only while Mom was down south with Lou, and each time I was not sure how to act because I had so feared her, like the rest of the boys.

I am not sure of any impropriety while I was there, but I do remember seeing a lot of blood on a white rag by the bed. I expressed concern that she might be in pain, and she said, "Not at all." It might have been a dirty handkerchief or a menstrual rag. It might have been the rag that was usually wrapped around my head (from me pounding my head against the wall), but then why would I ask her if it was painful? Nevertheless, the blood was shocking to see as a child, and any reason to expose me to that defies explanation.

Was there nefarious intent, or was she just wanting to keep an eye on me because I was so depressed and suicidal? Maybe she was protecting me from possible pedophiles that visited the boy's dorm. I cannot remember.

Trying to Tell Dad Something Was Not Right

These visits to the dorm supervisor's bedroom must have held some significance to me because when Dad eventually came to visit, I tried to whisper something to him about my experiences in her bedroom, but I could not find the words. Why? I can't remember. Had I gone crazy or were my thoughts based on reality? I am still not clear where the trauma and possible abuse stopped and the crazy began.

I'm not sure what I was trying to tell Dad, but I instinctively knew I could not talk openly to him about it in front of others, so I waited for an opportunity. The moment came when we were alone in a stairwell, maybe the same one where I had tried to bang my head to a pulp, and I whispered that something was not right. However, being so young, I did not have the language to clearly explain how I felt and what I knew. Then others began to pass us, and the moment was lost. The details of what I felt driven to tell him have been lost to time, but I do remember blurting out in an emotional whisper, with unexpected tears, "Please get me out of here."

He misconstrued my attempt at communication as a complaint against the culture of the school. He thought I wanted something trivial, like more music or something, and told me to straighten my back and try to be strong. He just could not see the depth of my pain and fear, and I could not communicate it to him. His solution was to arrange for Ruth and me to come home with him, because shortly after that incident we were allowed to go home for a brief visit.

A Visit Home Without Mom

When we finally arrived home, familiar sights and smells greeted us in the front porch, although there was a strange silence without Mom and Lou. I noticed that the red water yoke that Mom used for carrying water from the river now stood silently in the corner. The yoke was the cross that she had to bear each day, hauling water for our needs. I was reminded of Mom with that red yoke on her shoulders and two water buckets hanging at each end, and us three kids carrying our little buckets in single file behind her, like a mother duck and her three ducklings. It was such fun when the chore sometimes erupted into water fights, which inevitably happens when kids are close to water. I hoped that Lou's injuries would not prevent her from such water fights in the future. Now the yoke stood in the corner, as if waiting for life to be as it used to be. I felt Mom and Lou's absence deeply at that moment.

The porch also had a lively smell of home brew, the remnants of Dad and the clerk's attempt at making black currant wine. It was a welcoming smell – even better than that smell of communion wine in the chapel at school. Dad's homemade wine was not the blood of Christ, as was that in the chapel at school, but it was more important to me to be part of the lifeblood of home. I drank it in with my senses. It felt great to be home.

Dad curled Ruth's hair, and Ruth tried to help out with home chores, including caring for Mom's plants.

Ruth watering plants while home from school.

While Ruth tried to be helpful, I was not sure where I fit in, so I stayed in my bedroom for the most part, enjoying the silence and peace of my solitude. It was not the same with Mom and Lou missing. It felt empty, and the family dynamics were very different. Also, Ruth and I had become strangers because of the segregation at the school, which added to the emptiness.

Dad tried in his own way to make up for Mom and Lou's absence, including making us our home-cooked meals. Because Mom would normally do all the cooking, his attempts did cause us some concern, but we appreciated his efforts.

However, I could not contain myself when he made us porridge for breakfast. He put white sugar on it instead of brown sugar like we had at the school. But the white sugar melted into a clear liquid, and I refused to eat it because I thought he had spit in it; my experiences with the food at St. Anne's influencing my mistrust. He was so frustrated with me over that incident that he almost levitated. Call me sensitive, but I was having none of that porridge. He was trying to make a nice breakfast, and I ruined it. I was struggling with some internal demons that he simply could not see.

This was the difference between St. Anne's and home: I felt safe enough to voice my displeasure, even though it caused Dad to have a conniption. I intuitively knew that I had the freedom to refuse food without fear of the kind of corporal punishment handed out at school. Understandably, Dad was as upset as I was, but for different reasons.

Through all of this drama, Ruth just ate her porridge in silence, but her focused look in my direction suggested she also might have some thoughts on the matter. Maybe she was reminded of the challenges we kids faced when eating porridge at St. Anne's. Or maybe she was wondering if this was what boys were like since, she had not interacted with them for some time. Maybe she was noticing I was still the little hellion I was before we had been shipped off to school. My outbursts at home may have caused some drama at the time, but it was also an indication that I had not completely lost my voice, the very thing that St. Anne's was trying to take away.

Although I was quite troubled, just spending time at home with our simple facilities did wonders. It was certainly not like St. Anne's with its showers and running water, but enjoying a bath at home with our own water heated on our own stove felt glorious. Even the smell of our wood stove felt comforting.

We also enjoyed the little gifts that were waiting for us, such as beadwork brooches that we pinned proudly to our sweaters. It is now unclear who sent us these presents; likely Mom or Grandma Gosbee, but the symbolism is still quite clear. It is interesting that we received these tokens of beadwork as opposed to crosses; St. Anne's go-to symbol for hope and comfort. It is also curious that Dad did not bring us these gifts while we were in residence, as if he sensed that receiving gifts in residence, however comforting they might be, was somehow not appropriate. Though Ruth and I were innocent witnesses to the cultural genocide that was taking place at St. Anne's, while at home, we enjoyed wearing symbols of Native culture in the form of this beadwork, which the residential school was attempting to wipe out.

Ruth and Ron at home at the Fort Albany HBC post, with our beaded brooches.

Lou Is Finally Released from Hospital

After many months, Lou was released from the hospital, and the plane bringing her home stopped once again in Moosonee for refuelling on its way back to Fort Albany. Mom recalls that a Hudson's Bay man agreed to take them across to Moose Factory because the plane would leave from there. It was a float plane tied up at the dock close to the hospital. Mom remembers that when she and Lou got out of the boat to go toward the plane, the staff from the hospital were up there watching. They hadn't thought Lou would make it. They all came out to see the little girl who they had not given much hope for as she boarded the plane to fly back up north to her home. Lou recalls that the people just stared at her, not saying a word.

They landed late in the day at Fort Albany, and Lou remembers being in a motorboat going across water in the dark to the shore and home.

CHAPTER NINETEEN:
LOU IS ENROLLED AT ST. ANNE'S

WHEN LOU CAME HOME TO Fort Albany, Ruth and I were in residence at school at the time and so did not know she was back until she suddenly was there at school as well but moving very slowly. She had suffered burns to 80% of her body.

Our parents provided the nuns in charge with a box of medication to help her deal with the pain as she continued to heal. Lou had an unfamiliar haircut now, and big white bandages under her shirt and on her hands. Thankfully she was assigned a bed beside Ruth's bed, which helped to give her some comfort.

Although Lou was in considerable pain, she remembers the pain around her, including other girls screaming in the night. Lou remembers beds in the girl's dorm with footlockers, row on row on row.

Girls' dormitory, St. Anne's. Source: Archives Deschâtelets-NDC, Fonds Deschâtelets, Fort Albany residential school.

Lou Experiences the Residential School Food

Although Lou could withstand a lot of physical pain and be self-contained, she did find that the food at the school was hard to take. She remembers that sometimes when eating the breakfast slop, she was terrified when she got the sensation in her stomach that told her the food was coming back up. She would say to herself, "Just set it aside. Don't eat anymore." Sometimes when the nuns were not looking, she would push it over to Ruth next to her to finish. Luckily, she had Ruth to help her. Lou was so afraid, and so were all the other little kids, because it was so hard to keep it down; it was slimy like a raw egg. To this day, Lou can't look at an egg because of it.

Ruth and Lou Visit Ron in the Boys' Activity Room

When Lou first arrived at school, I remember occasionally catching sight of her and Ruth entering the lunchroom together and hearing their voices at times. However, I would lose sight of them as they made their way to the girls' side. We were so close but so far away. It was painful and a personal reminder that girls and boys were not to mix and blood bonds were not important. Eventually, I found it better to not to think about them anymore.

And then, a few weeks after Lou's enrolment, Ruth and Lou appeared at the door of the boys' activity room accompanied by a nun. They had been given permission to visit me. Imagine my surprise. I was in shock.

> **Ruth:**
> *"It was an unbelievably frightening experience. Absolutely no boy was playing with anything. They all sat or stood around the perimeter of the room and stared at us. The room was silent, and it felt very tense."*

For a moment, it was like I was seeing a vision that I could not make sense of; girls in the boys' common room, and my sisters at that was unheard of. It may as well have been a miracle. They looked like two little angels standing there. And if there is one example that we "whites" might be getting preferential treatment, this might be it, although there was likely a valid reason for them to be allowed to visit me.

I guess because of the seriousness of Lou's burns and her fragile state, the nuns broke their rule of segregation to let us three kids have a few healing moments together as a family. I was so surprised when the nun led Ruth and Lou into the boys' room. I had not seen Lou for about a year. We just stood there, not knowing what to do or say. Girls were not allowed in this room, so I feared that I would be faced with some kind of penance at the end of the visit.

The nun suggested we play with the toys in a box in the centre of the room. I stood frozen, so the nun led the way to the toys. However, we three just stood and looked at the toys. In exasperation, the nun urged us to play. She even reached into the box, handed us each a toy, and then held my toy and shook it, saying, "Play, play!" She did not know English very well but was white – so possibly she was French. She meant well, but I was too scared to play.

I was so scared what hell would rain down on us if Anna Wesley were to catch us playing with these toys – and with my sisters at that. The nun left the room, leaving us to figure it out for ourselves. My sisters looked to me for direction; it was almost like a first awkward date. We just stood holding lifeless toys as the hundred or so boys stared at us, some snickering, some curious, some indifferent. Feeling that we must do something, I whispered to my sisters, "Let's just pretend to play."

This incident left me with many questions. Would there be other visits from my sisters, or would this be the first and last? I was not sure what to hope for, and with Lou's weakened health, I feared she might be damaged further from any roughness that might happen from the boys in the room. Even innocently touching her bandages out of curiosity might cause her pain. I was also keenly aware of the pecking order within that large group and that our "whiteness" was suddenly spotlighted. I also worried because I knew I was powerless to protect my sisters, even from any possible taunts and teasing. We stayed quiet and moved very little, much as the Native boys were doing. The strangeness of this event might have been felt by the nuns as well – maybe that's why visits from my sisters never happened again.

Ruth and I could not see Lou's burns because they were covered. It was her fragility and cautious, slow movements that gave us a sense of the seriousness of her injuries. It would not be until we were older down south that we actually saw the extent of Lou's burns. We marvel at her bravery and strength to carry such pain without much outward expression.

Given Lou's vulnerability and hesitant movements, I whispered that we should attempt another escape home again with Lou this time – to get her out of harm's way. Thank goodness this was not to be, as I don't think we would have been lucky enough to make it home again – especially with Lou being so physically challenged.

Then an incident came as a warning that it might not be a good idea to try another dash for home. The warning came that winter in the form of two toboggans.

The Toboggans That Held No Warmth

One escape still claws at my memory, images and feelings separated by blanks; its adult importance was not clear to my child's mind at the time. I remember standing outside the school, milling around with some of the boys. Then a few nuns appeared in our play yard, looking east toward the nursing station building with great anticipation. This caused us to look as well. One of the nuns was the nice nun who had brought the letter from Mom to me some months before, and I was curious what might have brought her out into the open this time.

Ruth recalls that some nuns also came outside on the girls' side of the school to look intently toward the nursing station as well. All of us boys and girls were looking east, unseen by each other on opposite sides of the building.

Soon, two figures emerged from the forest, plodding through the snow and the cold grey fog, pulling their loads behind them. The two nuns shivering in the yard with us whispered concerned and anxious words to each other. The message gradually filtered down to us that the toboggans likely held the bodies of some of our missing fellow students. We were about 250 feet away, and those sleds looked to be covered with blankets that gave no warmth to the bodies underneath them. We watched in silence as the men disappeared with their loads by the nursing station.

The playground was very quiet. The scene was not lost on us kids. As prisoners, we keenly observed what would happen to us if we also tried to escape, but I do not recall any of the boys in the yard crying. We just stood around like robots.

Ruth recalls there were tears and quiet sobbing by some of the girls, but not loud. Kids were trying to control themselves, since the general rule was to be quiet at all times.

Lou remembers being inside playing with the orphans of her age when two girls came in from the outside, sobbing loudly and uncontrollably. Their crying broke the silence and was a shock, and she listened for any clues as to what had happened. Putting the pieces together, she reasoned later that the girls were likely crying over the loss of their brothers.

Ruth later described that day outside as being like a snow globe: a bubble in which we and our silence were all hermetically sealed. Afterwards, she recalls being in the girls' dorm and their loving dorm supervisor trying to comfort some the girls who were crying in their beds. But there was only one of her to go around, so the girls had to struggle with vulnerable feelings of loss by themselves.

I remember being very calm and disassociated from what was happening around me that day. We never directly saw their shrouded bodies, so I can't even say if I would have recognized them. Maybe they were older boys that I did not directly associate with.

During the writing of this book, I looked through records of students who died or went missing while attending a residential school. Although there were many records, many were incomplete, missing the school name and dates, so the search was inconclusive.

But we kids saw what we saw and heard the crying, and that was the only time that I saw men pulling toboggans emerging from the forest. It was also the only time when that odd black fire appeared in the woodlot during the frigid cold of the winter, when it is so cold that the ground was frozen like a rock. I'm still not sure if there was any connection to the events of that day.

Aside from the tragedy, the truth is that the residential school had already changed those two unfortunate kids, so even if they had been able to get home, they did not fully belong there anymore. Shattering their identities was the stated mission of the school: destroy the culture binding the children together. Strip or degrade the bond of family, the bond of tradition and skills, and especially the bond of language, and surviving children were trapped in a limbo between the "shameful" world of their parents and the all-powerful world of the priests.

Dismissed by "settler culture" even today, this genocidal disintegration was so traumatic that – despite all my later privileges – even my own life remains crippled by the haunting "lessons" of St. Anne's. Not only were we to be quiet then, but we were not motivated to talk about it later either. Trauma was so normalized. We tried to forget, and just tried to survive.

The Girls Maintain Silence

My sisters remember the silence of St. Anne's, which felt like punishment to them. With all the Native girls, they spent a lot of time on their knees praying with rosaries to be better people. The restrictive silence in the chapel was deafening. As Ruth and Lou recount, it was always, "Silence! You be quiet!" You didn't talk in class unless in response to a teacher's questions, or anywhere, especially in the chapel. When the nuns sang vespers, though, they had beautiful voices, and the sound carried through the silence in the hallways, which was a reprieve and somehow gave colour to these otherwise drab and dreary surroundings.

Lou remembers the nuns at St. Anne's singing in chapel. That sound became very familiar and comforting. As an adult, she can still sit and listen to that for hours on end and not be troubled by it.

But it is troubling. Why would she want to listen to the singing of the Psalms when she had such negative feelings about the mission school? She says it's because when the nuns sang, it was lyrical: "The 23rd Psalm set to music is beautiful." Lou does not have anything else positive to say about St. Anne's except the singing.

Lou Does Penance

Even though Lou was severely burned and quite fragile, suffering real pain, she did not escape the requirement for penance that the mission school environment demanded.

Oddly, she laughs when she remembers the nuns always making her do penance by kneeling and praying with her little rosary because she had been so "bad," and having to confess her sins about the naughty little things she did, like spitting into the wind or whistling. Typically, that was ten Hail Marys, or more prayers with repetitions on the rosary beads. "The nuns once threatened me with having to sleep in the boys' dorm to curb my desire to whistle," she says. "After all, only boys whistled, they said." And yet she remembers whistling with Dad, who was a great whistler. It was confusing to her that she was allowed to whistle with Dad at home, but not in the presence of the nuns.

The nuns would find things for her to do to keep her occupied. She was too young to help cook or clean, so Lou was given prayer duty much of the time. I would have thought that the pain she endured from her severe burns would have made up for some of the penance expected of her. She learned you never trust anybody, and you do as you're told. "Be quiet. Don't whistle." So many years later, Lou says she rarely trusts anybody, but she whistles whenever she wants.

Ron's and Lou's Classroom

Lou and I were in the same classroom because some grades were combined into the same room. I would have been in grade three and Lou in grade one at that time.

It was obvious that she was different now, though, from the sister I remembered from home. She appeared fragile. Her actions were subdued as if uncertain of how to take her next step. It was a shock to me to see her in such a state as she was led in with the rest of the girls to take her seat. Her slow movements were of course because of her burns, and although concerned, I was powerless to understand or support her in her struggle to integrate and adjust to life at school as an older brother might do in normal life. Here, in this stark landscape of suppressed emotions, there was no room or opportunity to communicate let alone express any empathy. We had to bear our pain by ourselves, and had no choice but to follow the strict rules of the classroom, looking forward at all times at the teacher. It felt strange to be so close and yet so far from a sibling who I had played with at home about a year before, and now was like a stranger sitting only a few feet away from me, a memory of her former self.

Whenever I managed to peek at her, she appeared to be on a faraway journey deep inside herself, which I presumed was from the pain of her burns. But despite her serious physical injuries, she excelled in school. It was apparent right from those first days in school together that her mind was not limited by her injuries.

Ron (left foreground), Lou (centre foreground), and classmates at St. Anne's Residential School, Fort Albany, circa 1960. This photo gives evidence of the overbearing school policy of cutting off each girl's long hair and braids, shaping it into bowl cuts, and shearing the boys' hair into brush cuts, stealing their individuality.

Even though Lou was excelling in spite of it all, it was definitely not the ideal school for anyone – let alone a child who was suffering from a life-altering, life-threatening event. She was also being squeezed into life at St. Anne's and feeling some of the pain and discomfort that the other students and dorm mates were experiencing as well. As she was to later recount, "I had been taken to a God-awful hospital, then another God-awful hospital, then came home to this God-awful school."

Holidays with Lou

Eventually, we were able to enjoy a more relaxed visit with Lou when Christmas holidays came, and we got to go home. She looked so different and stylish with her new haircut compared to the bowl cuts others had to endure at school. Thankfully, she was not subjected to such treatment, a privilege not recognized till the writing of this book.

Ron and Lou with her new haircut, coat, and mittens, Fort Albany.

Lou was more guarded and hesitant in her actions even in the safety of home. However, she still tried to interact with smiles, but understandably, had lost some of her playfulness. We were all under strict orders, including the clerk, to treat Lou with gentleness because of her injuries.

Unfortunately, holidays were over too soon and we had to go back to the strict environment at school.

CHAPTER TWENTY:
A CRUCIFIX AND CONFESSION

ST. ANNE'S WAS VERY DISPOSED to symbols, with lots of praying and giving thanks to them. One bright sunny day, a big wooden crate arrived outside the front door of the school. This curious crate was a welcome diversion for us kids, a change to the day-to-day routine of the place.

The crate was made of light, unpainted wood, about eight feet long by three feet wide, and three feet high. It was waiting outside in front of the school as we were all marched out to receive it.

Ruth remembers standing facing the school, over on the right-hand door, just kitty corner from where Lou and I were standing. I remember looking through the crowd to see the crate but was not sure what it was. Maybe it contained a casket that held a dead person. I wasn't sure. Was this going to be yet another student who had run away and died? I wondered if my sisters might know. I did not know how to get ready for it, how to feel, so I just braced myself.

One positive experience to student assemblies in the courtyard was that it blurred the lines of segregation. Brothers and sisters began to move toward each other. At least, those who remembered or cared whether they had siblings – including me. Regardless of the reasons for assemblies, it was a special treat to snatch a quick visit with siblings while the nuns were focussed on other matters.

In order to cope with living at the residential school, I tended to not pay much attention to the goings on around me unless they were threatening in nature, but this assembly brought me to my senses. I could hear whispers of "Jesus" and "Praise be to God," which hinted that it must be an important event and that there was some great power within the crate.

An ordained priest in black robes stepped forward to open the crate. He was the same priest who would occasionally be seen walking down the hallways holding a rolled-up strap and looking out of breath.

He reached out to lay his hand on the crate, as if trying to first get a sense of any power within it. Maybe he felt guilty about something. Maybe he had even lost his faith because his movements were more theatrical rather than in reverence. Interesting how insightful children can be.

His hesitation caused us all to focus on him, though, and the possibility, the hope that he might be struck down by some higher unseen power. But nothing happened in reaction to his touch. He gave a little nervous laugh and then began to pull at a nail in the lid with his brand-new hammer, acting as if his training and faith had led to this moment, where he, the chosen one, was entrusted to reveal whatever power was within the crate. One could see that he really thought he was special, but his religious, authoritarian zeal was not enough to loosen the lid.

Whoever had organized this spectacle had also arranged for a helper to be available, just in case. Compared to the polished appearance of the priest, the helper looked rough. He was dressed in an old, stained plaid bush shirt, grasping his trusted grimy hammer and sucking on a roll-your-own cigarette. He looked on with some indifference and impatience while hacking away with a deep, lung-ripping cough and sprinkling his cigarette ashes over everything in the vicinity, including the crate.

The priest finally gave up his struggle to loosen the lid and for fear of showing his ineptness, gave a nod to the helper to assist him. The helper approached the task without any obvious respectful deference to whatever or whoever might be in the box. After all, he was just another carpenter asked to pull out some nails. Eventually he was able to ease the lid off with his old, grimy hammer.

Nestled in a bed of wood shavings in the crate was a life-sized crucifix. Sister Marie Albert was the first to step forward to welcome it. There were emotional expressions coming from the nuns as they all swooned around. The event was extremely emotional for them, and they all fawned over this new addition.

If one looked closely enough, some of the shavings that covered the crucifix could be seen fluttering and moving in the breeze. To those with enough faith, hope, or even imagination, the figure looked like it might be causing the disturbance in the wood shavings. I found myself feeling somewhat unsure. I hoped this thing was real somehow, so as to validate our experiences at St. Anne's, and yet I did not want it to be real for fear of being confronted by such a power. Imagine the power of the universe coming to visit us in the back woods of Northern Canada at this residential school. For a moment, I thought that we must be very special to receive such a visit. I was not old enough, though, to be able to ask the why of it all.

On closer inspection, one could see that the crucifix came in two pieces, split along the length, which had to be assembled. The fragments of the figure seemed reminiscent of the broken body of Jesus after his crucifixion. The chiselled pain on his face was unsettling. If he was meant to be our saviour, he sure didn't look to be in a saving mood. Once assembled, though, the body was ornate, with blue and pink ribbons tied around the cross. Lou remembers that they looked quite beautiful and soothing. Maybe the symbol of the cross could not save her from her pain, but the ribbons had a positive effect on her.

We three kids were not aware that the crucifix was a "thank you" gift from Mom for letting her sleep over during some of her visits there. If I had known at the time, that it was a gift from Mom, the crucifix would likely have given me a comforting feeling too.

Going to Confession

We kids were all expected to go to confession. This happened every Saturday when part of our school day was reserved for us to confess our sins.

Tony:

"We had to go to confession on Saturdays so your soul would be without sin on Sunday. But what the hell kind of sin could we as young children do in that prison, having no freedom? I always found it somewhat stressful to ... make

up sins and [lie] to beat hell to the priest in the confessional booth, wondering if he would catch me making up my non-existent sins. I mean, what the hell kind of sins were we supposed to confess to? I realized later on in life that no matter what the staff did, they could [simply] confess to the Lord their sins, then the slate would be wiped clean. That way, no matter what they did, they felt that once their sins were forgiven, they didn't have a need to feel guilty. I remember one time being told that the priest basically had a direct line to the Almighty and thus didn't need to go to confession ... we wondered, who does a priest confess to? ... We would also go to school on Saturdays as we had nothing else to do. One day would roll into the next, with Sunday the only day being different, and on that day, we would go into a praying orgy."

There really wasn't anything I could think of that would merit a confession at the time, except maybe that little incident back home, a few years earlier, when we three kids had picked a number of kite frames that were growing right out of the ground on the other side of a tall wooden fence beside our house. It was a special, magical place we kids called "the gravy yard".

We kids were too young to understand the significance of the crosses but thought they'd be perfect for kite-making. Finding toys growing right out of the ground seemed totally magical to us. We hoped they were there for the taking and pulled out as many of the smaller, white, painted ones as we could carry. Imagine Mom's surprise and Dad's excitement when we presented them with our big haul. Words just can't describe their reactions.

That night, strange lights were seen flickering in that graveyard. Anyone seeing these lights might have wondered about the possibility of nightly spirits dancing around. But it was actually Mom and Dad replanting the little crosses, guided by the light of their flashlights. If anyone had actually seen them, they might have thought these white HBC Anglican people were a bit nuts crawling around there at night.

In our innocence, we kids had no idea of the trauma and pain that our greedy "harvesting" might have caused families in the community.

I did not think it was necessary to confess to the Catholic priest, though, since we had done this deed in Anglican territory, and a few years before being enrolled at St. Anne's. So why bring up the past after all the crosses had been replanted? Where was the harm? We had also been reprimanded by our parents – so why risk receiving further punishment by telling the priest? I hoped that the "sin," if it was one in God's eyes, could just fade away with time.

CHAPTER TWENTY ONE:
VISITS FROM MOM

ALTHOUGH THE WALL OF SEGREGATION at the school kept us apart, we three kids did get to see each other every few months when we were given permission to visit together with Mom – but for some unknown reason, this special treatment (of us kids visiting together) was not permitted every time she came to see us.

One time for example, I had outgrown my shoes and so Mom was allowed to take me to the little church-owned store on the grounds of St. Anne's to look for new ones. Although it would have been a great outing for we three kids to experience together with Mom, it was not allowed. Maybe the staff felt that it would not be fair to the rest of the students if they saw us three white kids walking around St. Anne's with our Mother.

Shopping at St. Anne's

Although Mom had received permission to take me shopping, venturing out to that store was also a concern for me because I had to go outside the boys' yard and onto the grounds where there were mean staff roaming about. I hoped that Mom could protect me. I was so afraid that we would get in trouble, and held her hand tightly for fear that our visit would be cut short. Thankfully, no one appeared to challenge us.

Once we were within the safety of the store, it soon became apparent that the shoes in the store were not new and had likely been donated to the church. However, it was exciting all the same to get to pick out the pair of shoes that caught my eye.

It was interesting that Mom was expected to pay for my shoes with special tokens – St. Anne's money. However, she didn't have any. But after a tense but friendly conversation, the nun managing the store accepted her real money.

I have always remembered that moment when Mom allowed me to exert my will and make my own choice. That freedom felt so empowering, especially against the backdrop of the prison that was waiting to swallow me up again.

I was too young at the time to fully realize that most, if not all, of my fellow students did not get visits from their parents, and likely some of them never saw their families again. Come to think of it, I never once saw Native parents visiting with any of the kids – except during Christmas celebrations.

Maybe we three white kids were privileged for being allowed more visits at the time, or maybe it was the seriousness of Lou's burns that helped to soften the rules of segregation for us.

Whatever the reason, we so appreciated the visits we did get to enjoy together. And even though there was a strange unfamiliarity between us at those times, and we were less able to intuitively sense what each other was thinking and feeling, we treasured each other and our precious time together.

Mom Comes to Chapel

On one occasion, Mom attended chapel and asked the Mother Superior to let her children sit with her. The Mother Superior said, "Of course," and sent instructions accordingly. My sisters were then brought into the chapel to sit on the bench next to Mom.

Anna Wesley, who brought me, pushed me firmly toward Mom, and I stumbled into the pew. Mom looked at the nun, thinking at first that I had just tripped, but the anger on the nun's face was unmistakable.

Perhaps she did not mean to push so hard, but in hindsight, I would consider this to be a very passive-aggressive act, suggesting that the nuns were accustomed to issuing punishment at will, with no repercussions or anyone to whom they needed to explain their actions. She also didn't stop to introduce herself to Mom. Since enforcer nuns never interacted with parents, she likely felt it unnecessary and just walked on. Mom may have not realized the full significance of the moment, but what she was observing was the flaw in the system of parents never having the opportunity of confronting the enforcer nuns.

I distinctly remember hoping that my fall would send a hidden message to Mom that not all was right between the dorm supervisor and we boys. The look in the nun's eyes definitely held some anger toward me for making her look bad in front of Mom. She was particularly strict with me after that, and I moved about in fear for some time as a result.

Aside from the meanness of Anna Wesley, I am not sure if the staff saw us as Catholic children who were expected to know better, or just children to be controlled. Whatever the objective was, we certainly felt the controlling grip of the place. After all, it was a monastic religious centre as well as a school, so strictness was the order of the day.

While in chapel, I am not sure if Mom saw any signs of religious coercion as she sat in that chapel and listened to the same sermon of hellfire that we kids were used to hearing. She seemed happy and content just to be there with us kids – although a concerned look would cross her face when the sermon expressed conflicting and confusing ideas of theology and morality far beyond our understanding.

Having such a moral framework being forced upon us, there definitely was some form of coercion going on – but what could we do as it was the price to pay for our education at the time.

I am sure that some Native parents, if they had been allowed to be in attendance, might have had similar concerns as well; that their historic, complex social and cultural customs were being erased by this aggressive form of evangelizing.

Mom Breaths Happiness into Us through Music

It was only when Mom came to visit that I sensed any relief from being imprisoned at St. Anne's. Sometimes Mom would be allowed to use the piano located in the main building, something I enjoyed much more than our time together in the chapel. The music she played was more uplifting and hopeful in its nature.

The piano itself was nothing special. It was just a dark, old, dusty thing in the shadows. But with Mom, it came alive. Mom packed our time with the kind of love and nurturing that we kids were missing. The whole experience gave us a sense of belonging to a family again and a reason to want to survive a little longer.

Mom would sometimes have a pensive look on her face at these times though. We were to learn that she was remembering her own precious piano that her family had sold years before, in spite of her pleading with them not to sell it. This personal pain surfaced while playing for us kids. One does not realize as a child that one's parents have childhood hurts and memories that they also still carry with them.

Mom would mostly play fast-paced hymns. Her joyous way of playing breathed life into us and also expressed the joy she felt in getting to have some time with us. She played as if our lives depended on it. Occasionally a nun would appear and put her finger to her lips, signalling us that we were getting too loud and interrupting vespers or some such religious activity next door. Experiencing the two modes of religious expression colliding, with us in the middle, caused us kids concern that we might get into trouble, but Mom's confidence in playing in the face of adversity gave us kids courage as well.

The nun would remain in the room standing rigidly in the shadows watching us with a pained smile painted on her face, raising a finger to her lips each time the sound of the piano got too loud. This suppression even got to Mom, from the look of resignation on her face as she slowed the music down and pressed the piano keys with a little less pressure each time until the passion was squeezed out of her and she stopped playing altogether – which also signalled that our visit was over.

There was the feeling that we were being given permission to feel happiness, and that it would be allowed to last only as long as our mother was there. I am forever grateful for her efforts and sacrifice to come and give us her loving presence during those precious times. Our time at the piano gave me hope to cling to from one visit to the next. She seemed to sense it as well, in the way she would pack as much of herself into the time we had together before sadly preparing us for her departure.

Mom's Courage and Sacrifice

On one of these visits, Mom stayed a little later than planned and then had to trudge home the five miles through the bush and across the river by moonlight. The next morning, a visitor who had followed the same trail to the HBC store and our home told Dad that he had found polar bear tracks over top of her trail on the frozen river, exactly where Mom had walked the night before. When Dad told her, she went outside with our binoculars to scan the river for any evidence of the bear, and there it was – still lurking in the area, walking on the far side of the river. It was hard to see because of its white coat against the snow and ice, but there was no mistaking it. It was a close call, but as Mom says, that was part and parcel of living in the North.

Adult polar bears average around 1,000 pounds and stand about eight feet high on their back legs, with some as tall as twelve feet high. They can eat up to 200 pounds of food in a single meal. Mom's Remington shotgun would likely have not been able to save her if the bear decided that she looked like a possible meal.

There was a unique awareness about one's surroundings in the North. It was like thin ice; it is something to be aware of, but it is not going to stop you from living and functioning.

It was not like a normal situation in the South where one jumped in the car and drove a few miles down the road to see us. This was my mother on her own with her shotgun, trudging through five miles of bush on foot, keeping an eye out for wolves and bears.

Sometimes she got to stay overnight with Sister Marie Albert in her quarters at the mission, but not very often. The personal risk and effort Mom made to visit her children speaks to her devotion and the deep feelings of separation she felt as well. I am grateful to finally have this insight and to know how much she really loved us, and still does.

The thing is that it was all normalized. The abuse was normalized. The risk was normalized. So, looking back, Mom needs to be celebrated for the things she did do right. How many moms would be able to rise to that occasion in such isolated wilderness? Most women might think, *I've been to the movies, I know what happens when the woman goes into the dark woods, and it's not going to be me! That is the beginning plot of every horror show, so forget that!* But it did not even cross Mom's mind; she just had our welfare on her mind.

I can imagine the conversation Mom might have had with Dad when she would arrive back home, with Dad saying, "Hi, you're back. How was your day with the kids?"

"Well, okay, I guess. I braved a polar bear to go see them, that's about it ... and how was your day at work?"

Years later, I came to learn how lonely she was without her children at home, and therefore she was willing to risk her comfort and safety to come visit with us.

CHAPTER TWENTY TWO:
MOVING OUR HOME

THAT SAME YEAR THAT MY sisters and I were in residence at school, the HBC decided to move the post, including our home closer to the Roman Catholic Community near St. Anne's. This was because all our Anglican neighbours, our immediate customer base on Albany Island, had moved north to the new community of Kashechewan. Although the HBC had set up a satellite store there in the form of a wall tent, the decision was made to relocate the main HBC post closer to Roman Catholic territory where there was more economic potential. A store operated by Bill Anderson was already enjoying a successful business in the area there, and it was decided to move the post to compete with him.

The house was scheduled to be moved over the ice in the winter. One of the necessary steps was to make a break in the cliff and river bank where the house could be pulled down to the river. Dad filled the dried pussy willow stalks along the route with gunpowder, then set them on fire to explode them and create the path. In the process, he discovered cannonballs in the cliff, evidence of the historic battle between the English and French when they had battled over control of the land and its resources in 1688.

There was also a lot of preparation required at the new store. Dad and Chris, the HBC clerk at the time, would walk over to the new location whenever possible during the winter to do this work. Given the number of wild animals in the area at the time, they talked loudly, shouted out the biggest words they knew, and sang songs as loud as possible to scare off any danger along the way. Of course, Dad also carried his pistol in his pocket to protect them if necessary.

Rupert's Land Construction (part of the HBC) was contracted to move the house. The Caterpillar tractor and swamp buggy were on loan from St. Anne's. They pulled the house down the bank to the edge of the river but stopped there because the ice was still too thin to cross. And so it sat there for several weeks, waiting for the ice to thicken.

Our house at Fort Albany being moved onto the Albany River, circa 1961.

Our house being moved, circa 1961. The house looked like it had dug its toes in, as if in fear of the unknown.

Eventually, when the ice was thick enough, the house was eased out onto the frozen river by the Caterpillar tractor and pulled to the new location. During the move, Chris the clerk remained in the house trying to keep things from crashing to the floor on that bumpy ride over the ice. I shudder to think now what his chances of survival would have been if the house had crashed through the ice and sunk into the icy depths. Thankfully the house reached the new location without incident, with all involved breathing a sigh of relief.

The old ship anchor in our front yard unfortunately had to be left behind because there was no place for it where we were going. It had become a symbol of our family unity, but according to the HBC, it was just a novelty item and not representative of the company, and therefore, was not included in the move. Having to leave our anchor behind was somehow symbolic of leaving our haven and being set adrift in the larger world.

At the time when our house was moved, Mom was allowed a rare extended stay at St. Anne's. She slept in the building where her friend Sister Marie Albert stayed. Dad had to fend for himself and likely slept on the floor in the new store, or else at the radar site where there were lots of beds available. I was not old enough to understand the full details of what was going on, but the occasion was marked with more frequent visits from Mom that I so appreciated.

After the house was moved, we three kids (and Mom) never went back to the old location where we had enjoyed so much fun as young children. Dad still had the responsibility of going back to retrieve the inventory of explosives and bullets in the dusty confines of the gunpowder shack. This stock was used by the Natives for their hunting purposes – so it was important to continue to stock it in the store.

Some time after our move, Mom walked over to see Mr. Anderson (our old neighbour and competitor) to find him leaning against his store counter smoking his pipe. He pointed to a bag sitting at the end of the counter and said in a gleeful tone, "What do you think I have there?" It was a bag of gunpowder. Mom was shocked – not just that he had nicked it from our abandoned gunpowder shed, but that he was smoking so close to it.

She also noticed that he had transported our precious anchor to his place. It was a surprise, and she didn't know whether to think he had stolen or was preserving this symbol of our past. At least it ended up in the possession of someone who would appreciate and care for it.

The Danger of Spring Break-up

Even the change of seasons and our appreciation of nature changed in the new location. Mom remembers the spring break-up that year. We lived close to the river channel that separated the Native village from the residential school, an almost-dry riverbed for most of the year.

One lovely spring day, while we kids were at school, Mom went for a walk along the river and stopped at a little point that was nice and sunny. She put her trusted gun down against a tree and sat there on the riverbank enjoying the peace and beauty of the moment. The river channel, with its sparkling trickle of snow melt and rounded stones, lay about twenty feet below her and spread out about one hundred feet across to the other bank. It made a sort of miniature valley with rounded shoulders.

Suddenly, she heard loud, cracking thunder and a rumble. She looked upstream and saw that some of the snow on the surface of the frozen river was moving. Next came a swelling flow of muddy water, and then the ice dam broke. To her astonishment, an enormous rush of muddy flood water, huge, jagged chunks of ice, trees, everything, came roaring down the valley right in front of her and rose within seconds, right up to where she sat on the bank. This was not beautiful nature; it was destructive nature. As she stated, "It happened so fast and quickly that I was afraid to move. I was just stunned. I was worried that the force of the water might undermine the ground beneath me."

The river roared down on her like a tsunami. A twenty-foot wave filled the bare riverbed instantly. "If I had been in that hollow when the water rushed through, I would have been swept away, and no one would have ever found me again." Instead, she sat there on her safe perch and watched as the swirling water went roaring past her toward James Bay.

I wonder now if some of the kids who ran away from St. Anne's over the years and were never found might have met such a fate.

Photo of the mouth of the river channel after spring break-up, Fort Albany.

The power of that flood was astounding and awesome. But when Mom returned home and tried to describe the experience to Dad and the clerk, they did not react with much excitement. They continued to concentrate on their work, with only token comments of relief that she was home safe and sound. It seemed that the new location and environment, with its demand for business and commerce, left little room for appreciating the wonder of nature around them – or the possible death of my mother!

To Mom, a natural event like that was awe-inspiring – with the crash and roar of the wall of water moving like a freight train right before her eyes. She was indeed lucky to see it happen, and luckier still to be out of its way.

Our New Community in "Civilization"

With our house so close to the school now, one would think that we kids would get to go home each day after school. Unfortunately, it did not happen because the simple stone and dirt road across the river tributary between our new home and the school was washed away each spring due to the flooding. The water was not very deep there, and only about a hundred feet across, but in the spring especially when the water level was relatively high, there was no way to cross it other than by boat. It was decided, therefore, that we kids would continue to live in residence during the week and just come home every Saturday after school for a sleepover. It was a disappointment, but at least we got to enjoy a day at home once a week.

The river crossing was a great way to meet some of the local people in the community, especially the many labourers who worked at St. Anne's. Each time Dad or Mom would use our canoe to cross that stretch of water, there would be people waiting for someone to give them a ride as well.

The Catholic staff, including the priests, also had to commute from St. Anne's to their church in the community. In those days, because the religious communities were quite insular, the greetings Dad exchanged with the priests' as our boats crossed paths were initially quite formal. Although they were likely pleased that the HBC post was now in Roman Catholic territory, the fact that it had come from Anglican territory and was being run by my dad, an Anglican, was an obvious concern for some of them. But as they got to know each other while contending with the natural barrier of the river, they became quite neighbourly and began to smile and wave friendly greetings.

As the water subsided, the road was built once more across the shallow water between St. Anne's and the Roman Catholic Community.

[Looking south from our new HBC post location to St. Anne's across the river, Fort Albany, circa 1961. This photo shows the road across the river, and on the far bank, a lumber mill on the left, with the brothers' building on the right. Further back, past the brothers' building, was the nursing station. On the right is St. Anne's Residential School.]

Looking in a northward direction toward our new home and the radar station, circa 1961. This photo is taken from St. Anne's side of the river.

We kids gradually got into the rhythm of visiting home once a week, and Ruth even began to associate with friends she had met in St. Anne's whose homes were located close to us.

Ruth with friends (Georgette and her younger sister).

Although I was more of a loner and did not seek out friends, I enjoyed being able to see Mom and Dad and my sisters more often now. This resulted in school not being so traumatic for me, to a point where I started to try harder and even excelled.

Although Mom was enjoying seeing us kids on a regular basis, she didn't like the new location of our home.

> *"The new location was terrible. It was horrible. There was no place to go where you could be alone. It was so bad. We had moved from the complete peacefulness of the country to the slums of a town. For example, at our previous home, our outdoor toilet was situated within the privacy of our yard, and it was well-built, and I put ashes in it so it never smelt. It was nice, and I could scrub it out. But here anyone who walked*

across our yard could use our toilet. It was unbelievably hor-
rible having strangers use it like a communal washroom and
leave their filth for someone else to clean up. When I think of
it, even now, my stomach just goes sick."

She remembers that carpenters and workers who had been shipped in
to do construction work for the HBC made the place intolerable.

"As well as cleaning up all their filth in the toilet, I was
cooking for the whole gang and it was just getting me down.
And some of the young carpenter helpers (snotty little boys,
as she calls them) *sometimes didn't like what I cooked, and*
they would just send back the plate untouched."

Sending one's food back was certainly not an option for us at St. Anne's.
Mom also recounts that the workers would have women coming into
their sleeping quarters, and she was so fed up with the whole situation.
The workers shacks' were nearby, and Mom could see and hear the ladies
wandering into the men's barracks at night. In an effort to protect us from
witnessing such sights and sounds, she would make sure that our windows
were closed and the curtains tightly drawn.

"If I could have gotten on a train or plane or boat and gotten
out of there, I would have gotten out with you kids, but I didn't
know how to go. But I had had enough, and I was losing my
marbles a little bit. I was tired and frustrated with the way of
life closer to the 'white' civilization that we suddenly found
ourselves in. We went from homesteading, in a way, to a more
populated suburbia, and it was terrible!"

My two sisters and I were now also confronted with the challenges
and conflicting morals and habits found in larger populations. I had the
strange and unique experience of standing in my actual childhood home,
where I had enjoyed such promise and freedom, while the world outside
my window now was different and unfamiliar. Our white picket fence, our
line of defence, had disappeared. It was like the house was floating in an
alien world that I had never encountered and that my young eyes did not

really understand. It was troubling to witness such strange goings on while peeking out of the very windows of my once-safe home.

At my young age, I could not recognize all of the immoral acts that now infested the surroundings of our new home. But I could see that the situation was not a happy or even a healthy one. I observed strangers wandering around with no regard for us, or our space, or our land. It is ironic that I had thought of our white picket fence at our old home as a border to keep the Natives away from me and now was wishing we had a fence to keep these workers, who had the same skin colour as me, out of our lives. I began to wonder and worry if everyone in the South was like those workers.

I wanted to go back to a more peaceful place, to go back to the land. To make a safe, quiet place where I could hide. My sisters likely felt the same because on one of our visits home, we decided to build a play fort, so we started to chop down a very large tree one evening when it was dark enough for no one to see us. Our mother agreed to help. Instead of using trees that we could manage, we hammered and chopped and sawed away at that monster, and eventually cut it down. It's a wonder we didn't kill anyone, as we were now living in an organized community.

That tree was so big we didn't know what to do with it. In fact, we couldn't do anything with it. Looking back at that incident, I think that we were all crying out at our loss of freedom. Our choice of such a large tree somehow symbolized the size of our concern with the situation we now found ourselves in. We were excited about the creation of the fort, but as it turned out, the fort would never be, and our safe place, our precious home, seemed farther away than ever before. On subsequent visits home, I would walk over to that now-dead tree and sit on it, even talking to it, as it slowly rotted away.

There was nowhere to hide from the disrespectful white people from the South with their aggressive customs and habits. Mom says she didn't know how to handle them.

She still wonders whether any of those people were spies sent to see how Dad was running the place. Maybe her reactions alerted the HBC upper management because on one particular day, a lady flew in and questioned her about everything: how she was doing and what she was feeling in this new environment.

"I feel now that she was some kind of a psychologist coming in to see if we were nuts or not. I remember telling her, 'Moving into this new location somehow makes me afraid to think that should we ever be out in the open, living down south again, I might not be able to function in a neighbourhood with other ladies and children, because all I have ever had up to this point are my children and my chores.' I couldn't seem to think beyond it. And the lady said, 'Oh, you'll do fine.' But now I feel she wasn't just a tourist taking pictures. Now I think that she was sent in to assess something for the HBC. Maybe to deal with the immoral actions of all of those scumbags, the HBC labourers, and their treatment of the local Native women."

Whatever the assessment was by the higher powers of the HBC, the construction work continued and the store was eventually opened for business.

Shopping at the New HBC Store

Although the HBC post was now located close by St. Anne's, the school staff were still concerned about leaving their relatively sheltered world in order to shop at the store. They were obviously aware of the ignorant and immoral acts that Mom was witnessing, but the opportunity to shop obviously outweighed the dangers.

Tony:

"From time to time, the staff would take us summer inmates for a ride to the local Hudson Bay store. Of course, we never entered the store and merely waited in back of the truck while a brother went in to purchase whatever. Funny thing to me was that the nuns made us pray before we left the compound for a safe journey on the highway. To this day, it boggles the mind to think that they would consider that rough mud / gravel road, a highway."

Kids on truck, St. Anne's. Source: Archives Deschâtelets-NDC, Fonds Deschâtelets, Fort Albany residential school.

Tony Tourville standing in front of a nun. Extract. Source: Archives Deschâtelets-NDC, Fonds Deschâtelets, Fort Albany residential school.

The truck was only operated during the summer months when the land had dried out from the spring floods, and it could be used on the grounds as well as driving the short distance between St. Anne's and the HBC post.

Anna Wesley in the driver's seat. Extract. Source: Archives Deschâtelets-NDC, Fonds Deschâtelets, Fort Albany residential school.

Watching the Game

With the warmer weather, there were opportunities to enjoy more outdoor activities as well. On one occasion, we were assembled in the boys' playground to see a baseball game between some of the older boys at the school. All of us boys and girls, as well as some of the staff, gathered to watch. Everyone milled about together in anticipation. Even the dust in the air, kicked up from so many people, added to the excitement.

As the game began, it was a surprise to see the boys play in such an organized way, and with such a frantic focus on winning. These older boys must have been allowed to practise when we younger boys were not in

247

the play yard, likely when we were in our forced naps, because I had never seen such activity before. Even though I was now eight years old, I was not used to seeing such friendly aggression, and was not sure whether I liked it or not. The fact that each player had a baseball glove was not lost on me either. I wondered why we younger boys were never provided such gloves during our playtime and felt the injustice.

Boys and girls were now mixing together and enjoying being allowed so close to each other while watching the game. Nuns and priests stood together at the back of the crowd. They looked out of place in their dark robes, like judges at a picnic. It was odd to see them actually enjoying such an event, because as a rule, so many of them gathered together meant some sort of religious activity. But here they were, trying to fit in, but not too much. After all, they were our guards. All had smiles pasted on, but the eyes of the mean enforcers still darted around looking for victims to reprimand if we showed too much joy. The presence of their power also radiated out from them in the form of strong starch smells from their clothes and the rich odour of cologne filtering through the crowd and mingling with the dust in the air, reminding us all of their presence and the larger game in play of power and control.

Because the HBC post and our home was now just a few minutes' walk away, Mom was also invited to attend the game with her nun friends. This was hard for me to deal with. I always associated her appearances with visits, and now here she was enjoying a common activity, and with some of the nuns instead of me, and it looked like she was actually enjoying herself. It was hard for me to share her. I still needed her for my emotional lifeline, even if I was getting to go home to visit once a week. Maybe Ruth and Lou did not miss her as much because they had each other, but I was on my own.

I hoped I could pull her away as she innocently watched the game with her adult friends, but I knew the dangers of challenging the authority of the place, so I dared not. I did not even turn around to look at her for fear of meeting the evil eye of one of the priests or having a nun notice my actions, which I might have to pay for later.

Over Visiting

Because of the proximity to St. Anne's, Moms visits became more frequent. Not just with us kids – she would say hi to me in the schoolyard – but she would also come to visit with her nun friends. However, it soon became apparent that she was starting to overstay her welcome. She began to see some aspects of the school that troubled her. One memory that still remains with her was the time she visited her friend Sister Marie Albert in the nuns' residence, who had invited her to dinner at the last minute. A special meal was requested for Mom, their dinner guest. When her meal appeared, Mom caught her breath. It was a jumble of turkey guts – as if to emphasize that apparently some of the other nuns or workers did not want her there. Sister Marie Albert asked from her position further down the dinner table, "How do you like your meal? Isn't that good?" Mom disposed of the guts in her napkin and into her pocket.

Mom says that finally she had some clarity that there was more going on behind the scenes at St. Anne's than she had originally thought. This incident was the point at which she began to see the different worlds operating at St. Anne's and to connect the dots.

Mom Offers a Word of Warning

It was around this time that Mom met a white woman from Moosonee who was bringing her two white boys up to enroll in St. Anne's, after which she would return home. This woman was hoping to give her boys the promise of a good Catholic education.

She asked Mom, "How do you like St. Anne's? It's so beautiful."

"Well, I sincerely hope you get a better experience than we have had, because something is not right, and my children are not happy there. I wish we could leave this place," our mother replied, trying to offer the warning she had not received.

CHAPTER TWENTY THREE:
THE END OF THE NIGHTMARE

OUR TIME AT FORT ALBANY and St. Anne's ended relatively quickly. In the spring of 1961, the Hudson's Bay Company informed Dad that we were being transferred out of Fort Albany.

When Dad appeared on the last day of school to collect us, he said, "Today is the day. Time to go!" My fear of being left behind was so great that I asked for clarification that it was the last day of school at St. Anne's, and he said, "Yes, today is your last day here. "Forever?" I asked. "Yes, forever and ever," he said.

Realizing that St. Anne's was not going to be forever after all, a feeling of relief began to flow through me. It was like I had been holding my breath for the three years I had been imprisoned there and could now lower my guard and breathe normally again.

To mark the historic moment, Dad took a picture of Lou and I with the nuns who had delivered us to him, while another nun went to get Ruth.

Ron and Lou and two nuns on the day we left St. Anne's for the last time, in 1961. Notice Lou's discomfort and Ron's irritated reaction to the hand of the nun on his shoulder.

One can see Lou (in the picture above) protecting her side where her burns had made her sensitive. When Dad saw her obvious pain, he asked for the medicine that he and Mom had provided a year earlier in a sealed box when Lou was first enrolled at St. Anne's. There was a frantic search for it and eventually it was found and brought to Dad, still sealed. To his surprise and anger, she had not been given any of the drugs. It left questions in all our minds: Did the nuns not know what the drugs were for? Did they think the drugs constituted some kind of special treatment that was forbidden under school rules? There was no explanation. Both internal and external wounds apparently went unnoticed at the school. This is highly indicative that special, caring treatment for the children at the school was rare to none, no matter their colour, age, or physical condition.

I do not think that it was malice that the nuns withheld her drugs, or ill will. Rather, I believe it was ineptness, a lack of due diligence and empathy. Perhaps that amounts to the same thing. Anyone aware of Lou's burns would have known she was in pain, and any caring person would have tried to alleviate it. Maybe there was a fear of being held accountable in some sort of malpractice charge if they had actually administered the drugs, but I doubt it.

As can be seen in my body stance, I was feeling quite troubled. I still remember tensing at the moment that nun put her hand on my shoulder. It was like a message to the future, to anyone that might care, that the nun was mean. Maybe she was not perverted, but she was overly strict.

One would think that my two sisters and I had lots of emotions because we would be leaving St. Anne's forever, but it all happened so fast that day. Initially, it was like a weight had been lifted, the prison gates had opened at Dad's command, and we were being set free. Unfortunately, the parents of my schoolmates did not possess that same power to free their kids on demand, and so could only watch as we left them all that day.

As we three kids walked over that little bridge for the last time, we were strangely silent, but happy inside to be leaving. For me, it was like I was disentangling myself from the school and its religious morality – which (like a cult) had become my world. It was like walking out of a black and white illustration and back into the world of colour. As we walked across the field past the screeching sound of the sawmill and toward home, the wind on my face felt like the wind that had given me that peace of mind prior to my enrolment so long ago. Its soothing power danced around me as if in celebration of my survival, giving me a fresh feeling of better things to come.

There had been a flurry of packing activity during the previous month while we kids were still in school, so most of our belongings were already in big crates to be shipped out on the next supply ship. All that was left to do was to pack the remaining clothes and items in suitcases. As part of my packing process, I also crammed the memories of the residential school experience into spaces in my mind where they would lay festering till many years later.

In a final act of disgust with how our lives and home had ended up, Mom burned any remaining clothes that would not fit in the suitcases. It was like she did not want to leave any trace that we had been at the new location, given all the perversion she was witnessing there.

As the flames flickered in the burn pile, and the construction workers wandered about in our yard still making a mess of the place, Mom's nun friend Sister Marie Albert braved the troubled and confused scene to come to say goodbye to her. To mark the heart felt moment, she also signed our guest book with a date of July 1961.

The Final Canoe Ride to Say Goodbye

On the day before we flew out of Fort Albany, Mom and Dad took one final canoe ride over to the old HBC post on Albany Island, to say goodbye to what was left of it. However, Dad did not let Mom walk up the riverbank to where the old store still stood because without the house there, it was not the same anymore.

Don and Margaret Gosbee on the shore at the Hudson's Bay Company post at Fort Albany, 1961.

Although the old HBC store still stood on the hill with its memories, facing an uncertain end, it was to live on in another form. Years later, it was dismantled, and its large timber beams were used to construct a dock.

Our Last Flight Out of the North

On our last flight out of the North, we landed at Moosonee. It was obviously a bigger centre because there were two HBC stores in the area; one down town, and one about a mile away on Moose Factory Island. We landed on the river and taxied over to this island and tied up at the dock.

My family and I then made our way up the path to the store where I immediately asked how I could find a Native friend with whom I had gone to school with at St. Anne's. Mom remembers that the store manager was shocked that a little white boy would want to visit a little Native boy. He looked sternly at me and then said something to Dad like, "No, you are not doing that!" So, I was not allowed the chance to say goodbye to my friend that day.

Dad also tried to maintain some separation between the Native kids and me. While waiting for the train to take us south, we decided to do some shopping in the Moosonee HBC store. That is where I saw a jacket I wanted, but Dad said no, and the tall, young clerk said, "But it looks rather good on him."

Dad said, "Oh no. Look, all the Native boys in the store are wearing the same style, so that just would not be acceptable."

Mom remembers that her toes curled up in embarrassment when Dad said that. She felt that we were not better than anybody; we were used to a more comfortable lifestyle, but that was all. That didn't mean that we were smarter or better.

Tony Gets Released from St. Anne's

Coincidentally, fellow student Tony Tourville was released at about the same time we left the North.

Tony:

*"After eight long years, in the summer of '61, my brothers
and I were finally released from St. Anne's. We flew out on
a pontoon plane and never in my life had I been so happy,
as I realized that finally I was leaving this very brutal and
evil place. To this day, I still have nightmares about trying
to escape! You see, my siblings and I had been basically
kidnapped by the Church and shipped off to Albany, and
after three years, we were made wards of the Children's
Aid, who in turn left us there to rot for another five years.
We arrived in Albany in '53, and in '61, we left with just the
clothes on our backs.... However, I remember being given
rosary beads and holy pictures, which I promptly threw
away upon landing in Moosonee."*

While Tony and other survivors were integrating back into society in
the North, my family and I boarded the train to the "settled lands" of the
south. It was such a great adventure, swaying back and forth on the Polar
Bear Express. With its white tablecloths, polite staff and yummy food, it
was a refreshing and exciting experience as we travelled towards the better
life we were anticipating.

Fate Intervenes

Our plans were to go for a holiday to Cape Cod with our friends (Hans
and Louise, who had met us up north while on a canoe adventure). But
before joining them, Dad had to find out where his next posting would be
by visiting the Hudson's Bay Company head office in Montreal.

In that interview, he was hit with devastating news instead. He was let
go by the company, with them saying they had nowhere to transfer him.
The news left him stunned. Our vacation plans were abandoned, and we
found ourselves standing on the streets of Montreal in shock, with no
home and only $5,000 in severance pay.

For us, the streets of Montreal may just as well have been another
country. Mom and Dad did not fit in, as they had been away from southern

society for so long. And Dad had no job and three little kids and a wife to worry about. Mom recalls that he walked out of the HBC headquarters that day, held her hand, and said, "Well, where do you want to live?"

Margaret:

"[It was] very traumatic! And Dad in his younger days – his growing-up years were all with the company. He was a company man! And the HBC betrayed him, for whatever reason. And that broke his spirit in some way. Although he never talked about it, being let go hurt him deeply. We never talked about it at all. Never! We were just too busy and too afraid to. And when I read memoirs of other Hudson Bay men, they talk about the wonderful pension plan that the company had. Dad never got any pension, and he was up there fifteen years. Unless his severance pay included a buyout of his pension, but he never mentioned it."

Dad was only seventeen, not even shaving yet, when he first joined the HBC as a clerk. He was just twenty-one when he met our mother, who was still a girl of eighteen. Mom and Dad's coming of age in Canadian society was actually in their thirties when they emerged from the North.

Dad's dismissal hit them hard. His fifteen years in the North had been for half his life. But in the end, that didn't count for anything.

What was the real reason Dad was let go from the Hudson's Bay Company? Could it be that he had become too friendly with the Natives, not cutthroat enough? His HBC work record indicates the company felt he was not aggressive enough in sales, so that might have been a deciding factor.

Another possibility for letting Dad go is that the HBC might have preferred the simplicity of hiring an unmarried man at the time, since Dad's replacement manager was a single man.

Living Down South

Mom says that when we came out of the North and found ourselves without a job on the streets of Montreal, we were like refugees. We were not used to the culture, and those around us did not understand us. We just didn't fit in, and of course there was no money. And as a further reminder of our loss of class, Louise, Mom's friend who had planned to go on holidays with us to Cape Cod, came to visit us in Oakville instead, and brought Mom some of her used clothing to help with the transition. But it was obvious that we were not the same class anymore. We were now essentially immigrants without any money or prospects. Mom and Louise were never to see each other again.

> *"We may as well have been in a different country. I felt unsure, unseen, and incompetent like the rest of my family. We had the gentle, polite demeanour similar to the Natives we had lived beside up North. But now we were at a disadvantage trying to adapt and learn to compete in the relatively more modern world down south. I felt like I was always struggling to catch up to my new friends in order to fit in. The possibilities of what to see and do seemed endless."*

Ruth says in hindsight now that the North was a great place for people who liked their own space, but isolation is not necessarily good, because it does not force you to grow or teach you how to compete in the world. We had to learn to speed up, and this point was highlighted when Dad took lessons to get his driver's licence. When the instructor directed him to drive on the big highway, Highway 401, Dad kept the car's speed at a respectable fifteen miles an hour. The instructor yelled, "Get going, hit the gas!" Dad obviously was not used to being in the "fast lane."

We first lived in a rented cabin in Oakville in a little orchard. One of our favourite activities was knocking down the apples from the apple trees whenever we wanted one, as kids do. But occasionally we knocked down more apples just for the fun of it, which upset the landlord and also our parents. Concerned about fitting into our new surroundings, and fearing there were no other options if we were not accepted, our parents did not have as much patience as they used to and reprimanded us more than usual. I could feel the strain and urgency to learn how to fit in as fast as possible.

Dad went out each day looking for work, and we cringed each day when he came home without a job. Even at my young age I could feel the stress he was under to support us, and it was so scary and sad to watch.

Eventually we moved into a house in another suburb of Oakville where we were enrolled in the school located only a few minutes walk from our home. In retrospect, I don't think I was ready for school, as the sights and sounds of the boys and girls freely mixing together was overwhelming to me and I was unsure how to interact. The lessons in the classroom also seemed to be beyond my comprehension.

Likely all us northern residential school students were struggling to varying degrees, trying to integrate into the standards and school curriculum of the South.

Tony:

"In the fall of '61, I went to my first normal, all-white school and what a culture shock that was ... After years of watching brown-skinned kids being silently led to the residential school, here I was on the first day of school in a strange French town listening to the excited shouting and loud laughter of the kids. [It was] something which just really amazed me. I agree that our schooling was guaranteed to make us failures, as scholastic achievement was secondary to the daily life of prayer. When I left Albany, I used to feel really stupid when listening to the white kids answer what seemed to be very hard questions from the teacher. However, when it came to prayer, none of them knew more than me, even though they were all French Catholics."

Although my sisters and I experienced the same bewilderment at subjects that appeared very easy for southern kids to grasp, we three kids at least had the advantage of having white skin which helped us to blend in with the largely white population at the time. However, the daily pressure to integrate still left us terrified.

As part of our integration Dad and Mom enrolled me into Cubs. But I was too wild to sit still and learn to tie knots and all the tasks that cubs are expected to learn. I did not want to be in any kind of structured environment anymore after my experience at St. Anne's. Eventually things came to a head, and I was sent home and told by the Cub master, "Don't bother coming back." Mom was really upset at the time that I was expelled from Cubs, although I was happy not to have to attend such an organized activity any longer. Years of not being allowed to think critically made the effort of just learning how to tie a knot unbearable. My mind had been shaped to follow rules not to think for myself.

As I continued my integration into the ways of these new lands, my sister Ruth found pleasure in learning to play a strange instrument I had never seen before: the accordion. Lou had bigger challenges as she continued to recover from her burns while excelling at school – her strength and scholastic abilities shining through.

Relocated Again

Dad struggled to find adequate employment for about a year in Oakville, but was not successful. So, we decided to move to Barwick, Ontario, where Mom's mother lived. Living within the safety and security of Grandma Rahn's home, we three kids began to rediscover the joy of play. However, St. Anne's had replaced most play with structured, religious practice. So, with the residential school experience still fresh in our minds, all our play had a religious context to it. We set up Grandma's ironing board as an altar in the basement and played "Communion" all the time. We did not pray for the forgiveness of our sins so much as to just be kept safe and secure.

Playing Communion was more important to us than playing house at that time. We did not want to play pretend house, because we were desperate to feel safe and secure. From our experience, the chapel at the residential school had been the safest place to be, and observing Communion in the chapel had been the most important activity there.

Using theatre, using play, we summoned that familiar environment that we associated with safety. We hid in the basement, our pretend chapel, and on our pretend alter, we had pretend Communion, which hopefully was summoning God's presence and power as well. We collaborated, acting out this ritual together, because our identities had been stripped away, and now we were in an incredibly alien world, and we got through it by summoning a feeling of safety.

If Grandma had come down into the basement to see us acting this out, we would have likely stopped. Not because we felt like we were being bad but rather that it was private. We were conjuring up a power, a familiar comfort that no one but us kids likely understood. Our actions when giving each other Communion were not gentle and polite, but rather tinged with authoritarian commands like, "Here is the glass – drink now!" This was likely the result of the highly authoritarian conditioning found at the residential school.

We also played church; my sisters were the nuns, and I had to pretend to be the priest. We knew many Bible passages and hymns, probably even more than most of the adults in the community, but were in fear of being seen as different. Feeling out of place, we tended to hide away as much as possible.

A Special Goodbye

We all struggled as we tried to adapt to our new world in the South, but one experience that helped Ruth to draw a line on her past was when she went with family to see the religious movie *King of Kings* in the nearby town of Fort Francis. When the movie was over and everyone was leaving the theatre, a group of nuns turned towards her and there stood her dorm supervisor, Sister Catherine, from St. Anne's.

Fort Francis is in Southern Ontario, hundreds of miles south of St. Anne's Residential school. Sister Catherine was probably there because the local La Verendrye Hospital was being run by the Order of the Grey Nuns at that time – the same order of nuns at St. Anne's. Their eyes met, and for a moment, as Ruth recounts, they looked into each other's souls and not a word was spoken. Then the crowd swept them apart. Ruth's hesitation of pushing through the crowd to say hello was likely because of her shock at seeing someone from another world, time, and place. Ruth still regrets that lost opportunity but treasures that special hello and goodbye that they shared with each other from afar. It was a precious, poignant moment and would mark the closing chapter of her life at St. Anne's Residential School. Who better to wish her well than the nun who had treated her so well? She was never to see Sister Catherine again.

Ruth wanted to be a nun at the time, likely from her fond memory of Sister Catherine and her experience at St. Anne's. But her growing interest in boys eventually caused her to see there were alternatives to living a reclusive life. She recalls that when she was around twelve years old, she looked up the word for "kiss" in the Cree dictionary ... for some reason, the word was really important to her at that age.

Trying on a New Identity

It was during our church-playing phase in the basement that we also learned about the special kids' day called Halloween, when kids were allowed to play pretend by dressing up in costumes and visiting the neighbours, who rewarded them with candies.

Such a celebration was new to us three kids. Since we had lived an insular life behind our white picket fence up North, we were not aware of such a celebration. Our Native neighbours might have welcomed such fun, but since they were living so close to the poverty level, I am sure there were no treats to exchange anyways. So, we knew nothing of such a celebration like this one in the land of plenty.

With the help of Mom and Grandma, we three kids were dressed up in variations of the same kind of disguise. I was dressed up in a dress, wig, and even had some lipstick plastered on my lips. Yuck! But with the lure of candies, I complied. Likely this was the cheapest costume possible – to use what was available and out of the norm. By helping me with my costume, Grandma must have been reminded of her first experience with Halloween, years before, when she and Grandpa immigrated to Canada and arrived in Halifax on the evening of Halloween. They had never experienced such a sight before, having come from Russia, and were shocked and concerned when they observed crazed kids walking around in costumes and carrying pillowcases to hold all their treats.

Although I was initially uncomfortable wearing a dress, I convinced myself that it was okay to do this one time, since it was like a uniform, similar to the robes the nuns and priests wore at the residential school. And so, dressed appropriately, I went out into the night, to get my share of sweets, as the other kids were doing.

Months later, though, in the summer, with an urge for sweet treats again, I had a brilliant idea. I thought, well, I got sweets last time when I dressed up in my Grandma's dress, so I decided to do it again. I also found Mom's lipstick, put a few dabs of it over my mouth, and put on her high heels for good measure. I then walked very slowly and carefully to the neighbour's house. A young boy wearing his grandma's red dress and walking in his mom's high heels is not a sight one normally sees in a sleepy little farming village.

I knocked on the door and Mrs. Black, the neighbour, greeted me, wide-eyed in surprise at the spectacle standing before her. "Hello, and who are you?" she asked.

"Hi," I replied in a high pretend voice. "Could I please have a cookie?" She was gracious and invited me inside – probably to get me out of sight before anyone else saw me. Being freshly out of the North I had no sense of the frequency of Halloween; dressing up was just a means to get treats. There were some pieces missing to my jigsaw puzzle. Thankfully, she played along and asked in a voice one uses when they are playing house, "Would you like some milk too?"

I said, "Yes, please," in a girlie voice to match my outfit. And as I munched away, I got thinking, *Now that I got a cookie, do I still have to sit politely like my grandma did?* After all, I was wearing her dress. Eventually, with the cookie eaten, we said goodbye.

About a month later, I felt the urge for more cookies, so I dressed up and shuffled over to visit Mrs. Black again in Mom's high heels. This time when she saw me standing at her front door, she said with a stern face, "No, no more cookies! You should go home." Apparently, I was cut off.

She then asked, "Does your Mom know what you are doing?" She must have had a little chat with Mom because all of Mom's makeup, her high heels, and Grandma's dress disappeared soon after that. I had to figure out how to get cookies and sweets without dressing up anymore.

It was great to have the love and gentle support of family and community to figure things out – to play, as it were, to experiment in a safe environment where there was an answer to any question I could form. Experiencing so many new things at that time, though, was overwhelming. I did not know the difference between a quarter and a nickel. I even had to learn what a bicycle was for and how to ride one.

Having to attend school also pulled us out of our hiding, but it was weird and scary. Even though I complained about having to go to school, at least I was not crying any more as I had done when going to the residential school up North, which was a relief for Mom and Dad. There were still challenges, though, with integrating into the new school system.

Fitting into the New School System

Since we were living in Mom's home town now, we were enrolled in the same school that she had once attended. Although I wanted to make her proud of me, I was unsure as to how to conduct myself.

My new teacher and those around me thought from my actions and reactions that I was disturbed and stunned for some reason and likely quite dumb, as expressed by some fellow students. My academic skills were also assessed as inadequate (since the focus at St. Anne's had been on religion, not academic standards). So, I was sent back two grades, back to grade one, and made to start over. To further complicate my sense of identity, I was now in the same class as my sister Lou.

Unfortunately, I was not assessed for learning disabilities. It is likely that in addition to being a visual learner, I was wrestling with some dyslexia and had trouble reading. For example, what else could explain why when my teacher asked me to write the word "cat" on the blackboard, I would sometimes write the word "dog"? I suspect my difficulties also came from having integrated some Cree words into my vocabulary, leading me to further confusion in my new solely white environment where Cree was not used.

It was also hard to understand how to respond to the spontaneous laughter and shouting of my new classmates. I was not used to experiencing so much unchecked expression, or seeing so many white faces, for that matter. I hid my face in my arms when sitting at my desk, hiding from the world of strangers and strange actions around me. The teacher would try to pull my head out from under my arms where I was hiding while the rest of the class laughed at me.

I was so stressed out from all the changes in my life that I could not even hear the teacher talking to me at times. When Dad was informed of my struggles at school, he thought I was daydreaming too much, when in fact I was still retreating from the trauma in the residential school.

I was even afraid to ask to go to the bathroom for fear of reprisal, another result of my time at St. Anne's with its repressive rules. I felt broken somehow, walking with subservient stooped shoulders like an old man, but I was only about ten years old.

Moving Again

Although Dad wanted to be available to help us on a day-to-day basis to integrate into the Barwick community, it did not hold any opportunity for work for him. So, he had to look elsewhere and finally found a job in Dryden, about 250 kilometres away. He came back once a week to visit, but it soon became obvious that to stay together as a family, we had to be living together, so we moved to the outskirts of Dryden where we three kids were also enrolled in the local school.

Lou Remembers All the Words

Lou remembers that in grade three, she was asked to write out "The Lord's Prayer," "God Save the Queen," and something from a biblical passage or a hymn. She was the only one in the class who could write out all three, word for word, with perfect sequence and spelling. It was part of our training at the residential school to learn by rote, not substance. The only thing missing was that we hadn't been taught cursive writing, only printing, so she quickly caught on in order to fit in.

Ruth Acting Out Her Learned Authoritarian Behaviour

Ruth recalls when her teacher made her the class monitor, charged with watching children in the earlier grades (which included Lou and me) during lunch hour. While watching over us all, Ruth snuck a look into the drawer in the teacher's desk and found a strap. She took the strap out and hit the desk with it, yelling at us kids to be quiet. One day, not long after that incident, she was startled to see the teacher watching her. That was the last time she was ever asked to be a class monitor.

Ruth had learned the attitude and behaviour from the nuns at St. Anne's. Her St. Anne's style of control remains one of her most shameful memories. She would think, "How cruel you were to those little children. They probably went home and cried and told their parents, saying, 'Our monitor at school is so horrible.'" This is a clear example of how conditioning can influence even those with a different set of conscious values. That memory of using the strap would stay with her for years.

Lou did not voice any complaint about Ruth's actions as our class monitor. After all, she was used to the St. Anne's style of teaching and control. As for me, I was like a leaf in the wind, taking whatever came my way, including the familiar sound of a strap smacking against the teacher's desk.

I was just living each day as it came – just trying to make sense of the many voices and emotions rattling around in my head. I can see now how a lot of that "noise" was the result of the trauma I had experienced at St. Anne's, living in fear, frustration, and confusion.

The legacy of my experience at the residential school still continued to plague me and could be summed up in a comment expressed by one of the teachers a few years later, who mentioned to my parents during a parent-teacher meeting that, "I would likely never amount to anything."

Getting the Strap

Although that teacher might not have seen my potential, for me, in retrospect, I was still in my residential school mode of not trying to learn anything. One event that snapped me out of my stalled and stunned state, though, was when our school needed some urgent construction and our grade-five class was relocated to the historic one-room school in the area. In that relative tranquil setting, I received more one-on-one attention from my teacher Ms. Cairens. She caused me to want to start learning again, for which I will be forever grateful. I think she was more than a teacher. She was a special teacher who recognized some of my challenges and helped me with her patience and extra attention to a point where even my marks improved.

That amazing school year, though, also holds my most shameful memory. One winter day, Ms. Cairens was not able to teach and a supply teacher was sent instead. This teacher was young and bubbly, but her clothes reminded me of a nun. Or maybe she actually was a nun. I forget. When she went to use the outhouse, I locked her in and began throwing snowballs into the air vent above the door. I heard her crying and pleading with me to open the door, but I continued to throw snowballs in for several minutes. A number of other boys joined in the fun, as kids are prone to do at times, but I had been the one who had started it.

It is chilling to me now just thinking about it because I had no feeling when committing the deed – just a conscious thought that I was driven to do what I was doing, and hoped she wasn't too upset.

When she finally convinced me to open the door, she was completely soaking wet from the snow, cold, almost frozen, shivering, and crying her eyes out. Because of her frozen state, her skin looked unnatural, almost like marble, and with her makeup running down her face, she looked disfigured. She had been reduced to just a humiliated young woman stripped of her authority, and her appearance shocked me. I suddenly felt embarrassed and confused at the damage I had caused her. She ran to her car and drove away, and we never saw her again.

Not only did I ruin her day, but I fear that might have also caused her to leave the teaching profession forever due to my malicious actions.

This memory has haunted me ever since, but I am not quite sure what to do with it. We got the strap for that one, and even at the time, I felt I deserved it. We received five smacks of a ruler on each hand, which seemed to be a light punishment. But is a strapping in any form ever appropriate, especially if the past is influencing us and we are not aware of our motivations?

I was never mean or malicious like that ever again. Maybe that one act was enough to satisfy any subconscious anger I was still carrying from the residential school and the mean nuns there. Who knows?

Needless to say, I had a lot to think about, but there seemed to be no time or safe place to do it.

CHAPTER TWENTY FOUR:
WE MOVE TOWARD A CONCLUSION

AS WE KIDS STRUGGLED TO fit into the unfamiliar challenges of the south, and with the residential school experience still fresh in our minds, our parents struggled as well, trying to create a new life for us and to fit into a world that had evolved during their time up north.

Eventually Mom and Dad purchased a place in the country. It was an old, rundown farm, but that didn't matter since it was about 200 acres, full of trees, and with a 40-acre private pond in the centre. After cleaning out the old dump and knocking down the rickety barn, it turned out to be a beautiful place. Finally, we had some privacy again and could relax. We began to put down roots. Little did we realize at the time that, compared to how most others lived, we had lucked out with a magnificent property that offered seclusion and space. It allowed us to relive the peaceful country life that we had enjoyed while up North.

Mom and Dad did not have the confidence to consider borrowing money though, to fix up our home.

Margaret/Mom:

"It is normal to think that if you buy an old house and you see that it needs repairs, well, you go to the bank and get a loan. I mean, it's just commonplace – you go get a loan, and you hire a carpenter [or whoever is required], and they get it done. Or if you need to dig a well, you go to the bank and say, 'I've got to dig a well, but I haven't got all the ready cash.' There is no shame in it. You just explain what you

need it for, and they say, 'Well, here it is, and the least you have to pay is this, but you can pay it off as fast as you want.' So you budget for it. It is now just a commonplace thing. But when we came out of the North, we didn't know nuts from anything. We didn't know that there was a financial system, a safety net in place that could be an alternative to what we had been used to with the HBC."

We all enjoyed the property in our own ways, but I came to treasure the pond especially where I would float around in the canoe looking up at the sky, relaxing, reflecting, and getting a different perspective. I had finally found my safe place.

Holding Onto the Past

As my sisters attempted to adjust and be forward thinking or at least engaged in the present, I tended to be stuck in the past. I was not just dwelling on the horrors of St. Anne's, but longing for the life we had enjoyed at the HBC post on Albany Island. I felt driven at times to unpack our past treasures – the last vestiges of our life of privilege up North – now stored in a trunk upstairs in our parents' bedroom. To save them the pain of old memories, I would wait till Dad and Mom were not at home before opening the trunk. Ruth and Lou would occasionally join in, but usually I would sit by myself and remember. However, there was always an empty feeling, as if those treasures could not speak anymore – like they had lost their power and were just trinkets now.

Now here were these lifeless relics that I tried to breathe life into by touching, rubbing, and even wearing them, like my beaded mitts, but they had no place in our new life. Dad and Mom must have noticed that the contents of the trunk were disturbed at times, and maybe they feared that the little hellion in me might eventually destroy the treasures with my curiosity. Dad eventually donated our family's mementos – furs, carvings, and beadwork – to the local museum in Dryden, Ontario. In this way, he managed to safeguard them, as well as our good memories of that time past. Here is one familiar item now on display there.

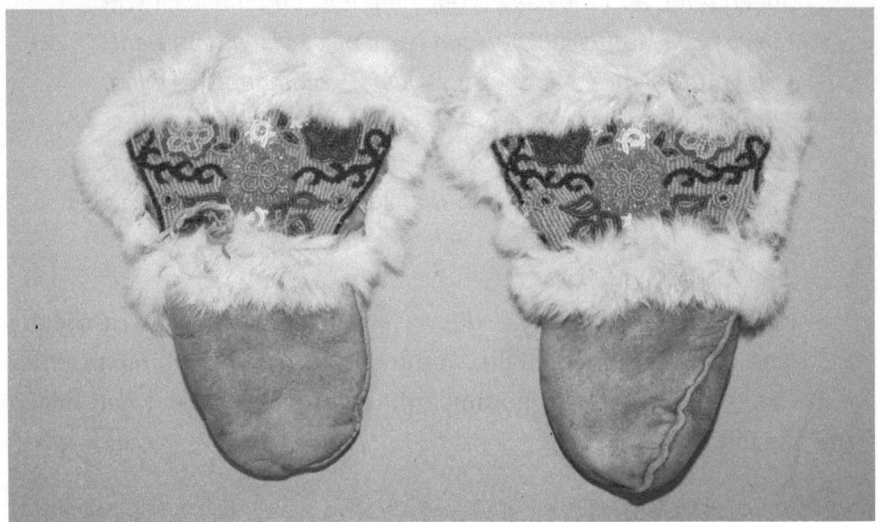

The mittens that Ron wore while living at Fort Albany.

As I grew older, I would occasionally stop by the museum to visit these treasures and imagine and remember my past life when I wore those mittens as the privileged little HBC boy.

Ron wearing the mittens while living at Fort Albany.

Fellow visitors admiring the beadwork in the museum would be unaware of who they were standing beside. I was never sure whether I wanted to smile or cry at those times. Some visitors would be inspired to talk about past memories, while others would just comment on the craftsmanship of the object of interest. Everybody sees what they want to see in life. They are limited by their upbringing. Some just see the veneer, the beads sparkling in front of them. Who knows whether it is better to be stuck in the past, present, or future? At least there are places like museums that attempt to record the past, even if some can only see the veneer, being unable or unwilling to dig any deeper.

The Burning of St. Anne's Residential School

Illustration of St. Anne's Indian Residential School burning, Fort Albany.
Credit: Bill Slavin

St. Anne's Residential School burned down in 2002, the end of an era in Fort Albany. It was representative of many acts of cruelty and was a symbol of a cultural genocide. It was where we three white Gosbee kids went to school and where we stood with our fellow Native classmates and hoped that our parents would come and rescue us.

It is where two cultures collided; one culture presuming that it was superior and had the right to dominate and eliminate the other. Ironically, it was our fellow Native students who showed such humanity toward my two sisters and me, and who sought to comfort and even protect us against the injustices of the white settler culture at the school.

For those kids who attended the residential school, and who are still trapped and struggling in their minds, I ask the reader to acknowledge them by pausing for a moment to consider their experience. They are looking to you to at least do that.

As I imagine St. Anne's Residential School burning down, my memories of our time there are dimming too, like stubborn embers gasping for life. I cannot get my childhood back and must now move on, taking whatever lessons with me. Hopefully, like all the survivors, we can evolve out of the ashes to a better place.

Although the buildings of St. Anne's were wiped away with fire, it was sad to learn that none of the buildings are left of the community and our home on Albany Island either, where we enjoyed such happy days before being sent to St. Anne's. It is a reminder that the world we create is all a construct – from the buildings we build to the rules and morals that we live by.

Everything is in constant flux and evolution; one moment it is there, and the next it is gone. Some new thing takes its place, and all one has left are the memories. But it is also a lesson that we have the ability to change what is wrong.

Old Fort Albany is no more. The Anglican Church and community where we visited with fellow Anglicans is gone. Our home is gone. The HBC store where our dad spent so much energy representing the will of the company in return for security for him and his family – also gone. They are not real anymore. The crumbling foundations stand in stark witness of the past.

Where we lived is now a field where, I am told, Native people gather again to beat the drum.

Let's learn the lessons the past teaches us so they can help those who come after us.

Thank you for coming on this journey of truth, reconciliation, and survival.

AFTERWORD

I THINK BACK TO THE BEGINNING of this memoir when I was taken on that canoe ride and enrolled at St. Anne's. I was filled with such apprehension on that fateful trip. Now, so many years later, time is more behind me than ahead. And with the passing of time, the chances of ever achieving what might have been prior to attending St. Anne's fade as well. But I still persevere, fighting against the past with its savage undertow, thankful to feel at least that I have found my voice.

As I attempted to collect the threads of this story into one final knot, one thread kept breaking free, demanding attention. It was the question: "Why share this horror story with the world? Hasn't everyone heard enough about the sins of the residential schools by now?" Some people say, "Why dwell on it? Just get over it. What does that experience have to do with us now?"

Here is one reason.

Tony:

"For most of us, the trauma and brutality we were subjected to at St. Anne's would haunt us all our lives. I oftentimes read comments on social media by ignorant people telling us to get over it and to quit feeling sorry for ourselves. I know that people who have had a traumatic experience in life never get over it, try as much as they can, and the best they can do is to try and cope with this pain and lead as much of a normal life as possible."

273

Not being able to talk about one's experiences can be personally harmful, and the push to sanitize the past is not healthy for society either; the danger of forgetting the lessons of the past invites us to repeat these errors.

Four things stand out for me as I finish this memoir:

1. Psychological damage

As students at St. Anne's Residential School, we experienced stressful mental entrapment to varying degrees. That deep trauma still leads us to attempt to recreate past incidents at times by imagining scenes, smells, sounds, and sights. It is like we feel we have forgotten something and so return to the familiar, to the past, to find more resolution, to try to make sense of it.

However, few if any words are stored to describe this type of experience, and the memory can only be triggered by a visual cue, a smell, or a sound. For example, some survivors found that the sound of jingling keys triggered a memory of the nuns at that school and the rings of keys they carried.

Trauma may also produce long-lasting behaviours and sensitivity to specific types of situations. Some find that the threatening silences of the nuns left them with a weakness – a fear of receiving the silent treatment in their relationships – and being exploited by those seeking to control them.

Other symptoms that survivors live with include having disturbing or intrusive dreams; loss of intimacy; feeling detached, sadness, and anxiety, to name a few. Likely most survivors also suffer from PTSD. These are just a few examples of symptoms that affect their daily lives, limiting them and causing them discomfort. As time goes on, and survivors pass, the trauma will live on with their descendants, in what is known as multigenerational trauma. This might also help to answer those who ask, "What does it have to do with us?"

To speak of my own symptoms, I would say that the mental entrapment of the residential school affected me in two significant ways: being withdrawn and unable to communicate – in other words, a loss of words, a loss of voice – and a fear of abandonment. Both these symptoms really became apparent after I moved down south and attempted to integrate into southern society.

2. My Path of Resilience

Although the story of St. Anne's Indian Residential School is not our story; we three white kids were there too. We slept side by side with other kids who came into the "civilized" world at St. Anne's, trying like crazy to adapt but getting smacked if they didn't get with the program. A lot of our fellow students came straight from living off the land to that insane authoritarian freak show. Day after day, their identity and voices were sucked out of them. In their natural world, power lay in knowledge and community. At St. Anne's, power meant, "I can do this to you." The message of the school was: "You kids will do and think what you are told! You better be quiet and follow the rules."

For my sisters and me, we had less of a cultural leap, but were affected negatively just the same. To a child surrounded by other fearful children the lesson was to be fearful, to accept control over our bodies and our wills.

And so, when my family moved to full immersion in Southern Ontario, I not only lacked the words I lacked anything to say. I was in a traumatized state of being, without my voice and an understanding of my own identity. The extent to which I was no longer a healthy little boy was on full display, which proved to be a frightening and frustrating experience for me.

Like others from the residential school, including my two sisters, we all struggled to rise above those troubled times, and followed various paths in an attempt to fit into the larger world.

My path included spending many years obtaining various degrees and diplomas. However, looking back at that time, I realize now that I was really just trying to find myself without any idea of what or who I wanted to be.

As I struggled to adapt to an unfamiliar and complex world, I began to focus on my work life and personal emotional evolution followed.

I eventually founded a business in Toronto. Ironically, it was a digital printing business. I was not conscious at the time of this irony, that as

I was struggling to find my own words to express myself, I was helping others to put their words on paper.

I enjoyed seeing people bringing their great collection of words to me to print out for them. But it was also frustrating and weird that I had no adequate words to express my own thoughts. So, I would depend on my friends to help me express what I could not. My relationships with most of my friends at the time were predicated on this typical interaction where they would have the words for what I meant. I think of it now as "word therapy," and it helped me to learn a broader range of expression to better describe the thoughts that were swirling around in my mind.

I also had the fortunate experience of meeting some of Canada's cultural icons through my work at the time, who inspired me when I observed that every one of them exhibited a common personality trait: they felt they had the right to express themselves, and they had the drive. That was a revelation to me of how much my voice had been silenced by my experience at the residential school.

As time went on, I continued to concentrate on my business. I did not become an alcoholic as some other survivors did. I became a workaholic. This workaholic lifestyle helped to build a comfortable life but not a rich life with any great depth. And it helped me to disregard my memory of the residential school.

One seemingly insignificant incident occurred while I was living the high life, and it might have made me start to consider the past. One night when I was walking by the Silver Dollar Tavern in Toronto, a voice called out from the darkness in the alleyway.

A Native person was sitting there in the shadows, politely asking for spare change. I remember clearly how polite he was. His approach caused me to strike up a conversation with him. I gave him what change I had and asked him where he came from.

He said, "Fort Albany, about a thousand kilometres north of us." I told him that I used to live there as well, but he didn't seem surprised or curious.

It sounded like just a normal conversation, but between two cultures and two lifetimes ago. It was eerie hearing this voice with its familiar Cree accent coming from the past and coming out from the shadows on a street in downtown Toronto.

The experience lasted only a moment, and I wonder now since we were both about the same age, whether we had known each other as children at St. Anne's and had both been standing on the school steps in the pictures I have of my time at the school.

I did not think to ask him whether he remembered the white boy at that school. He might have even been the boy that I had the blood brother ceremony with that one summer there so long ago. However, at the time, I was still intent on avoiding my past, so I said, "Good luck," and walked on, just as people always do. How many people have just walked on in our lives? We need to do less walking on. Although I did not seize the opportunity at the time, the memory of that Native person continued to haunt me over the years, as if inviting me to revisit my past.

While I was still running my company, Lazerline, located close to that same corner in Toronto where I met him, another significant event occurred. That day a young, articulate musician came into my printing business. His name was Charlie Angus, and he later became the federal Member of Parliament for Timmins–James Bay Territory. Little did he know that I was a survivor with personal experiences and a visual record of the residential school of St. Anne's, located in the territory he would come to represent.

He would also write a book called Children of the Broken Treaty, which would inspire me to write my account of St. Anne's.

As I began to piece together my memories of the residential school for the purpose of writing my account, I came to understand that knowing one's roots and how they affect one is important. Writing such memories down, not only helped to create a conceptual roadmap to resolve the trauma of the past, but the clarity also helped to guide me to a more meaningful life. I began to imagine something different from the deep-seated, limiting self-image I had been carrying from my experience at St. Anne's. If you can't imagine a better world, then you just get the world you got.

I was so fortunate there were friends around me to help me realize a constructive direction and perspective so I was not picking at the old wounds with no resolution.

Part of that perspective was realizing that finding a permanent self-image is impossible because one's identity is always evolving. I learned to regard any of my failed attempts at becoming better at something new as just evolutionary steps, and not to see them as failures. As my sense of identity grew from these efforts, so did my voice and confidence.

I also began to understand that there was a lot of make-believe in my social relations, because I was not exerting an equal will; I was just being a supporting actor for the wishes of others as I had been conditioned to do at St. Anne's. With that insight, I began to look for relationships that were more nurturing.

And now, I am thankful to have reached this place where I am able to communicate more effectively and with relative ease, and I am choosing relationships where I can bring my thoughts, opinions, and emotions into them without a fear of abandonment.

Here's to creating our own possibilities and opportunities, and living a life of our choosing. It seems so long ago now when we kids thought that life at St. Anne's was our only option, when we could not imagine much more than just following the rules, and praying for forgiveness.

Justice for the Abusers

Although a lot of damage was done under the auspices of schooling, to the point of being criminal, the deeper crime is that the entire residential school premise was wrong. All involved may have felt that they were "doing good," but just because they thought they were doing the right thing does not make it right. And without adequate checks and balances, the system also allowed some bad people to remain hidden and exert their will on the weak.

There were a number of suspects who were the cause of the trauma experienced by the students of St. Anne's. Those suspected of offences were brought to account. However, only a few of them were convicted. That is in part because most of them were only known by nicknames the kids had given them, so they were hard to identify according to law.

It is bewildering to contemplate that there were loving nuns working at St. Anne's while at the same time there were nuns and other staff inflicting so much pain and suffering on the students – so much so that students were willing to risk their lives to escape. Some died in their efforts to leave St. Anne's.

In this story, so much has been shrouded in the past and behind closed doors. But some facts have emerged that are now on record. In a 2018 article for CBC News, Jorge Barrera listed those charged with offences under the Canadian Criminal Code that included, Anna Wesley. As he states, "Anna Wesley, a Cree nun born in Attawapiskat, who attended St. Anne's as a child, was convicted of three counts of common assault, three counts of administering a noxious substance, and one count of assault causing bodily harm. She received an eleven-month conditional sentence" (Barrera, 2018).

Significantly, it seems likely that her cruel nature was learned in part during her "education" as a child at St. Anne's. Breaking this cycle of violence is another reason why I felt the need to write this book, and to share our experiences.

Tony:

"It is my belief that every boy that was there during Anna Wesley's tenure was irrevocably destroyed for life and that a great part of them died in that hellhole.... That place destroyed you day by day, and unfortunately, you end up trying to overcome this your entire life, and for many without much success.... Many of us unfortunately found self-worth at the bottom of a sixty-ouncer. However, thank God, we forget a lot of bad stuff or for sure we would all end up in a looney bin...."

Apparently, Anna Wesley's violent reputation was also well known in the Native community.

Tony:

"When Anna Wesley died, she was buried in Attawapiskat, and the villagers didn't bother going to her funeral. She was really hated in this area, and in her old age, she became very timid and fearful of her fellow Natives. No longer was

she the holy terror that at one time instilled much fear and dread on all the children in her control.... I purchased an apartment building from the Catholic Church that she was living in. I could have easily kicked her out but instead did the humane thing and let her remain. To my knowledge, she never had any visitors and spent the last healthy years of her life sitting by a window watching people walk by. I sometimes used to wonder if her memories [harkened] back to the days when she used to sit by the window in her office in Albany watching us with her cruel eyes. Sad, wasted life."

I find the list of those charged rather short. In an authoritarian environment such as St. Anne's, where the priests were ultimately in charge, it is odd that so few of them are on the list of those brought to justice.

Tony:

"[In] my many years there, I met [various priests] and what some had in common was that these supposedly saintly pillars of Christianity were but mere child predators. I dare say that countless former inmates went to their graves keeping the dark secrets of what these evil men did to them.

Once in a while, you read of altar boys who were molested by deviant priests in Boston or other places, and while shocking, it's nothing compared to what was done to defenceless kids that were at their mercy in the middle of nowhere. You ever wonder why that prison was built in a very remote location with no contact to the outside world? ... I am glad your sisters didn't experience or see the brutality you did, but many girls were not so lucky as they ended up being sexually assaulted by the brothers. Do you remember the boys' cabin on Lac Ste. Anne? It turns out that at times the brothers would take the prettiest girls there."

Given what might have gone on at that cabin, one has to wonder what memories and secrets might still be buried there.

3. A Validation

An opportunity for personal validation materialized during the writing of this book. It was the formation of the Indian Residential Schools Settlement Agreement, the largest class-action settlement in Canadian history, which began to be implemented in 2007. One of the elements of the agreement was the establishment of the Truth and Reconciliation Commission of Canada "to facilitate reconciliation among former students, their families, their communities, and all Canadians."

For me, it did not really ease any of the trauma, but it justified and validated my testimony about my experiences at St. Anne's. Mostly I felt anger at what had been done to fellow students. We three white kids saw things that we were not supposed to see, feel, or experience. And I am bearing witness to that. We knew something wasn't right at the residential school. We didn't know what it was, but we knew it was not right. A little child's mind can't always articulate what is wrong.

What makes for significant trauma? From my experience, it is the frequency. All children everywhere experience trauma, but they are spikes in an otherwise normal existence. However, the daily trauma at the residential school was constant for all the students there. Other students experienced physical trauma as well. The combination of the threat and the reality of abuse is likely what motivated students to risk their lives and try to escape.

Tony:

"What we were subjected to and what we as children witnessed on a daily basis certainly contributed to many of us ending up with what mental health care professionals now refer to as Residential School Syndrome. I also thought, and still do, that we all suffered from Post-Traumatic Stress Disorder and have carried that with us all our lives."

All the children, collectively, at St. Anne's were afraid. It was a ball of fear. We were silent witnesses to a cultural genocide, a disappearance of a people. We were in an environment that suppressed our need to express the wrongness of a situation, and we were so young. We didn't have insight or vocabulary to capture the story, to recount it in words, and flesh out all we felt was wrong at the residential school. All we had at that age were feelings with no words and no story, and here we were, years later, trying to find the words to tell the story of our feelings in our statement letters and having to relive some of the pain in the process.

The St. Anne's experience has caused me to live a life of extremes. One day I strive for great adrenaline highs, the next I become withdrawn, fitting in when necessary, but largely invisibly floating through the mainstream of life – constantly on guard, avoiding those who seek to control.

Tony:

"In no way was this place anywhere near normal for children, and on a daily basis the staff, by their treatment of us and their countless rules and regulations, insured we all would come out of there screwed up in one way or other."

I was not forced to sit in the electric chair. I was not beaten or sodomized by the priests. I escaped the more physical punishments. But I learned about bureaucracy and hierarchy and obedience and a whole bunch of other things, including what it felt like to be shut down in my curiosity. To me, the most important part of a young mind is curiosity, something suppressed brutally at St. Anne's unless it promoted the school's agenda to present an image of holiness. And, somehow, I got through that and hung on to a little piece of my curiosity, despite the accusations of "daydreaming."

In response to our submissions to the Truth and Reconciliation Commission, we also received monetary settlements. It was meaningful to have official validation in the form of payment for wrongs committed so long in the past. More than any monetary amount, it was a long overdue acknowledgement of the wrongs that were done. And what better way, in a capitalist society, than to receive monetary compensation for pain and suffering – unfortunately, it is the only way our society has to right such things.

282

Even with monetary compensation, the trauma that had robbed us of our sense of identity still plagued some of us. I was to learn that as part of the healing process, it was important not just to be seen, but to feel seen, to feel rescued, to feel validated as well – and that it was through the heartfelt connections with others that the emptiness slowly began to be filled.

I know my memory is fallible, but my feelings are not. My heart goes out to all of my fellow students in St. Anne's and the other residential schools; those who remember everything that happened to them and are likewise flooded with painful feelings that monetary compensation cannot erase. And I am thankful to Tony and the other survivors who have reached out to me during the writing of this memoir to share experiences and be supportive. I had originally been thankful that they helped to give clarity to the story, but I realize now that their empathy has also been such a validation – an informal healing circle – that is so necessary in the process.

Another validation that I hold dear to my heart is my mom's heartfelt acknowledgement to me in 2016. During the writing of this memoir, asking her to help me recover my memories really opened up wounds of guilt that she carries for sending her children to that school. She could not know how she was misled in her consideration to enroll her children at St. Anne's, and she had few options in the North for schooling. Though I hold her blameless, she still carries guilt, like all parents who were forced to or made the decision to send their kids to a residential school.

> *"Once upon a time, there was a mother who had lovely children, and through her ignorance and insensitive nature made choices that turned her lovely family into introverted, insecure adults. As this mother ages and the sands of time take their toll in her health, she is suffering mentally and physically for her failures.*
>
> *Forgive me, Son, where I failed. My purgatory will not come at death. I am experiencing it now.*
>
> *Forgive me,*
>
> *Mother."*

Now in her retirement, she feels most comfortable going to the local First Nations' Centre in her community in Southern Ontario, where she has made many friends. It is fitting that she, with her sensitive nature, is finally able to freely enjoy the friendship of Native people, whose company she was denied during her early years in the North.

4. A Call to Action

The residential school system in Canada grew out of the government's plan to control and assimilate, and the Church's need to convert and fund their organizations. The combination made for the perfect storm, which left a lot of damage. It also resulted in a polarization of how to reconcile the past and right the wrongs that were done. To truly reconcile, it takes both parties to solve the issues together and, as a guiding light, all involved need to exercise enough empathy, so as to see clearly through the eyes of the other.

As the experiences of the residential school are viewed in a broader context, it is obvious how polarized the opinions are on the subject, both nationally and internationally. To avoid stating the obvious to an already supportive readership, I'd like to offer some useful tools for your next conversation with those who continue to defend the colonial mindset.

Aside from the ninety-four recommendations that the Truth and Reconciliation Commission proposed, and regardless of one's perspective, the fact still remains that Native culture is part of what we consider Canadian. So, along with any financial considerations, reconciliation must also accept that First Nations culture has had a defining role on our national identity.

For example, in Canada, we have a maple leaf on our flag. Why? Because settlers were taught by First Nations how to get sweet syrup out of a tree. We named our country after a Native name. We have four provinces with Native names. Two of our three territories have Native names. We have towns all over the country that are Native in their origin. If we can see how Native culture has permeated many aspects of our life, right down to the name of our capital, it would go far in informing our perspectives.

It will be interesting to see what form the national reconciliation framework proposed by the Prime Minister of Canada in 2022 will look like.

My call to action is to ask you to: understand the actions, motivations, and constructs that make up our world so our society becomes more responsible for the hell we ourselves create here on earth; to not repeat the sins of the past; to understand the need for adequate checks and balances as a guard against the powerful; and to leave our society in better shape for everyone, including generations who have not yet been born.

The thirst for profoundly unequal power is at the center of all injustices visited upon the weak and children. This can be observed everywhere: in our homes, businesses, institutions, and in all countries around the world. It is systematic evil that replicates authoritarian structures no matter who is in power. Maybe the problem is our belief that a top down hierarchy is needed at all.

The residential school system was born out of a perspective that might makes right. How is it, though, that the obvious misery of children could not be recognized or given any weight in the management of the residential schools such as St. Anne's?

Hopefully this account will cause some good to ripple through the minds of those who have the power to visit pain in all its forms upon children and the weak, innocent, and vulnerable.

Build it and they will come. Ron Gosbee sitting in a new circle.

REFERENCES

Angus, Charlie. *Children of the Broken Treaty: Canada's Lost Promise and One Girl's Dream.* Regina, Saskatchewan: University of Regina Press, 2017.

Barrera, Jorge. "The Horrors of St. Anne's." CBC News. March 29, 2018. Available from https://newsinteractives.cbc.ca/longform/st-anne-residential-school-opp-documents/

Mas, Susanna. "Truth and Reconciliation chair says final report marks start of 'new era'." CBC News. December 15, 2015. Available from: https://www.cbc.ca/news/politics/truth-and-reconciliation-final-report-ottawa-event-1.3365921

ADDENDUM

The Quality of Education at St. Anne's

Page 144 of the summary of the *Final Report of the Truth and Reconciliation Commission of Canada*, published in 2015, states that, "The residential school system failed as an education system." [Hereinafter, this volume is referred to as the Final Report, or as the Report.]

Further, the Report states that our forbearers based their curriculum on "racist assumptions about the intellectual and cultural inferiority of Aboriginal people ... consequently, for most of the system's history, the majority of students never progressed beyond elementary school."

Ignoring the "positive emphasis" on education that many families believed their children would receive in this system, "The government and church officials ... instead ... created dangerous and frightening institutions that provided little learning." The Commission goes on to say, "In their mission to 'civilize' and Christianize, the school staff relied on corporal punishment ...[which] often crossed the line into physical abuse."

History was to show that mean, controlling teachers were preferred by the management at St. Anne's and that the good, caring teachers were actually persuaded to leave. There were good brothers, good priests, good nuns, and good teachers, and they were pushed out.

One account from an old woman said that as a young teacher [at Fort Albany], she was told, "These kids are bad, don't be nice to them." Nevertheless, she would go in at night to comfort these kids who were crying, and she was kicked out after a year. Another woman said, "I was at that school, and they fired me halfway through the year because I would not put up with the abuse."

Looking back, I also wonder why St. Anne's, and the Catholic Church, for that matter, would create such an oppressive environment. Where did monastic life end and individual abuse begin? They did not seem to care about the value of individual thought, personal expression, or the larger world around them. We were cloistered within the confines of St. Anne's and taught more about how to get to heaven than how to live in the real world. We were taught to be quiet and pray for forgiveness.

Making Sense of Our Experience
and the Government of Canada Policy

The Government of Canada needed sovereignty in the North. To do that, they had to bring the Native people together to educate them. But they could not build and staff schools, partly because of the great expense, and partly because the Canadian Constitution gives the responsibility for education to the provincial governments, not the federal government. Yet the federal government is responsible for the Native people.

Their answer to this problem was the churches. The Roman Catholic Church especially stepped forward because they had the means and their own agenda. The nuns and oblate brothers at St. Anne's came as missionaries and did the work of building the residential school complex and teaching the children.

The nuns of St. Anne's had teacher qualifications; that was their ministry, and that's what they did. But they were also missionaries, so religion became the central part of the curriculum. They put religion first as the means of assimilating Native people, and education became secondary. That resulted in a system of northern education in residential schools.

The Province of Ontario had minimal oversight of the educational process in the North – or at least had no adequate checks and balances in place at the time. The Church, therefore, had a free hand to do as they pleased to a great extent. Also, because Native parents were hundreds of miles away, and few white people lived and worked in the North to become advocates for the children, it made for the perfect storm.

I am speaking of what we experienced at St. Anne's in Northern Ontario, but this scenario was being played out across the country in varying degrees as well.

ACKNOWLEDGEMENTS

ONCE I SET OUT ON this journey to tell about the past, I had many helping hands along the way.

Thank you to my mother, Margaret, and my sisters, Ruth and Lou. Without them, I could never have pulled out so many memories and fleshed them out to a usable form. Their love and support are priceless. Thank you also to the rest of my family including, my younger siblings: my sister Helena and her son Mason (a budding writer); my brother David and his wife Lindsay, who gave me encouragement and advice during the process.

Thank you to my fellow schoolmates from St. Anne's, especially Tony Tourville, who helped enormously to add to this account. His no-holds-barred way of speaking provided details of the past and also helped to transport us back to that time and place emotionally, to feel what it must have been like to be imprisoned at St. Anne's.

Thank you to Ted Dyment. He helped me to rearm myself, to find the words, in order to understand my position and to be able to defend it as well. His friendship gave me a safe and quiet place to retreat and have the time to get serious about writing. He encouraged me to voice my thoughts, dig deeper, and also provided suggestions and encouragement throughout the project.

Thank you to Lawrie Gulston for his editing, writing suggestions, research, and clarity in initially helping me to pull my fragmented memory together. His music and friendship also provided a welcome break along that road of recollection.

Thank you to Jim Slavin for edits and suggestions during the final stages of the book. His unwavering support and enthusiasm in proofreading the book several times to catch any mistakes was so helpful, and his attention to detail was so instrumental in helping in the polishing of the book. Thank you also to Elizabeth Irwin, for her advice and overall support. They both also made the process fun and interesting over lovely dinners and conversation.

Thank you to Bill Slavin for his illustration of a very important point in the story: the burning down of St. Anne's.

Thank you to Deborah Carew for her support, research, and editing suggestions. She was my co-pilot in the early stages of the project, helping me to arrange the initial segments and to stop repeating myself. She also introduced me to Stephen King's writing lessons that taught about the "show, don't tell" approach to writing.

Thank you also to Deb Luchuk for her interest in the project. Ironically, she also drove me to eye doctor appointments to deal with my eyestrain, the result of writing this book. Thank you also to George Luchuk, her father, for his time and interest in sharing his experiences as a Hudson's Bay Company employee at Moosonee and Great Whale. By the way, he was the tall HBC clerk in Moosonee who had helped me consider a jacket when we had travelled out of the North for the last time. Almost sixty years later, and during the writing of this book, I found out he was now living about a block away from me. Talk about six degrees of separation.

Thank you to Wendy Chesworth for her encouragement and suggestions. Wendy was also instrumental in organizing a talk for the Kiwanis Club in London, Ontario that gave me an opportunity to tell my story, which proved to be a positive, cathartic experience.

Thank you to the many others who offered their advice and encouragement, including: Linda and Alan Slavin; Genevieve D'Souza; Michael Flynn; Slavka Marcincinova; Sullivan Dyment; Margaret; Susan; Joan; Brad; Bill and Yvonne; and Amy.

Thank you to the FriesenPress team, including Dahlia, Jodi the designer, and Rebecca, the editor who helped to organize the manuscript into a more cohesive account that improved the flow and clarity of the story.

Thank you to my friend Janette Irwin Shean for her belief in the project. Her encouragement and assistance was key in producing this book.

Thank you to the many other supporters I have met in my travels. When the topic of one's past invariably came up, I noticed that my own story sparked great interest, and their reactions informed me of its unique value and also inspired me to keep writing.

UPCOMING WORK

A BOOK RECOUNTING OUR LIFE AT the HBC prior to being enrolled at the residential school is in the works, with plans to publish it in the future.